Flying Stumps and Metal Bats

Cricket's Greatest Moments – by the People Who Were There

Foreword by Simon Lister

thewisden
cricketer

Aurum

First published in Great Britain 2008
by Aurum Press Ltd, 7 Greenland Street, London NW1 0ND
www.aurumpress.co.uk

This paperback edition first published in 2010 by Aurum Press

Photo credits: p. 1 Clive Lloyd and Prince Philip: Patrick Eagar; p. 43 The Oval,
16 March 1970: Hulton Archive/Getty Images; p. 79 Mike Procter and his
Gloucestershire team: Patrick Eagar; p. 117 Michael Holding at Dunedin: Getty
Images; p. 159 David Steele at Lord's in 1975: Getty Images; p. 237 Dennis
Lillee and his aluminium bat: Hulton Archive/Getty Images; p. 267 David
Shepherd and Saqlain Mushtaq: Patrick Eagar; p. 313 when snow stopped play in
Buxton: *Buxton Advertiser*

A catalogue record for this book is available from the British Library.

ISBN 978 1 84513 530 0

10 9 8 7 6 5 4 3 2 1
2014 2013 2012 2011 2010

Typeset by Saxon Graphics Ltd
Printed by CPI Bookmarque, (

Contents

Foreword

The articles from the *Wisden Cricketer* that make up this collection are a bit different from other parts of the magazine. The reason, I think, is because they are stories that the players tell by themselves. When it works well, 'Eyewitness' (as regular readers of the *Wisden Cricketer* know it) has the feel of a group of people talking around a pub table while enjoying a pint. An anecdote here, an interjection there, a contradiction, then perhaps a joke followed by a put-down. The task of the compiler is to place together these jigsaw pieces of recollection to come up with a colourful picture.

That's the theory. The trouble with 'Eyewitness' is that some of the eyewitnesses themselves have a terrible habit for making things up. Now, I'm not saying that the ex-cricketers of the world are a collection of mendacious obfuscators, it's just that a portion of them don't have great memories. Here's one example among many. It was an interview with a former county captain who insisted forcefully for several minutes that he had been caught at midwicket by a fielder who in actual fact was not playing in the match. The discussion only ended after he put the receiver down and went to the next room to look up the game in *Wisden*. Even then he suspected a printing error.

So the memory can play tricks – when it's working at all, that is. I was recently left slightly short of material by a player who was one of seven victims in the middle of a record-breaking spell of bowling by Pat Pocock. Despite the day's momentous events, he had absolutely no recollection of taking part in the game. So I rang his brother who had also been bowled for nought. He couldn't remember a blessed thing either.

If only they were all like Raymond Illingworth. Raymond is something of an 'Eyewitness' favourite, partly because he's played in some dramatic cricket matches and partly because he can remember almost every leg-bye and off-break he witnessed.

'It was Scarborough,' he might begin. 'I was slightly delayed because of a tailback outside Filey. There was light drizzle until about ten past twelve, then I brought myself on from the Trafalgar Square End and had four for 12 by lunch. Potato salad and ham it was.'

The other thing about Raymond is that he's never too busy to talk. I once interrupted him while he was cleaning the car outside his holiday home in Spain ('I dunno,' he grumbled, 'it was bloody spotless when the kids took it out . . .'), but he still gave chapter and verse. When I mentioned this to a colleague, he told me of a phone interview he'd done while Raymond was in the bath. On the tape, he had an account of the Ashes tour of 1970–71 as well as an intimate collection of sploshings and latherings.

Raymond is helpful, articulate and generous when he's describing his career (although to be mischievous for a moment, his recall for games where he took nought for 112 is slightly sketchy), and he is the rule rather than the exception. Only two out of the dozens of people who have appeared in 'Eyewitness' should have been forced to stand in the waste-paper bin with their backs to the rest of the class. One was a former England captain (and former personal hero) who took great exception to answering the phone to an ignorant stranger. The terse and spiky interview that followed, laced with sighs and sarcasm, took weeks to recover from.

The second naughty boy was a bit-part player who demanded hundreds of pounds for his muddled contribution, made over a mobile phone in a garage forecourt outside the village of Liphook in Hampshire. I was in the middle of explaining the constraints of the magazine's budget when he cursed loudly, announced that I'd caused him to fill his tank with diesel rather than unleaded, then hung up.

But these moments are very rare. I can't speak for Lawrence Booth, Nick Hoult or Huw Turbervill, but I suspect that, like me, they find it a bit of a treat to be able to talk about great cricket matches with the great men who played in them and to get, just for a quarter of an hour or so, a feel for their character away from the crease. And occasionally you receive more than you expected. I will always keep the recording of the moment that Mike Gatting was attacked on his sofa by his dog. At first I was horrified, thinking I was listening to a violent burglary taking place.

Mike: . . . So Steve Waugh somehow got his hands under it and caught a bloody good catch actually.

Me: Was that a pull, Mike, or a shot on the off side?

Mike: OI! OI! . . . ARRGHHH! . . . (*sounds of a commotion and barking*) GET OFF! DOWN!!! YOU BAD BOY!!!

Me: Mike? Mike? Hello . . .?

Mike: (*GRRRR!*) Sorry about that. I've got some biltong knocking around. Nightmare! Away! Bad boy! Anyway, yeah, so um, as I say, I pulled it . . .

The explanation turned out to be that Gatt's meaty mid-morning snack had proved too much of a temptation for his slavering pooch. Hard as I tried, it was impossible to work this part of the interview into the final copy. It might have distracted the reader from the game. And that, I suppose, is what Eyewitness is all about. The game. It celebrates the cricket match rather than the cricketer. It's not about the individual, but the individual's role in a greater thing. And there are few greater things than a cricket match vividly recalled by those who best knew the moment.

Simon Lister
June 2008

CHAPTER 1

Great Occasions

I thought: 'That's all I need after that –
a speeding ticket.'
The policeman said: 'I told my mate
that was Knotty and Denness – we'll
stop them and ask them what
happened at Headingley.'
They let me off a ticket.

**England captain Mike Denness following England's semi-final defeat
to Australia in the inaugural cricket World Cup, 1975**

overleaf:
Clive Lloyd picks up the first World Cup trophy from Prince Philip

The short and sweet World Cup entrance

West Indies win the first World Cup, England, 1975

The 2007 World Cup was widely panned for being too long – a far cry from the inaugural competition in 1975. The Prudential Cup, with its two-week, eight-team format, was more akin to today's Twenty20 World Cup. And it was greeted with similar ambivalence by most involved. One-day games had been part of the English county scene for more than a decade but for most other countries limited-overs cricket was a dubious novelty. India and Australia were wary of one-dayers, and Ian Chappell's main focus that summer was on the subsequent four Tests against England, although Australians never like losing . . .

Keith Fletcher (England batsman): We'd been playing the Sunday League for six years and the Gillette Cup for twelve, so we had more one-day experience than some of the others. There was lots of global interest but not as much hype, television and media coverage as now.

Chris Old (England bowler): Lots of the older players said one-day cricket wouldn't last. Certain players were having trouble adapting. There was a tremendous atmosphere for the tournament. We had a reception at Buckingham Palace just before the first game.

Mike Denness (England captain): I was playing for Kent at
Colchester and I walked off with Asif Iqbal because it was snowing
– two inches fell – and I thought: 'What a shame with the first
World Cup five days away.' As it turned out, it was 80°F at Lord's
for the opening match and a terrific summer. Most players were
supportive of the 60-over format. It had spectator appeal and the
players preferred performing in front of a crowd. We didn't practise
specifically for the format but we did work out some strategies,
unlike the Australians. Chappell wasn't a fan at all but they still
made the final.

Anshuman Gaekwad (India batsman): I was at college and it was
my first overseas tour – at Buckingham Palace it was the first time
I'd seen those Scottish skirts!

Farokh Engineer (India wicketkeeper): India had no experience of
one-day internationals but I'd played for Lancashire in the Gillette
Cup. We went into the tournament in optimistic mood,
determined to play well and have fun.

Bishan Bedi (India spin bowler): The competition doesn't hold
pleasant memories for us. We weren't used to the concept at all.
We were brought up to believe this one-day nonsense wouldn't last
long – how wrong we were.

*Surprisingly, Bedi was left out of India's first match, against England
at Lord's. England made 334 for 4 and India replied with 132 for
3, Sunil Gavaskar carrying his bat for a paltry 36 not out. One
disgruntled spectator threw his lunch at Gavaskar's feet.*

Old: It seemed there was more to Gavaskar's innings than meets
the eye. Maybe something happened on the field or when we were
batting. It seemed like a protest. It stopped the match being a
spectacle. This was a really special occasion. It was almost like he'd
said: 'We're not going to get 335, so I could do with batting
practice.' It detracted from our batting; we paced it beautifully.

Engineer: I don't know what got into Sunil's mind, I don't even think he knew. He's very single-minded and thought nothing of it. He's a great friend but we got very cross with him at the time. Even if we thought we were unable to chase down England's total, we shouldn't have been defeatist; we should have made a game of it. Venkat was too weak a captain to speak to him, but I told Sunil: 'It's not on.' He actually outscored me in our next game [65 to 54] when we opened and defeated East Africa by 10 wickets.

Bedi: It was terrible – our response to England's innings was so outlandish, a perverted effort. Only recently Sunil made the comment that he nicked one early on. He now says he wished he'd walked. But for all these years he seems to have had a mental blackout. It seemed to be a deliberate attempt to make a packed Lord's crowd look like a houseful of idiots.

Denness: I'm sure there'd been a dispute about the line-up – just about one player, I believe. We were trying to work out what was going on in his mind. It was a worry: what effect would it have on the tournament?

Gaekwad: Our approach was that 60 overs is a normal game, that you have to build an innings and in India we were of the opinion that the quality of runs was more important than the quantity. It was also not easy slogging in England: John Snow and Geoff Arnold didn't give us anything to go at. We had no special planning or instructions. I don't think Sunny had any agenda; to me it looked as if he was trying just to get a feel of the tournament. He was probably concentrating too hard.

England romped through, beating New Zealand by 80 runs and then East Africa by 196. West Indies nearly came unstuck against Pakistan at Edgbaston but last pair Deryck Murray and Andy Roberts put on 64 to win.

Asif Iqbal (Pakistan captain): The format was also new to us and it's clear how much the game has changed; the fields set then and the approach were totally different but it was a World Cup so we took it seriously. I missed this game as I was having a minor operation so Majid Khan was skipper, but it wouldn't have been allowed to go to the wire nowadays. The bowlers would have been rotated, more pressure put on tail-enders, the runs squeezed. It was a shame, as we'd been the side named as most likely to upset West Indies, Australia and England.

West Indies hammered Australia by seven wickets at The Oval. Glenn Turner struck 171 not out against East Africa. India had to beat New Zealand at Old Trafford but lost by five wickets.

Bedi: We had no chance after that inauspicious start. Our intensity was low – it didn't seem to matter where we finished. For us, Test cricket was still the ultimate.

In the semi-final at Headingley England were destroyed by Gary Gilmour, who took 6 for 14. England had Australia at 39 for 6 but Gilmour and Doug Walters saw them home. At The Oval, West Indies beat New Zealand by five wickets.

Fletcher: Batting at Headingley first thing in the morning wasn't fun. We were eight wickets down by lunch. England lost that game in the first hour and a half.

Denness: You'd never know what type of wicket you'd get there. We'd spent all winter ducking and weaving against Dennis Lillee and Jeff Thomson, now we had trouble adjusting to getting on the front foot.

Amiss: It was seaming and swinging all over the place. We put down two catches – I think it was Tony Greig and Chris Old, very unlike them.

Denness: I travelled back with Alan Knott and we were pulled over by police. I thought: 'That's all I need after that – a speeding ticket.' The policeman said: 'I told my mate that was Knotty and Denness – we'll stop them and ask them what happened at Headingley.' They let me off a ticket.

In the final, on Midsummer's Day, Clive Lloyd made 102 as West Indies scored 291 for 8. Viv Richards had three run-outs, with five in total in Australia's innings. They looked finished but last-wicket pair Thomson and Lillee took them within 18 runs of victory.

Iqbal: It was an exciting end to a tournament enjoyed by players and public. No wonder Kerry Packer embraced the format soon after.

Derek Underwood (England spin bowler): A packed crowd of 26,000, record receipts and a game that finished at a quarter to nine at night on the longest day of the year – just the way you would want it. The organisers certainly got it right for that tournament.

Interviews by Huw Turbervill

In the beginning ...

Durham's first season in the County Championship, 1992

Durham's victory in the final of the 2007 Friends Provident Trophy showed just how far they had come in 15 years as a first-class county. It was in 1992 that they left the Minor Counties, recognition at last of the immense passion for cricket in the north-east of England. Local boy Geoff Cook, the former Northamptonshire and England opener, was given the task of shaping a squad and Durham took the field that first season with a mixture of old and young and Ian Botham as talisman. It was a brave new world but the ground at Chester-le-Street was not ready and the campaign proved testing.

Brian Hunt (Durham scorer): I've scored for Durham for 32 years – 17 seasons in the Minor Counties and 15 in the first-class game. I didn't know what it was to lose from August 1975 till August 1982 – 65 games undefeated. We steamrollered sides. Without first-class cricket, however, the lads had nowhere to go. Talent fell by the wayside; they became teachers or took nine-to-five jobs. The north-east needed a first-class county.

Geoff Cook (Durham director of cricket): My first-class career had finished with Northants in 1990 and Durham appointed me here in 1991. They were in the final throes of applying for first-class status. I played a season of Minor Counties for them that gave me the chance to run my eye over the recreational and amateur players. David Graveney was playing for Somerset and was chairman of the PCA [Professional Cricketers' Association], so he could advise us; he was the ideal man to captain Durham in that first season. He was terrific with the media and did a grand job. The signing of Ian Botham received financial backing from Scottish and Newcastle Breweries; that was a real coup. I knew Ian fairly well from my county days and he was a terrific presence. David was in charge of the first team and it wasn't too regimental; there was no point with players of that experience. Ian, Wayne Larkins and so on fancied one last challenge; they enjoyed the razzmatazz and the circus.

Simon Hughes (Durham bowler): Some big names were on their list of potential recruits: Chris Lewis was one, I believe. My contract had ended at Middlesex and I'd been at university in Durham so was aware of the depth of passion for cricket there. It was a new challenge and exciting. It was better paid than at Middlesex but, of course, there weren't many win bonuses.

Hunt: We needed those older players for credibility. I had private reservations about big names coming in but they were all as good as gold. Ian still looks me up now when he comes to the Riverside.

Ian Botham (from *My Autobiography: Don't Tell Kath*): Looking back, the decision to leave Worcestershire to join Durham was one of the worst decisions I ever made. There were of course great attractions. It was a new county, apparently full of ideas and ambition, and the prospect of playing home matches only an hour's drive from where I lived was appealing. But I should have known better. Quite early on I became aware of major problems behind the scenes. I was actually offered the captaincy. However, when later I met Geoff Cook, he told me he had already promised it to David Graveney. I was not happy but I shrugged my shoulders and accepted that Cook had not wanted me at the club in the first place.

Hughes: How would the club wickets stand up to four-day cricket? What size might the crowds be? How many toilets would need to be installed? Everywhere there were fresh and not always pleasant discoveries – the biting wind off the moors at Gateshead Fell, the thieves at the Racecourse, Chester-le-Street's shirtfront wicket, the perilous scorers' crow's nest in Stockton's pavilion. Actually, playing on those out-grounds added to the interest; it felt like going back to my roots in club cricket.

Paul Parker, Larkins, Dean Jones, Phil Bainbridge and Hughes had been parachuted in to complement the home-grown talent like opener John Glendenen, off-spinner Phil Berry and left-armer Simon Brown, who was born locally but had played for Northamptonshire. Durham made a dream start, beating Lancashire by nine runs in the Sunday League on 19 April with Jones making 114. And soon they were celebrating their first Championship victory, by an innings at Cardiff. Brown took eight wickets, Stockton-born seamer Paul Henderson, aged just 17, took three in the first innings and there were centuries from Larkins (143) and Parker (124).

Steve James (Glamorgan batsman): It was us playing particularly badly rather than them playing well. They had a pretty old side, with a few youngsters, and not much in the middle – quite similar to now: some England players and good youngsters but they have had to bolster their side with Kolpaks.

Cook: Henderson made a terrific debut but it was tough for those youngsters. The dressing room was full of strong characters and the youngsters needed education. Now the counties have their own academies. We knew Grav, Botham, Parker and Larkins wouldn't be around for long, so we needed to put in place a sustainable youth structure. Jimmy Daley was emerging, while Paul Collingwood first appeared on my radar in 1994.

Hunt: After beating Lancashire, the one-day kings, and then the innings victory at Cardiff, we were on the crest of a wave; it was a fairy tale.

But Durham managed only one more Championship win. Before long some of the older players were running out of steam and the young were struggling to keep up.

Hunt: The step up from Minor Counties to first-class was colossal. That's why we were whipping boys.

Botham: [Cook's] big idea was that there should be no star system at Durham. It was his dream to build a kind of socialist cricket republic where all players would be equal. If he'd had his way, we'd have stood up before the start of each match and belted out a couple of choruses of 'The Red Flag'.

Hughes: Cook and Botham fell out a bit. Botham wasn't prepared to compromise; he relied on the methods that had brought him his success. He was incredibly generous that summer. He had a lovely home which I think he'd seen in *Country Life*; he hosted us a lot, particularly when we played near Darlington, letting us raid his wine cellar.

John Emburey and Phil Tufnell shared 17 wickets as Durham lost heavily at Lord's, although Berry took 10 wickets in the match.

Hughes: The youngsters were finding it hard. I'm not sure many had the appropriate dedication; they lived for their Saturday afternoon matches, then for going out afterwards. There was a big socialising culture and they found it hard to adapt.

The wheels were truly off in the last days of that first campaign: Somerset won by eight wickets at Taunton, Lancashire by 10 at Gateshead. Durham did better in the one-dayers: joint eighth in the single-division Sunday League, the NatWest quarter-finals and third out of five in their Benson & Hedges group.

Cook: With Parker, Larkins, Jones, Botham and Bainbridge the batting was OK but, apart from Brown, we were short of wickets.

Botham: I got on well with most of the playing staff, sharing some good times with the likes of Jones, Hughes and Graveney, but my real problems were with members of the committee. Initially promises were made that were never kept and the level of in-fighting grew and grew.

Hughes: I think it was probably the right way to go. If Durham had just plumped for the local players, I think they would have been annihilated; it would have been like boys versus men. The youngsters, even Collingwood, in the juniors, learned a lot from seeing how Jones and Parker prepared.

Cook: I wouldn't have changed anything, in hindsight. We had a lot of people to satisfy, the cricketing public in the north-east, the sponsors; ideally we'd have liked a fully professional approach and been able to sign players with more longevity but it was a different system then. Players were either Category A or B and you could sign only two Category A players in two years. It was a tough system. We owed a lot to the members who put in voluntary work to get grounds like Hartlepool, Stockton and Darlington up to scratch. It was a difficult yet romantic time.

Interviews by Huw Turbervill

Serious celebration

MCC v Rest of the World, Lord's, 1987

Twenty-two of the world's greatest players gathered at Lord's to play in a one-off match to mark the MCC's [Marylebone Cricket Club] bicentenary. England held the Ashes, West Indies dominated the world game and only one Australian was deemed good enough to get in the Rest of the World [RoW] side.

Mike Gatting (MCC captain): The calibre of players on show was amazing. The greatest thing for me was that Malcolm Marshall was on my side for a change.

This was not a one-off match for the RoW. They had played a couple of warm-up games with Dilip Vengsarkar and Desmond Haynes scoring hundreds against Gloucestershire.

Clive Lloyd (RoW manager): We had been together for a while and built up a good team spirit. We had a star-studded side. Some players would perhaps relax when not playing for their country but not those guys. They were very keen to do well. It was good to see them as a team together.

Dean Jones and Maninder Singh were left out of the RoW team at Lord's. Allan Border was captain and Sunil Gavaskar opened the batting in his final first-class match.

Lloyd: The MCC chose the sides and we had a very good run-up to the game. The guys had clicked. We ate together the night before and enjoyed the moment.

Gatting: We had a very good team spirit. I had a chat with them all the night before the game and it was very encouraging. Everyone wanted to do the right thing.

The MCC lost Martin Crowe and Ian Botham through injury and Viv Richards opted to play for Rishton in the Lancashire League rather than at Lord's.

Clive Rice (MCC allrounder): I broke Martin Crowe's hand the game before in a county match between Somerset and Nottinghamshire. It was just an accident.

The MCC decided to call in Rice for Crowe, sparking fears of demonstrations at Lord's over the inclusion of a South African.

Rice: They were really concerned about me playing because of the links with South Africa. They did not want any demonstrations on such an occasion. In the end there weren't any and the atmosphere was fantastic. I was a bit worried, though. Nottinghamshire were also a bit worried because we were going for the Championship and had five players disappearing to play at Lord's.

Gatting won the toss with a Spade Guinea coin first minted in 1787, the year of the first game at the ground. A bright sunny day and a pitch perfect for batting brought a stack of runs for the MCC.

Graham Gooch (MCC batsman): The match was pretty much a who's who of international cricket. I had not been having a great season for Essex and I didn't play many international matches. But I got my chance in this match and took it. The first-innings hundred got me my place in the World Cup squad that winter.

Gatting: It was a nice atmosphere to play in. People were coming along to watch good cricket rather than to support one side. As for the players, though, nobody was taking it easy. Players wanted to go out there and win.

Gordon Greenidge reached his fifty off 91 balls but shortly after lunch lifted Abdul Qadir over mid-on only to be caught by 6ft 5in tall Roger Harper. It was not his only piece of brilliant fielding.

Rice: Mike Gatting played brilliantly that day. He made batting look easy. Everyone, though, was demonstrating their fantastic skills. There was not an overuse of short-pitched bowling and the players used their ability to get wickets or runs.

After Greenidge's dismissal Gooch carried on and helped himself to 117, making the most of a perfect batting pitch.

Gooch: It was a very flat pitch and Malcolm Marshall was the only bowler to be really effective. Although I scored runs it was not my best batting performance at Lord's, which was a good ground for me over the years.

Gooch's innings is perhaps remembered for its ending. He departed when he drove a ball straight back to off-spinner Harper, who threw the stumps down before Gooch had time to react.

Gooch: I tried to dive in front of the ball but I wasn't even quick enough to do that. It has got to go down as one of the great fielding moments. My momentum just carried me forward but before I could get back he had thrown the stumps down. It all happened in a split second. I was well and truly stuffed.

Gooch's dismissal brought Rice to the wicket. With South Africa banned from world cricket, it was a rare chance for Rice to perform against world-class opponents.

Rice: Put it this way: there was no way they were going to get me out. It was as simple as that. It was a fantastic opportunity for me and I couldn't wait to show off my skills. The politics had been forgotten and the match was a true reflection of the countries playing international cricket at the time.

On the second day Rice and Gatting took their fifth-wicket stand to 201. Gatting was in the form of his career, scoring his fourth century of the month.

Gatting: I got a reprieve early on and it was such a good wicket I knew I had to make the most of it. I just went on after that and the guys supported me very well.

Rice: When you are with someone who is playing out of his skin you give him the strike as much as possible and that is what I did. I gave him the strike and let him dominate. I just stood back and watched the show. It was the only time I faced Qadir in my career. He was a lovely guy and he used all his tricks.

Gatting enabled his team to declare and put pressure on the RoW, for whom Javed Miandad was injured. Gatting dropped Haynes in the first over but Marshall struck back.

Rice: Malcolm bowled very quickly at Dilip Vengsarkar because of an altercation they had when Malcolm first started playing Test cricket. He felt Dilip claimed a catch on the half-volley. He never forgave him for that. When Dilip walked in Malcolm changed. He went around the wicket, asked for another slip and bowled some very quick deliveries.

Gatting had one of the most potent attacks in the world at his disposal. Marshall and Hadlee took the new ball with Rice, Emburey and Ravi Shastri making up the attack.

Gatting: It was nice but I got a bollocking off Richard Hadlee for polishing the ball. 'Only I polish the ball,' he said. It was a great privilege to be playing with such amazing talents.

The RoW innings was moulded by Gavaskar. He scored 188 and his stand of 180 with Imran Khan thrilled the sell-out crowd.

Lloyd: We had some very good performances and the batting was beautiful. Imran and Sunil batted really well together.

Gavaskar had announced his retirement the previous evening and looked as though he would mark the occasion with a double hundred. Border's declaration left the onus on Gatting to set a target. Greenidge had missed out on a hundred in the first innings but was not going to make the same mistake in the second. He scored 122, over five hours and off 223 balls, and was supported by Gooch (70 off 118 balls).

Gatting: We were able to declare and then get Gavaskar before the close. It was well set up for the final day.

Lloyd: It was set for an intriguing finish and we felt we could win.

The RoW had been set 353 to win but rain washed out the final day. It was a sad end to the match.

Rice: It just wasn't to be.

Gatting: It had been a good match and four excellent days. On the fifth, though, it rained and it was a real disappointment.

The match had been played in such a good spirit that the MCC increased the prize money to be shared by the teams in the event of a draw. Gavaskar was named batsman of the match, Marshall won the bowler's award and Rice was named the fielder of the match.

Rice: Denis Compton gave me the fielding prize and I can see it on show in my living room now.

Interviews by Nick Hoult

'Welcome to the revolution'

The birth of Twenty20, 2003

A warm summer evening in 2003 at Worcester. The first sight of Twenty20 cricket in England. One of five games played that night to mark the start of a new project in county cricket. Across the country there were girl-bands, carousels, bouncy castles and spit-roasts. How did they come to be there?

David Sales (Northamptonshire batsman): It was a packed house. There were local DJs commentating, a hot tub to jump into …

John Carr (then ECB [England and Wales Cricket Board] director of cricket operations): Work cricket, school cricket – there'd been 20-over games going on since the year dot. What we added was the concept of the best cricketers in the country getting involved.

Lord MacLaurin (ECB chairman 1997-2002): Let's get it in perspective. We've all played 20-over cricket. Everyone has. This wasn't rocket science.

But it was different. By the turn of the century cricket's administrators had become very worried that fewer and fewer people were watching the county game. Could a three-hour match played at night after work bring them back?

Carr: It was one of my hobby-horses. We wanted to make the most of the appeal of county cricket, bring in a new audience and not lose the interest of the game's long-term supporters. In 1999 there was actually a sort of trial match between Worcestershire and Glamorgan at New Road. 25 overs a side. It was a one-off game but a thousand people turned up.

The problem was that the county chairmen needed convincing. Why take a punt on something that might fail? Perhaps they would be reassured by some expensive research.

Stuart Robertson (former ECB marketing manager): We had some money and had been helped out by Channel 4 – it cost nearly £250,000. We found that people thought cricket was inaccessible. It was played when they couldn't watch it. If four-day games began on a Tuesday, why should we be surprised if only retired middle-class white men watched? People also thought it was socially inaccessible. Don't I have to be a member? Don't I have to wear a tie?

Not in the jacuzzi at a Twenty20 match.

Robertson: We wanted cricket in the evening, after school, after work. Would people go? They said they would.

By April 2002, with the answers from 4,000 interviewees who were questioned for 15 minutes in their own homes, the ECB eventually put their findings to the counties to vote on.

MacLaurin: The meeting was, well, very, very interesting. The 18 counties of course as well as MCC would have the final say. It was going to be nip and tuck. I phoned a number of the chairmen before the meeting to try to persuade them. Many of them weren't happy. This new competition would replace the Benson and Hedges Cup. 'We like the B and H,' they said. 'That's when we do our membership drive.'

The modernisers won the day but only by 11 votes to seven. MCC abstained. The new game would go ahead. But would the players like it?

Robertson: What we found was that the best players, the international Test players were the most sceptical. I think they already got their buzz from playing in front of thousands of people. The first-class pro, though, he was really excited. These guys only knew playing in front of a few dozen and, when they saw the proposed audience, they liked it a lot.

David Taylor was not even a first-class pro. He ran a building company and played league cricket in High Wycombe. He could hit a cricket ball, though.

Taylor: I had always scored quickly. I didn't mind going over the top early doors. And I knew that, if I was hitting it out of the middle, I could take people apart.

The Worcestershire coach, Tom Moody, through his contacts liked the sound of that. He offered Taylor a contract for the county's Twenty20 games.

Taylor: It's what books are written about, isn't it? A bloke goes from the building site to playing cricket in front of thousands of spectators. I was absolutely delighted because five years earlier I'd completely given up on the game because I had thought I'd never get anywhere.

In the Worcestershire dressing room Taylor looked around for familiar faces.

Taylor: It was freaky because actually I don't really follow first-class cricket – I couldn't tell you which county sides the England team play for. So I didn't really know that many people.

Then at last he recognised someone. Graeme Hick perhaps?

Taylor: I grew up in Australia. And there sitting across the room was a kid I hadn't seen since I was six in Perth. Matty Mason. His dad had owned a garage and my dad had once bought a car off him.

In front of 4,005 spectators, Taylor, Mason and the rest of the side went out to bowl at Northamptonshire. Games were starting at other grounds too. 'Welcome to a revolution in cricket,' boomed the announcer down in Hampshire.

Robertson: I remember standing just behind the bowler's end at the Rose Bowl. I think James Kirtley of Sussex bowled a wide first ball and it was a bit of a deflating moment but then, realising the situation, he ran back to his mark for the next ball and everyone knew that the players thought this was something different.

Carr: I took my family. Hampshire had booked the girl-band Mis-Teeq to play there after the cricket. I think they wanted a bit of a safety net in case the game didn't turn out to be so popular. But actually we discovered that most of the crowd had just come to see the game.

Back at New Road, Worcestershire were doing pretty well against Northamptonshire.

Sales: Our coach, Kepler Wessels, told us that anything near 160 was very good. If you got to 180, you had to do something very wrong to lose.

Northants made 150 from their 20 overs. David Taylor got padded up.

Taylor: It wasn't quite what I expected. These guys were playing cricket every day, so they weren't pumped up like I was. There was a bit of a feeling that it was another day in the office. As for me, I had no idea who Andre Nel was, for instance. My first scoring shot was a four, so that helped.

In the field Northants were trying out their new tactics.

Sales: We'd had a lot of conversations. How to bowl slower balls, variations, yorkers. We even had code names for different deliveries. I remember that 'Koala' meant bouncer, so the bowler would say to mid-off 'Koala next' and he would spread the word. What else was there? We had signs. Stroking the ball on the trousers was one – can't remember what that meant, then there was rubbing the hands through the hair …

The sign they saw most often, though, was the umpire signalling 'four'. It was as if David Taylor was still batting for High Wycombe.

Taylor: I told myself to do what I always did but maybe do it a bit quicker. Quick hands and feet.

The pep-talk worked. Taylor hit nine fours and a six. He made 46 in 19 minutes from 20 balls.

Taylor: I was out in the fifth over. So I was seeing it pretty well. In fact you could say I missed out on the chance of a big hundred.

From 60 for 1 Worcestershire slipped to 84 for 6. But Stephen Moore and the lower order got the home side closer and closer.

Taylor: We were all out on the chairs. It was getting very tense. I was sitting next to the coach and thinking, 'If we lose this, my innings won't have counted for anything.'

With three balls to go, Worcestershire needed one to win with one wicket in hand. Mark Harrity, the Worcestershire No.11 was hit on the pads.

Sales: We all thought it was out. It was an lbw shout and, while we were appealing, he ran. We felt pretty hard done by.

'This game had just about everything,' decided The Times. 'When Harrity dived to make his ground at the bowler's end for the winning single, he crowned a thrilling victory in front of a full house. The victors

leapt for joy as hordes of youngsters invaded the field; the defeated looked utterly dejected.'

Taylor: Graeme Hick was really funny. He was injured but he was in the dressing room and he was walking around with a mobile phone to his ear pretending to call people, saying: 'Yeah, come and play in the next game. No, it doesn't matter if you've not played before, just turn up and hit it out of the ground.'

Taylor's innings got him the man-of-the-match award.

Taylor: What did I win? Well, I'll let you into a secret. I got an envelope and took it into a corner and quietly opened it, hoping for a few extra quid. But it was empty – there was nothing there. I went to the chairman and said: 'Sorry to bother you but I think the cheque may have fallen out.' And he said: 'No, there's never anything inside. It all goes straight to the players' fund.' It was all just for show.

But what a show it had been. Thousands of tickets had been sold on that first evening. By the competition's end about a quarter of a million had been bought.

Carr: It was great. Really satisfying. A lot of hard work had been done. I remember getting a couple of texts that night from various county folk saying it was a real shot in the arm for the game.

MacLaurin: Did anyone call me? Er, no. County chairmen are often of a type and reserve is one of their qualities. There were no plaudits from that part of the world. However, I'm sure that, if they looked at their profit and loss columns after the first season, they would have been very happy.

So Twenty20 grew. Internationals. The World Cup. Stanford. The IPL [Indian Premier League] and the ICL [Indian Cricket League]. Do the men that brought it to life still like the look of it?

MacLaurin: I should say that I count myself among the traditionalists who didn't want any lessening of the game of cricket. Twenty20 should be kept in its box. It mustn't be the be-all and end-all of cricket. That should be Test matches. I would hate to see Twenty20 become the biggest form of cricket.

Carr: Successful products have to be very carefully marketed. The challenge for us is to complement, not destroy, cricket. But it is a wonderfully adaptable game. What other sport can be as exciting over five days as it can be in 2 hours 45 minutes?

Robertson: I love two innings. I love the longer game. I don't want to see it disappear. But the decision will be made by people with their wallets and their feet. A mix would be brilliant. We're part of the entertainment industry, not a trust set up to guarantee the future of 250 professional cricketers. Surely we're obliged to play the games that the public want to see. If Twenty20 is all there is in 10 years, so be it. The customer will decide.

For David Taylor the competition's first night was his best night. He would never again open an empty envelope in a quiet corner of the dressing room.

Taylor: Perhaps I was too aggressive. I realise now that it's all right to have a look at, say, Waqar Younis for a few balls before trying to put him out of the ground. I started to put myself under too much pressure. So that was it. Oh yeah – one other thing. Tell people that I'm available for Twenty20 this summer if they're looking.

Interviews by Simon Lister

How the county cousins cracked the capital

Somerset win their first trophies, 1979

For more than a hundred years cricket's trophy engravers never had cause to write the word 'Somerset'. However hard the county tried, the only cups at Taunton came with saucers beneath them. In 1978 not one but two trophies were surrendered at the last moment. The players were determined that in 1979 things would change.

Peter Roebuck (Somerset batsman): Somerset was a rural club that had won nothing – and seemed doomed never to do so. But alongside these crusty old cricketers, and a handful of doughty locals, there then came four or five unknown properties, two of whom, Ian Botham and Viv Richards, became giants of the game. In all sorts of ways it was a remarkable collection of characters to have at the club.

Brian Rose (Somerset captain): When I first came to the county in the late '60s it was struggling. We were often bottom of the Sunday League and the Championship. Yet there were signs that things could happen. Peter Denning, me. Two years later Vic Marks and Peter Roebuck, then Ian and Viv.

Vic Marks (Somerset allrounder): It was soon apparent that Viv was astonishingly good. No one knew Both was going to be as good as he turned out but we had a wide variety of characters:

Denning and Rose, both dashing blonds from Weston, both bright but Denning in particular doing his utmost to disguise it; Pete and myself, view as you like, Oxbridge types or whatever. I don't suppose we knew it at the time but it was a situation to cherish and certainly made for a lively dressing room.

The young hopefuls were skippered and swan-songed by that famous old 'Bald Blighter', Brian Close, who had moved to the county after being sacked by Yorkshire.

Rose: When the county signed Closey they got a completely different animal than anyone at Somerset had been used to – toughness, mental strength and a man who refused to accept defeat.

Roebuck: Brian Close captained the side on the field. The idea that he was constantly raging in the dressing room is wide of the mark. He was either drinking tea or whisky. On the pitch he was alive every ball – a great man to play cricket with. I never batted with anyone who tried as hard as Brian. It reeked from 22 yards away. Not even Viv tried as hard as him and Viv was a passionate cricketer.

Rose: I changed next to him. I was the only bloke who was stupid enough or brave enough to do it. So he talked to me for two or three years and I learned a lot – he taught us all that it was horrible to lose.

Derek Taylor (Somerset wicketkeeper): I was his vice-captain. I respected his ability but he did some crazy things on the field. A few times in limited-overs games he'd put the batsman Mervyn Kitchen on to bowl and Mervyn didn't even bowl in the nets.

Marks: Closey was a bit of a legend. I don't think he knew which of us was which, but he was certainly larger than life.

Roebuck: He was a gambler on the field and that meant he was a good captain for three-day cricket but not so hot in one-day games. In one-day games it's good when nothing's happening. Closey would always try to make something happen.

Taylor: Yeah. Things did happen. Like the ball going out of the ground.

Close brought inspiration to Taunton but no pots. In 1978 Brian Rose succeeded him as captain.

Roebuck: Brian Rose was much more methodical, self-contained. A strategist as opposed to a tactician.

Marks: Looking back, it seems obvious that Rosie was the perfect successor to Brian but at the time it was far from clear. I don't think he was even the favourite. Partly because he never used to say anything. He'd be in his corner of the dressing room and keep his own counsel and he got on with the job of scoring his runs. As it turned out he was very tough, determined, prepared to take hard decisions and very soon he commanded respect. He was also prepared to take a bit of a punt on the young guys. He understood them.

Joel Garner (Somerset bowler): Closey wanted me to bowl a lot. I mean a lot. I was thinking to myself that if I went on like this I'd be dead in a couple of years. I had to let Brian Rose know this. I couldn't bowl all day. He knew I needed a rest now and again.

Nobody got much rest in Rose's first season in charge. Somerset reached the final of the Gillette Cup and on the last day of the John Player League, had the chance to win it.

Roebuck: We'd never won anything and we tried to win everything – and it drained us.

Garner: We played exciting cricket, we made all the running. And that worked against us. Teams didn't play against us. They just sat back.

Roebuck: The Gillette final at Lord's was a big, big thing for us Somerset lads. You walked round the corner and you'd bump into Jim Laker or Richie Benaud. A big thing and we froze. But it was the Sunday League that killed us. We sat in the dressing room for two hours afterwards; Viv broke a bat against the wall.

Marks: He smashed his Jumbo to smithereens. The game was lost by two runs to Essex. A silent dressing room. And then an old bloke Jock McCombe, a disreputable Scot who was Viv and Both's go-fer, said: 'You've got to go on to the balcony because there are people there.' He kept pestering us and we eventually went up and there were about five thousand fans there, cheering, clapping. You see, there was a real bond between us and the spectators and we were taken aback by the warmth. We only thought we'd let them down. And that was the moment it really got to people.

Rose: That's when the tears came, I'd never really seen players cry before. We learned a lot from that year. A very difficult weekend – what it did was make us ruthless.

So ruthless in fact that in the following season Somerset were kicked out of the Benson & Hedges Cup for deliberately losing a game, knowing that a swift defeat would see them through to the next stage with a better run rate.

Taylor: That was a mistake; it was wrong. What it showed was that in 1979 we were keener than ever, having failed twice the year before.

Roebuck: There was a sense of this rural county wanting to go and take on the Londoners, the Northerners and the Midlanders. The binding force was that desire to go out and take on the rest of the country.

Despite the misjudgement in the B&H Cup, Rose's county were playing great one-day cricket and in the John Player League the captain himself seemed particularly blessed.

Rose: I could cope with the pressure and I could express myself. I was a player just below Test cricket. Boycott, Gooch, Gower and Gatting were ahead of me and I was pressing for a place. Sunday League cricket I was good at because I played overs well. 50, 40 or 20, you have to have someone who can bat three-quarters of those.

Taylor: We always won more games than we lost. Controlled bowling, that was the thing. We could bowl to our field with length and line.

Roebuck: We all liked it. The crowds were big, you see. The Sunday league found us playing in an excited atmosphere with a compelling team. We weren't used to that feeling. Taunton wasn't a big ground, and I suppose it was quite intimidating for some sides, especially with Garner playing.

Marks: The locals were fantastic and Taunton could be a bit of a cauldron. We used to joke that we should put a sign up in the old pavilion saying 'This is Taunton', just like Liverpool FC had in the tunnel at Anfield. I saw sides quake there. I remember we bowled Kent out for 60-odd; the ground was full, cramped, the noise was huge and each player looked whiter than the last coming out to bat. We loved it that they made a bit of noise and got up a few people's noses.

Garner: They were loyal because they knew we were trying hard.

By September, the fans' loyalty was rewarded with another trip east to the capital – the Gillette Cup final versus Northamptonshire.

Roebuck: We arrived the night before and Brian Rose was looking fresh and awake; Viv was looking fiery. Joel was being Joel and the rest of us were lifted by that.

Marks: We were less intimidated by Lord's this time and we were determined to be more relaxed. I think we even wore our scruffiest jeans on purpose to take on the surroundings. And more of us played properly.

Richards and Garner played very properly. The Antiguan batsman scored 117 and the Barbadian bowler took 6 for 29.

Marks: We'd had a team meeting, a waste of time because all we ever decided was that the opposition weren't going to be able to play Joel.

Garner: A decision made much to my detriment! I had a lot of responsibility. I knew I had to take wickets at important times. Lot of responsibility. But if you're gonna go to work and not like it, change your job.

Marks was right. Northants could not play Joel. Somerset won by 45 runs. The county had been waiting for 104 years and one month for such a moment – the first trophy. Cue enormous celebrations?

Taylor: Well, not really. We had another game the next day.

Roebuck: No late night partying. A glass of champagne I think before we drove to Nottingham. Lots of Somerset cars going past us hooting and hollering.

Garner: No, no, no. I walked straight from the ground and into the Tavern bar. A lot of big drinks. I wasn't driving.

Later that evening the sober drivers and the relaxed non-drivers headed north. The final match of the John Player League v Nottinghamshire awaited them the next day. Kent, who were two points ahead with a game to play, would take the title if they won their game against Middlesex. Somerset sped up the M1 in hope rather than expectation. On the way the captain felt peckish.

Rose: I remember pulling up at Watford Gap services on the M1 with Peter Denning who was my pilot. I didn't want to leave the trophy in the car, so we had the Gillette Cup on the table and we were eating our eggs, beans and chips when a coach load of Somerset supporters from Frome turned up, also on their way to

Nottingham. They couldn't believe it. The captain, the opening bat and the trophy all there, having a fry-up.

The next day the biggest crowd of the season at Trent Bridge gathered to see if Somerset could make it two trophies in a weekend. The innings started slowly.

Roebuck: I got a 50, I think, but it wasn't a huge score.

185 for 8 from 39 overs. Then, when Nottinghamshire batted, Clive Rice and Tim Robinson added 68 in 12 overs. Fortunately, down in Kent, the favourites were making a hash of things.

Roebuck: I didn't field so I was following the Kent game. It was live on the radio. Wickets kept falling there and each time a huge roar would go round the ground at Trent Bridge.

Marks: That's right. Lots of cheering for no apparent reason which meant another Kent wicket had fallen. It seemed the force was with us.

Taylor: I don't remember that. I was concentrating on my wicketkeeping. I do remember Eddie Hemmings being bowled by Viv and he accused me of whipping the bails off. The ball had just gently lifted them off, you see.

Nottinghamshire lost seven wickets for 46 runs in the end. With similar news coming from Canterbury, it looked as if Somerset were about to snatch the title from the favourites.

Roebuck: They say the trophy was down at Kent but with a helicopter ready to take off if necessary. We were definitely second favourites. But that last hour at Trent Bridge, when we knew we were likely to win, really did become a happy hour.

Rose: Suddenly we were winning easily and Kent were losing badly. By the time 70 per cent of the game was over we knew we were going to win it. Fantastic.

About this time the helicopter must have taken off. Soon afterwards Kent had lost by 55 runs. Nottinghamshire lost by one more. The trophy was flying north.

Marks: So, we'd done it. A fine weekend, you could say. They've got these hanging baskets on the dressing-room balcony at Nottingham, and I do remember Graham Burgess, who'd been in the side since the '60s, getting his boots and he hoisted them up off one of the baskets. He literally hung up his boots. 'That'll do I,' he said. And he retired there and then.

Roebuck: There was a great satisfaction in winning both of them because of '78. We wanted to win both to make it right. By Sunday night we really felt we'd put something to bed.

Marks: We had lots of good players who got increasingly good in the tight situations that present themselves in one-day cricket. But of course the Championship eluded us. It still has. If you want the critical view, it's this: we should have won the Championship as well but we were temperamentally suited to the one-off big days rather than the long haul of the three-day season.

Roebuck: We were left-field, an unusual bunch. The fans liked that too. They played up to the image of county cousins going to London and getting the better of others. The cider flowed. And being captain was a bit like being president of Russia – all these different federations inside and of course in years to come they would battle away and then war would break out. But the point is we weren't a tight, conforming, uniform team.

Garner: We were friends and our success came because of that friendship.

Interviews by Simon Lister

On top down under with Elton and the axis of evil

England retain the Ashes, Australia, 1986–87

England had spent 1986 losing away in the West Indies and at home to India and New Zealand. Their record as they reached Australia to defend the Ashes was eight defeats in 11 Tests and no victories. They had a new captain and – for the first time – a proper coach. As *Wisden* put it, 'they flew from Heathrow carrying the prayers rather than the aspirations of their countrymen'.

Ian Botham (England allrounder): It was the longest tour I've ever done. An Ashes series, two one-day competitions. About five months away.

David Gower (England batsman): You couldn't have been entirely sure how a lot of the side would play. There was the 'axis of evil' of course – Gower, Botham, Lamb – but it was a real mix of experience and yet-to-be-proven talent.

The man charged with making that mix work was the manager Micky Stewart. He was not in Australia for High Commission small talk. England had got themselves a proper coach.

Mike Gatting (England captain): Micky came in, he'd played football, played cricket. He knew what it took to prepare thoroughly for a tour. We were like-minded people.

Micky Stewart: I was appointed in August. They wanted to call me assistant manager, I said, 'No, it's cricket manager.' The committee said 'Sorry' and I said 'Forget it then.' They backed down. I went as team manager.

Chris Broad (England opener): Gatting was my kind of captain. Get up and go, loved a challenge.

Stewart: Gatting was red, white and blue through and through – so was I. He was determined. Loved playing the Australians; loved stuffing them.

Gatting: Micky had a very friendly exterior but underneath there was a harshness, a steeliness and he wanted to be a part of something successful.

Gower: The trickiest problem that Gatting and Micky had was how to work with the various factions within the squad. That is the art of leadership. They managed pretty well and approached people differently and got the best from them. The stark contrast came when Micky went back to Australia with Graham Gooch in charge. They then came up with one plan for 16 players, which, as we now know, is a complete disaster.

A more immediate problem was England's play in the warm-up games. They were beaten by Queensland and outplayed by Western Australia.

Allan Border (Australia captain): England's early form was below par. On the other hand, Australia's preparation had been pretty good – we'd drawn a series in India – and we fancied our chances.

Botham: The first three or four weeks we were playing against Western Australian young farmers and the crop-sprayers of Queensland. I found that pretty hard to get motivated, and as a consequence we got hammered.

Broad: I soon realised that the senior players didn't take these games too seriously. They were acclimatising to the wine and the socialising.

Gower: Personally, the first month of that tour was a nightmare. It felt like the worst build-up to any tour a side could have had. I exaggerate only slightly when I say that the top four had single-figure averages.

Gatting: I had a basic confidence in the side. All that stuff about 'worst team to leave England's shores' – how could it be when you had Botham, Gower, Lamb, Edmonds?

The early scorecards made depressing reading. Then, with the first Test in sight, came news of a more sinister distraction.

Gatting: We had three girls from a tabloid paper fly out to try to trap one or two of the boys just before the first Test. We got wind of it so Micky took on the heroic task of chatting to them in the hotel bar for two nights before the first Test so we knew where they were.

The tabloid teasers were foiled, but a second wave of attack came from the Australians.

Stewart: At the pre-series lunch, some senior bloke from the sponsors, Benson & Hedges, made this big speech saying how sorry he felt for England having to take on the Aussies. The boys were really wound up. The result was I didn't have to do much of a motivational speech the next day.

Botham: One of the British broadsheet papers wrote on the eve of the Brisbane Test that the only problem with the England side was that they can't bat, bowl or field. That really fired us up too.

Gatting: In the team meeting that night Both said, 'Don't worry about what's happened before. The Tests are what count. Eleven v eleven, so let's get out there and take them on.'

Apart from raising morale, Botham had been charged with looking after one of the tour youngsters – Phil DeFreitas, who was only 20. The management had gambled on Beefy thriving on the responsibility. It just about worked.

Phil DeFreitas (England allrounder): As we checked in and got our room keys Botham said, 'C'mon, you're with me.' I went, 'Oh my God.' He was one of my heroes. I was so nervous.

Gatting: I gave Beefy express instructions not to go drinking with him. DeFreitas was a good lad. I remember Botham brought in tumblers of Scotch at one point and Daffy said, 'I can't – the skipper said so.' He was as good as his word. The next morning the two glasses of Scotch were there, untouched.

DeFreitas: I'd gone to bed. Beef came back a couple of hours later with a bottle of whisky. He said, 'You're on tour – pour.' I was so knackered I soon fell asleep. Good job too. If we'd have started he'd have probably made sure we emptied the bottle to teach me a lesson.

The first Test was at Brisbane. Australia won the toss and put England in.

Geoff Lawson (Australia fast bowler): I was 12th man but I should have played. I'd been injured but the opening bowling attack had a total of nine Tests between them. Really inexperienced. I said to the selector, Greg Chappell, 'Mate, I'm not pushing my own barrow here, but you've got it wrong.' We bowled appropriately badly.

Gatting: I was still a little bit nervous about our batting. David Gower hadn't got so many runs and I decided to do three and he went in five. That decision was made after the toss.

The first innings – and the match – was defined by a fifty from Gower and a hundred from Botham.

Gatting: They dropped Gower horribly. He sliced one to third slip and they spilled it. As good a player as him doesn't need a second chance and he and Both put on some runs.

Gower: It helps every now and then to have a bit of luck, whatever people say. I started to rediscover what it was all about. It was my most important innings of the tour – even though I was to get a hundred at Perth. By battling away to get fifty-odd at the Gabba, I actually rediscovered some confidence.

Botham's 138 included 22 taken off one over bowled by Merv Hughes. Wisden compared the innings to his century at Old Trafford against Australia in 1981.

Border: The couple of hours that Botham batted was a key moment in the entire series. It went from bad to worse for us and set the tone for the tour.

Five wickets from Graham Dilley in the first innings made sure the Australians followed on, and five more from John Emburey in the second meant England needed only 75 to win the game on the last day. The bowling had been as good as the batting.

Stewart: It used to drive me barmy that England bowlers that summer would beat the bat twice, try a yorker which was actually a half-volley, beat the bat twice more, get cross and throw in a bouncer that was top-edged over the slips and suddenly they had eight runs from the over. The idea now was to make them fight for every run.

Gatting: We bowled tremendous lines and the two spinners kept it very tight. Edmonds and Emburey didn't get many wickets but played a huge part in the series.

Gower: The result was a bit of a surprise. It was a tour of discovery because we had old and new with Gatt on his first trip as captain and Micky Stewart trying to find his feet as manager. There were lots of things to play with. A bit of experimentation going on. Lots of things to work out.

Stewart: I knew how a losing dressing room could get down and how one win could make such a difference. I thought it was a talented side, better than the Australians' in fact. But I'd never known such a bunch of talented people with such little confidence. I wanted to boost that confidence and get the big players performing.

The second Test at Perth was drawn. Chris Broad scored the first of his three Ashes centuries and Bill Athey showed what a good opening partner he was. Gatting became the first England captain to declare in Australia since Ray Illingworth 16 years previously.

Gower: To predict that Broad and Athey would have the series they did would have taken a bloody good crystal ball. Broad had been in the side then out of it; Athey had been round about the side without really making it big.

Broad: The outfield was so fast. It was like an upturned saucer. If you got it past the infield it was four runs. Bill and I got away to a terrific start.

Lawson: During the first Test I fell over the fence by the old dog track on the way back from nets. I shouldn't have played at Perth – let alone run in and bowled. I was on painkillers, had about four catches dropped. I was bowling line and length but not very fast.

At Adelaide, in the third Test, there was another first-innings score of more than 500 – this time for Australia. But England, growing in confidence, replied with 455. Another draw suited them – if not all of the crowd. 'A female spectator set up an ironing board and attended to her laundry throughout the fifth day's play,' noted the Wisden Book of Test Cricket. *Then came Melbourne.*

Border: The fourth Test. We were about to cop another shellacking.

Gatting: Graham Dilley came up to me 20 minutes before I had to toss up and said, 'I've done me knee in' and so we had to choose between Gladstone Small and Neil Foster all of a sudden. We chose Gladstone and after his first over, he'd hardly hit the mown track – one down the leg side, one wide on the off. I thought, 'I've picked the wrong one here.'

But Gladstone was just nervous. Botham, who had missed the third Test with a side strain, was back – but not back to his best. Even so, both Small and Botham finished with first-innings five-fors.

Botham: I was about 50–60% fit but we felt like it might do a bit, so I waddled in off a few paces and the Australian batsmen obliged.

Gatting: Beefy was still struggling – nowhere near the pace of Brisbane – and you wouldn't say it was his best five-for. But there were some unbelievable catches by Jack Richards behind the stumps.

DeFreitas: I bowled one of my best spells in Test cricket and didn't get a wicket – had no luck at all. Both came on, bowled a load of rubbish and got a five-for.

Gatting: Gower caught Dean Jones off a leading edge – that was very important. I screamed, 'Catch it David' and he casually jogged in and his first words were 'There's no need to shout.' The other big wicket came in the second innings when Gladstone got Border. I was thinking, 'third slip or gully?' I plumped for a slip and Border got a bit of width and absolutely kitchen-sinked this ball and Emburey had one hand round it at full stretch, and that was the moment I thought, 'We're gonna win this.'

Gatting was right. With Border out, Australia were heading for defeat by an innings. Their last seven wickets fell for 41 runs. Merv Hughes scooped Phil Edmonds to Gladstone Small at deep backward-square and the Ashes were England's. In the dressing room, a special fan arrived to help with the celebrations.

Stewart: Elton John had been in Australia for much of the tour. He had a good friendship with Botham and Gower. That was a surprise wasn't it? He was also a great red, white and blue man – a true sporting Corinthian actually.

Gatting: He got champagne thrown all over one of his silk suits which had cost him about five grand. It was great having a legend like him in the dressing room.

Gower: Elton had become our No. 1 groupie. He was not supposed to be on tour in Australia when we were but he had to have an operation on his throat, so he decided to stay. He knows his cricket and he's a clever bloke. We saw a lot of him. If it had been Joe Bloggs following us on tour we wouldn't have him in the dressing room but we didn't mind Elton there. He's not short of a bob or two, but he is a very generous soul and he looked after us.

Defeat for England at Sydney in the final Test was irritating, but as far as this Ashes series was concerned irrelevant. It did though provide a hint of what was to come in future Test series between England and Australia.

Broad: Australia weren't a poor side, they were an emerging side. The one thing we took an age to realise, and that Australia had started doing, was to pick players who they thought would be very good and to stick with them and make them better.

Gower: Even if Australia are below par, they're still not bad. Like there's no such thing as a bad champagne – well, there is actually, but anyway – there's no such thing as a truly bad Australian side. The fact was that during the tour we took control at the right moments.

Lawson: People tend to forget that we lost half a dozen of our best players to the South African rebel tours. Alderman, Hogg, Rackemann. People gloss over the fact that we weren't trotting out with our first-string side.

Stewart: We won everything. The Ashes, both one-day series which included West Indies. We wanted to win every session, every day. It was very satisfying. Hour by hour, over by over. Every ball was an individual match.

DeFreitas: Only when I got back to England did I realise what it was that we had achieved.

Gatting: Bringing back the Ashes was without doubt my best moment as a cricketer.

Border: It was probably the lowest point for Australian cricket in my experience. We'd had some pretty ordinary performances for a few years. I'll never forget being in the sheds at the MCG [Melbourne Cricket Ground] when we were drowning our sorrows. The tennis player Pat Cash was winning the Davis Cup for Australia on the dressing-room TV. Speaking at the tennis, the Australian Prime Minister Bob Hawke said, 'It's a pity there weren't more Pat Cashes at the MCG today.' There was this stunned silence and I thought a few beer cans would fly at the screen. Even the Prime Minister was having a go. Later that evening, after a thousand beers, we promised ourselves that it had to stop there and we made a pact that it wouldn't ever be that bad again.

Interviews by Simon Lister

CHAPTER 2

Politics (On and Off the Pitch)

I'm from the IRA. Can you show me to
the England dressing room?

Photographer Graham Morris during England's 1984–85 tour of India

overleaf:
**The Oval is ringed with barbed wire to prevent vandalism by anti-
apartheid demonstrators ahead of South Africa's abortive 1970 tour
of England**

The empire strikes back

England v Rest of the World, England, 1970

In 1968 South Africa refused to let Basil D'Oliveira into the country with the rest of the England team because of the colour of his skin. Two years later there was enormous pressure for South Africa's tour to England to be scrapped. Trouble loomed. Anti-apartheid protesters promised disruption and the England players had their lives insured for £15,000. At the last moment the tour was cancelled. It looked like the summer of 1970 would be without international cricket, so a five-Test series between England and a Rest of the World side was hastily put together.

Ray Illingworth (England captain): We were bitterly disappointed that South Africa weren't coming. We had a very good side with Alan Ward and John Snow – so I reckon we had them in the bowling department. Of course they batted right the way down and had just whopped the Australians. So it would have been a marvellous series.

Graeme Pollock (South Africa and RoW batsman): We'd just beaten the Australians 4–0 in South Africa. We were getting to the prime of our time. I think we did feel that we had the best side in world cricket – we'd been together since 1963 and had just kept getting stronger.

The South Africa tour wasn't called off until the middle of May. Huge demonstrations had been planned by anti-apartheid protesters. One of the organisers was a student, future cabinet minister Peter Hain.

Peter Hain: There was an escalating tension and pressure in the final weeks. When the tour was eventually cancelled I was relieved beyond belief. We had been determined to stop it and had lots of ingenious protests planned. We'd discovered that a disused branch line of the London Underground had an air vent that led directly up to the concourse inside Lord's.

Derek Underwood (England spin bowler): I remember that there was a lot of bad publicity. Talk of barriers being built at Lord's. It was the right decision to take but it was also very disappointing.

Illingworth: We knew about the changes very late – in fact it was so late that there was already barbed wire up around Lord's to stop protesters. Many things happen in the world today which are as bad as apartheid but cricket still gets played in those places.

Pollock: We all anticipated that there would be hassles. There was an awful lot of uncertainty. But we never thought we'd be away from Test matches for 22 years. There was always hope that we'd be back sooner not later, but we were wrong.

The first Test was at Lord's. England lost the toss on a humid morning and Garry Sobers ran through them. It was a heavy defeat.

Clive Lloyd (West Indies and RoW batsman): We had an excellent side – the near-perfect team. Spin and pace, great batsmen and two fine wicketkeepers.

Illingworth: I lost the toss in the first Test – if I hadn't, it would have been a nice match. That two-hour spell of swing in the first morning ruined it and after then we could only try to save the game. We were annihilated, but came back very strongly.

Mike Denness (England batsman): It was a pretty difficult morning – Garry Sobers was making the ball talk. I edged Graham McKenzie to slip, low down. There was a nod and a wink from Eddie Barlow who caught it. Of course I believed him. Later when I was fielding near the umpire, Arthur Fagg at square leg, he said: 'I wouldn't have given you out if I'd been asked.'

England won the next game at Trent Bridge thanks to a century from Brian Luckhurst. At the time the authorities said the games would be official Tests with caps awarded. Later, they changed their minds.

Underwood: When they took away Test status, that was a blow. I mean Brian Luckhurst – he grafted for that hundred at Nottingham. Against that attack, it should have counted as two Test centuries. And another thing – if the games had been official, I would have reached 300 Test wickets!

Denness: Why did all these lads suffer? It wasn't as if it was a Mickey Mouse set-up. Alan Jones never played for England again.

In between the matches, many of the RoW players returned to their English county sides, before meeting up two days before the next Test.

Lloyd: I remember we had single rooms, which was unusual. Normally just the senior players would get that treatment. I took some of the ideas when I became captain of West Indies. For instance we all ate together the night before each Test to discuss tactics. I'd never done that before.

Denness: The Rest of the World side took it very seriously. They were desperate to make sure it would be a competitive series.

Mushtaq Mohammad (Pakistan and RoW batsman): The night before the match we all got together for a meal. Usually it would be a time to discuss strategy. But how do you tell the best players in the world how to play? So it always ended up being a party. Garry would say: 'Do your best, let's enjoy it and have a drink.'

Clive Lloyd was hilarious. In the dressing room at Edgbaston there was a map of Britain on the wall, and Clive was pointing out the cities: 'Glasgow, Newcastle, Leeds, Manchester.' When he reached Birmingham he jabbed his finger at the map, saying 'And here – this is where the boys are beating that ball.'

After winning at Edgbaston, the RoW clinched the series at Headingley in the fourth Test. It was the closest of all the games – a two-wicket victory.

Illingworth: They were good. There'd never been a side like it. They had everything – but it was much closer than the 4–1 result suggests. We dropped two catches at Edgbaston that turned the game and at Headingley Arthur Fagg gave a couple of terrible decisions that cost us. We could have been going to The Oval at two each.

Mushtaq: I'll never forget in the last game at The Oval watching Sobers and Graeme Pollock scoring for fun. Someone on the balcony shouted: 'Lads, come and watch – you will not see this again.' They were matching each other stroke for stroke. It was like, 'whatever you can do, I can do better'. It was entertainment of the highest class.

Hain: I was a big cricket fan and enjoyed the series on television, although it had an element of unreality about it. I was a left-handed batsman and Graeme Pollock was my hero. Like him I was brought up in South Africa. It was a historical irony that I was responsible for stopping his career in mid-term.

Lloyd: The whole situation seemed so silly. We weren't allowed to take on South Africa, but here I was playing alongside half of their team in a Test match.

Pollock: It was embarrassing to live abroad and then have to go home and live a completely different way of life. You have to remember that in South Africa at the time if you criticised things your life became very difficult. In the end our conscience demanded that we had to show our hand.

Hain: The South African players were cross at the time – I was a hate figure for them. But I think they have come to accept that sadly their careers were a necessary sacrifice for the ultimate good. After he'd been released from prison, Nelson Mandela told me that the 'Stop the Tour' campaign was a decisive moment for the anti-apartheid struggle.

Pollock: We could have made a bigger noise about apartheid at the time – I think that's a genuine criticism. In hindsight, perhaps we should have done more.

Illingworth: We saw ourselves as cricketers – it began and ended there. We had a laugh and that was it. No one thought about colour.

Although the series would end up not counting towards the England players' averages, they were playing for a place on the tour to Australia.

Underwood: We can rightly say that we did pretty well in that series – especially given the result of the first match. And we had a very good captain. Raymond was tactically very sound and my goodness he was determined. He'd probably never played better in his career.

Illingworth: I thought that Colin Cowdrey was automatically being lined up to take the side to Australia that winter, but as the series went on, it became clear to me that most of the selectors wanted me to be captain – apart from the odd dissenting voice. The thing about Cowdrey was that the pros didn't trust him. He was a funny bloke. He'd promise you the moon and then nothing would happen.

Lloyd: I learned a lot. It was very interesting for me to look at all these players and see how great some of them were. It made me realise how far West Indies still had to go.

Mushtaq: After it all finished I was left with a funny feeling because we weren't playing under a flag. Despite the victories, there wasn't the 'feather in the cap' feeling when I was winning with Pakistan. It had been an honour, but at the same time the inner satisfaction was missing.

Interviews by Simon Lister

Lever swings and the gauze slips

Accusations of ball-tampering taint England's victorious tour of India, 1976–77

England had not won in India since Douglas Jardine's tour of 1933–34. The odds of breaking that sequence seemed slim as an England team minus Geoffrey Boycott took on India's legendary spinning trio of Bedi, Venkat and Chandrasekhar. By the end of the series Tony Greig had claimed a famous victory but it was a success tainted by controversy. Accusations of ball-tampering and cheating have left scars that are still felt today.

Mike Selvey (England bowler): Greigy told me two years beforehand that this was the tour to go on. He was right. Everything about it was great. We all gelled and the whole thing was fantastic. We met some great people and visited some amazing places. Greig was an extremely charismatic and compelling captain. I would have done anything for him.

John Lever (England bowler): I didn't really appreciate how hard a tour it was going to be. At the start Tony Greig said it was not going to be easy and that there would be days when we did not feel well. Alan Knott was fanatical about not getting ill. He said the last time he was in India he was ill because of the tiny droplets of water on the packets of butter. He did not eat any butter for the whole tour – he was that particular. Bananas on toast was our main meal.

Bishan Bedi (India captain): It was not a very pleasant trip. It was one of the forgettable moments of my career and not a great time for cricket in general. The controversies had a big effect. It was not very long after that trip that Packer was born and it was just not a great time for the game.

There were no one-day internationals, only five Test matches and warm-up games. Essex bowler John Lever played his way into the team and made his debut in the first Test at Delhi. It was to be some debut.

Lever: Tony was a shrewd cricketer. We used a lot of their cricket balls in the run-up to the Test series. I told Kenny Barrington that they were swinging all over the place and could we use them in the Test series. We had brought balls with us and we had the choice of which ones to use in the Tests but we went for the Indian balls and I think that pleased them. But the balls were hand-wound and were easy to get out of shape. That gave them an imbalance.

Dennis Amiss had given England a platform with his 179 but India started their reply confidently until the new ball went out of shape and was changed. India were 43 without loss when the match and series turned.

Selvey: The first ball had not gone off the straight. We managed to get the ball changed. I don't know whether it was out of shape. I think Knotty lost it and chucked it under the stand. The first delivery with the new ball hooped down leg side. Keith Fletcher was at second slip and told [Lever] to aim it out there.

Lever: This ball felt as though I could aim it at the slips and it would come back. It was great fun. What I had achieved didn't really sink in.

Lever took four wickets in 16 balls and went on to take 10 in the match. India followed on. It was left to Derek Underwood to mop up the following day. It was the start of his duel with Sunil Gavaskar.

Tony Greig (England captain): I did not think the great Sunil Gavaskar would be a threat. He had a real problem with

Underwood. He could not play him. If he did not get out to Derek Underwood, then he got out to another bowler because Underwood had put him under pressure. He could not pick Underwood's straight ball.

England's victory at Delhi set the tone for the next two Tests. In Calcutta it was Greig who was to be England's hero with a seven-hour hundred that paved the way for victory.

Derek Underwood: When Bedi won the toss he did a jig of delight because he thought that would mean they would win the Test but Greigy went on to play brilliantly.

Selvey: They prepared a complete road for the second Test. Just before the match they were scrubbing the pitch with wire brushes. We got them out for 150 but then Greigy got an outstanding hundred. He was very ill and had a temperature in the 100s. But he came out and batted all day in 90-degree heat.

Greig: That innings was a turning point of the tour. I got sick overnight but I got through it. In some ways I think it may have helped me. I also had a technique to play spin, especially Bedi. What also helped me was Kenny Barrington. He was a terrific manager who did not interfere too much. Whenever I looked up during that innings he would be sat in a chair on his own watching. He was a superstitious man and would not move in case something happened, so he sat in that chair for seven hours.

Claims of ball-tampering tainted the third Test. In Madras England struggled with the heat and Lever and Bob Willis asked the England management to help them stop sweat running in their eyes.

Selvey: The bowlers were complaining to Bernard Thomas [physiotherapist] that sweat was getting in their eyes. Boxers put Vaseline on their brows and it channels the sweat away from the eyes. Bernard didn't have any Vaseline; he only had some Vaseline-impregnated gauze. He stuck these to JK's and Willis's foreheads but when they bowled, the things slipped down over their eyes, so they took the gauze off.

Lever: I had these two white strips above my eyes but it did not feel right so I chucked it away. It was pounced on by Bish. He went to the umpires and he ran off to the press tent saying he had caught us cheating. We had not done anything different, though.

Lever was reported by the umpires for carrying the Vaseline gauzes, a breach, they felt, of Law 46 governing fair play. Bedi claimed he'd had his suspicions in earlier Test matches.

Bedi: When I brought it up my board did not back me up. John Lever was made a scapegoat and it was being done at the behest of somebody higher. If there had been an ICC [International Cricket Council] in those days, then a lot of people in the England camp might have lost their jobs.

Lever: Bishan Bedi was under a lot of pressure. He was a Sikh from the north, and when we went to Madras in the south, there was a lot of talk about the captain being changed. That was when it all blew up. He was grabbing at straws and looking for a way out. I had worked hard in county cricket and I wasn't about to let it all be taken away by someone accusing me of cheating.

Lever was cleared of intentionally breaking Law 46 after it was explained why he was wearing the Vaseline gauze but he still came in for heavy criticism from the crowd.

Lever: It was a fairly hard time for my parents. They had press people sat outside their house. My dad had a heart attack, which stopped him working – I'm sure it was linked. It is because of that kind of thing that I find it hard to forgive Bish and I only made up with him last year. I felt he really stuck the knife in on that trip.

England's victory in Madras ended the series but India struck back in Bangalore. The bad feeling between the two sides spilled over as accusations of cheating by the umpires were made. Umpire Mohammad Ghouse came in for particular criticism.

Underwood: They brought in the Butcher of Bangalore [Ghouse]. He was involved in a whole spate of decisions, especially in our second innings.

Greig: They had a bit of a problem in those days. [S.K.] Wankhede [Minister of Sports] had just built a huge stadium in Bombay and they needed a full house for the last Test. They were worried no one would turn up and I don't know whether he was under some sort of pressure. All I know is that he had a very bad game.

Lever: I had not seen umpiring like it. It was not even subtle. If we got hit on the pad and it went to short leg, then we were struggling. I bowled pretty well and had a few shouts for lbw but nothing was given. The umpire could not even look me in the eye. He was there to do a job and he did it.

Selvey: They brought in Yajurvindra Singh. He stood at short leg and equalled the world record of catches, some of which had hit the bat. Willis was last man. Singh needed one catch for the world record but as Willis walked out he said there is no way he's getting that record. He went down the pitch for a big mow and was stumped.

India won in Bangalore by 140 runs. England were exhausted by the time the fifth Test started. It ended as a draw.

Lever: I have so many fond memories of that trip. We were a close unit and still are today. County cricket was never the same again after that tour. I would play against people I'd toured with and stay at their house rather than the team hotel.

For Greig it was his last tour for England. Packer and World Series Cricket came calling 12 months later and the England team, which he had led so successfully in India, broke up.

Interviews by Nick Hoult

Murder for starters

Assassination fails to stop play during England's tour of India, 1984–85

Murder, violence and racial tension: England's tour to India was one of the most dramatic in recent history. The cricket was not bad either, with David Gower's team pulling off a remarkable comeback.

England arrived in Delhi in the early hours of Wednesday 31 October. The plan was a quiet night's sleep and gentle introduction to the tour. It was not to be. India was plunged into turmoil when the premier Indira Gandhi was assassinated by one of her Sikh bodyguards.

Tony Brown (England tour manager): I was woken up by the telephone ringing. I didn't really know where I was and the person asked for Graham Morris [photographer]. The caller told me Mrs Gandhi had been assassinated. I immediately woke up then. I told David Gower but we didn't wake the lads up straightaway.

Graeme Fowler (England batsman): I remember getting in the lift to go down for breakfast and an American in there said 'you guys have picked a great time to come to India'. I had no idea what he was talking about until he said Mrs Gandhi had been shot.

The squad were left kicking their heels in the hotel and friction soon developed.

Brown: The players called a meeting and Allan Lamb said they wanted to go home. I explained to them what we were doing and there was no reason for anyone to be frightened. I offered them their passports and said they were free to go.

Fowler: Tony Brown really lost it. He asked us what our thoughts were. We all sat down and had a chat and then called Brown in and told him that there was no point staying. We were willing to go anywhere to get some practice until it calmed down. We did not want to go home. Brown, who could be a lovely guy, came in with a pile of passports and said we could all f*** off then.

England were advised that it would be unwise to leave before Mrs Gandhi's funeral while there was civil unrest on the streets.

Fowler: We didn't have a clue what was going on. We ended up getting more information from people in London than in India.

Colin Bateman (*Daily Express*): We saw several incidents of Sikh rickshaws and businesses being torched. We went to the hospital where Mrs Gandhi had been taken and Graham Morris was taking pictures when the crowd turned on us. They grabbed Graham's camera and came after us. We ran round the corner and thankfully our taxi driver was waiting with the doors open and the engine running.

A two-week period of national mourning was announced. Unable to train, England were invited to Sri Lanka. They played two warm-up matches in Colombo before returning to India.

Brown: We realised we had to get out if we were going to prepare for the first Test. Once Mrs Gandhi's funeral was out of the way we slipped away. The moment we arrived in Colombo, though, somebody bombed the bus station. But at least we were able to practise for a few days. While we were in Sri Lanka we heard that Martyn Moxon's father had died.

England flew into Bombay before taking on India Under-25s in Ahmedabad. England were given their first glimpse of Mohammad Azharuddin and Laxman Sivaramakrishnan.

Brown: We flew to Bombay where the British deputy high commissioner Percy Norris threw a party for us. He was a splendid bloke. No one wanted to leave. We stayed until quite late.

The following morning Norris was shot dead on his way to work. The tour was plunged into crisis 24 hours before the first Test.

Brown: I had a running argument with Richard Streeton of *The Times*. He thought we should go home. But we felt that if you thought you were going to be at risk on the cricket field then you would never play anywhere. There is nothing to stop someone taking a pot shot at you at Lord's or Bombay.

Fowler: A few hours after the killing we got on a bus and drove through the spot where he was killed. We had no security. That was a great move by the management. We got a message from Lord's saying we were expected to stay in India. I thought bollocks to that.

Matthew Engel (*Guardian*): The England team were a much higher-profile target than Percy Norris and nobody knew if this was an attack on British interests. It was reckless to play that Test match and it was a decision taken by the lords in the Foreign Office.

Not surprisingly England were soundly beaten by eight wickets despite Mike Gatting's long-awaited maiden Test hundred.

Laxman Sivaramakrishnan (India spin bowler): I was brought into the team because England were considered to be weak against leg spin. There was a bit of tragedy just before the series when one of the English ambassadors was killed. It was a major problem at the time. We wore black bands on our sleeves but continued anyway.

Fowler: We had some shocking umpiring. I remember Sivaramakrishnan had an appeal against me turned down. He burst into tears. Gavaskar made a big play of handing him a handkerchief. Next over he had another appeal against me. Surprise, surprise, I was given out. Tim Robinson had two bad shouts as well.

Graham Morris (photographer): The security had supposedly been increased. On the first day of the Test I walked in wearing my camera jacket which had lots of pockets that could have held a bomb. Nobody checked me. I went up to the most senior security man I could find and said: 'I'm from the IRA. Can you show me to the England dressing room?' He took me right to the door.

On the previous tour to India, England had lost the first Test and were then faced with a series of flat pitches as India strengthened their hand. Gower feared the same again. He need not have worried. England levelled the series in Delhi.

Brown: The Bhopal disaster [a toxic gas leak killing thousands of people] had happened a few days before and that caused huge problems in India.

Fowler: They got me out of bed to bat. I lost half a stone in five days with Delhi belly.

The third Test at Calcutta was drawn due to bad weather. Gavaskar was booed for his cautious approach and the Indian side was riven with strife after Kapil Dev had been dropped.

Fowler: The crowd got a bit restless. There were about 110,000 in the ground who were fed up with dull cricket. When we fielded Lamby played up to the crowd. He threw an orange at a policeman's helmet. All of a sudden the crowd threw thousands of oranges at him. They were just giving him more ammunition. We were so bored we sat down while fielding at slip.

The fourth Test was England's finest performance. Double hundreds from Gatting and Fowler and 11 wickets from Neil Foster gave England a 2–1 lead.

Neil Foster (England bowler): I was not selected until the fourth Test. I found out on the morning of the match that I was in. I bowled a bit full to begin with but then I bowled Gavaskar a full toss which he missed. It all went from there. India had just won the World Cup and they batted as if they were playing a one-day game.

Fowler: I ripped the skin off my knee fielding in the first over and it went septic. I later did the same thing with my other knee. Neil Foster was a real hero. We then batted. I remember being 149 not out in the last over when Gatt said I'd done enough for the day and he would bat it out. That was a great gesture. When I got off my knees were stuck to my pants and my trousers to my pads because of the pus from my knees.

Fowler went on to make 201 the following day.

Fowler: It was over 100°F and I remember there was a fish market next to the ground. If the wind blew the wrong way, which it seemed to do a lot of the time, you got this overpowering smell that made your eyes sting. I had batted nearly nine and a half hours. When I got to 200 I remember thinking they can't take that away from me and that my dad would be pleased. It felt like a weight had been lifted off my shoulders and I was out within a few minutes.

Foster: Gatt and Fowler were given chocolate cakes by the manager of our hotel but I got nothing. They lionise batters over there. At least I got a share of the cake.

The final Test at Kanpur was drawn and England won the series 2–1. They left India to travel to Australia for a one-day tournament. England lost every game in the tournament.

Engel: The players were knackered. We were all knackered. I remember they were beaten by New South Wales B. I wrote a stinging article attacking their professionalism having spent the day asleep on the banks of the Manly Oval.

Fowler: I missed India when I got home. It had got under my skin. The Red Fort, the Taj Mahal, sailing down the Ganges and wandering around the cities. Great memories.

Interviews by Nick Hoult

The tale of five captains

England's dismal summer of 1988

England won the one-day series 3–0 and, with West Indies in transition, seemed ready to make waves in 1988. They did – but for the wrong reasons. Five captains, 23 players and four Test defeats later English cricket was again a laughing stock.

It all started so well. England ended their 10-match losing streak against West Indies when bad weather and the excellent Graham Gooch earned a draw at Trent Bridge.

That was the end of the good times. A few days after the Test the captain Mike Gatting had been sacked by chairman of selectors Peter May after tabloid revelations that a barmaid had been in his hotel room.

England committee statement: The selectors emphasised that they did not believe the allegations in the newspapers and accepted Gatting's account of what happened, namely nothing. The selectors were concerned, however, that Gatting behaved irresponsibly by inviting female company to his room for a drink in the late evening.

Mike Gatting: The selectors asked me for an explanation, which I gave. They tell me they believe my version of the events, even issuing a statement saying so, and then sack me. I couldn't believe it.

David Gower (England batsman, from his autobiography): Micky Stewart, England coach, was down in Swansea and was staying in the same hotel as two of the cricket correspondents. The two pressmen arrived in the breakfast room before him and had been choking on their toast at the front page of the *Sun* when Micky walked in. A scribe walked over and plonked the *Sun* on the manager's table, whereupon a large amount of coughing and spluttering ensued. Stewart hastily dismissed the waitress, scuttled out to find a telephone and set off not for the cricket ground at St Helens but Lord's.

Alan Lee wrote in *The Times*: There will be no smugness at his [Gatting's] fall from grace, no jealous chuckling, only a sense of sadness that one whose life has been wrapped up in cricket should have failed in a job he had never dreamed he could aspire to.

Gower: The players were stunned by what had happened and, as you can imagine, morale went from something approaching good to rock bottom overnight.

Gatting was replaced as captain by his Middlesex colleague John Emburey for the second Test at Lord's. Gatting did not want to be considered for the Lord's Test and scored three hundreds for Middlesex instead.

John Emburey: It was a difficult time for Gatt and his family. He wanted to keep a low profile but he wished me good luck.

After the Gatting affair Stewart cracked down on discipline.

Gower: We were told that we were not to be seen in public after 10 p.m. Given the West Indies' slow over rate this left us with an outside chance of being fined while still on the field. On the eve of a Test there were two or three of us having a drink at the hotel bar counting down the minutes and seconds as the clock ticked around.

Malcolm Marshall's six wickets gave West Indies a first-innings lead and they then made 397 to leave England needing 442 or to bat for two days. They managed one and a bit. Emburey took 1 for 79. It got worse at Old Trafford. Marshall's 7 for 22 in the second innings resulted in a thrashing for England. Emburey's reign was over after two matches.

Emburey: During that period I was not bowling well and after two defeats Peter May thought I should go back to county cricket and rediscover my form. I was disappointed that within a space of three weeks I had gone from the highest point in my career to the lowest. To be realistic, though, I was not bowling well enough.

Mark Nicholas of Hampshire, Bill Athey of Gloucestershire and Kent's Chris Cowdrey were considered as replacements. May opted for his godson and a Cowdrey was England captain again.

Chris Cowdrey: They were not going to go back to David Gower, so there weren't too many candidates for the job. We were at the top of the Championship with a side that had been written off; that gave me a good chance of getting the England job.

It was made clear that I would captain in the last two Tests and that I would lead the side to India later that year. I felt confident that I would have time to prove myself.

Cowdrey's captaincy began in an inauspicious way when a gateman at Headingley refused to let him into the ground.

Cowdrey: I had hardly played at Headingley because Kent's Yorkshire games were often staged on festival weekends at Scarborough or Harrogate. He wouldn't believe I was the England captain and I had to park next door.

Robin Smith came in for his debut and Worcestershire's Tim Curtis replaced Martyn Moxon. When Allan Lamb and Smith added 103 for the fifth wicket, England were in a good position on a ropey pitch but Lamb pulled a calf muscle and Cowdrey was quickly to discover what the job was all about.

Cowdrey: In those days we did not meet until Wednesday lunchtime, which seems ridiculous now. I ended up going in at No. 7. It was a hard thing to go into the dressing room having never played a Test in England and to start telling the likes of Gooch and Gower what to do. Once the match started I settled into the job.

For Gower it was his 100th Test but last of the summer. He was dropped after Headingley.

Gower: My memory from that match is of receiving a commemorative medal to mark my 100th Test and chatting to Brian Johnston in an interview. He asked me whether I would like to have any two words erased from my career ('laid back' being the two he had in mind) and I said, 'Yes, caught Dujon.'

Cowdrey was dismissed for 0 by Marshall, and as England slumped in the second innings, he was bowled by Courtney Walsh. It would be his last ball in Test cricket.

Cowdrey: I felt under more pressure in the first innings than the second. I didn't think I was out in the first innings as I thought the ball had done too much but in the second I was beaten by a quick ball that nipped back. Still, I was definitely going to play at The Oval.

Wrong. Cowdrey was struck on the foot by Somerset's Adrian Jones during a county match and was ruled out of the Test.

Cowdrey: I would like to have been given until the morning of the match as Allan Lamb was. But looking back it was the right decision because I would not have been able to play in a five-day Test.

Gower: By this time both PBH [Peter May] and Micky were beginning to have doubts about their original casting of Chris as the saviour of English cricket, and this came across in the differing nature of telephone calls from the England manager to his two wounded men. We had this bizarre situation in which the England captain was being persuaded to drop out two days before the match while the No. 4 batsman was given until the morning of the game. His [Cowdrey's] opinion of Stewart after that episode was not a great deal higher than mine.

Cowdrey: My initial appointment was for the two remaining Tests against West Indies. I was never officially appointed for the Sri Lanka Test but, as I had been selected before, I felt I had a good chance of getting picked for that game. I did not go to the West Indies Test as I was having treatment on my foot but I expected to hear from England at some stage.

It was not to be. Stewart and May turned to Gooch, who the year previously had stood down as Essex captain. England took a first-innings lead at The Oval and set West Indies 225 to win. Gooch split his finger fielding in the slips. Enter Derek Pringle – captain No. 5. England lost by 8 wickets, and when they played a one-off Test against Sri Lanka, Cowdrey had been forgotten.

Cowdrey: I was supposed to have a chat with Micky Stewart but I never heard from him. I was playing at Chesterfield when I heard Graham Gooch had been appointed captain for the final Test of the summer. That hurt and it all ended in a very sad way. When I look back I was never given a chance to prove that I could have been captain for three or four years. It just came at the wrong time for me. Kent were chasing the title but I could hardly have turned England down. A year later it was my benefit and I had a golf day at Sunningdale. Gooch, Gatting and Emburey all turned up to play and we remain good mates to this day.

Interviews by Nick Hoult

Rebels take a step too far

The English rebel tour of South Africa, 1989

The 1980s was the era of rebel tours. In 1989 Dr Ali Bacher, South African cricket's leading administrator, planned one more trip. A tour by an English team was proposed. As Australia regained the Ashes in style the England team was being torn apart by the lure of the South African rand. An English team had already toured South Africa in 1981. They were followed by the biggest coup of them all, a West Indies team in 1982, and an Australian side under Kim Hughes in 1985.

Ali Bacher: In the 1980s I felt that apartheid would be around for the rest of my life, which meant we would be isolated for life. I was also a professional cricket administrator and it was my job to keep the game alive in South Africa. The game was stagnating in my country.

The summer of 1989 began with England favourites to retain the Ashes. Australia were dominant from the start and the summer was played out against a backdrop of innuendo over the rebel tour, recruited by off-spinner John Emburey.

Bacher: My first contact was with John Emburey in Johannesburg in 1988–89. He was the first point of contact for me but thereafter he quickly handed that responsibility over to David Graveney. It took about a year to plan and execute.

Angus Fraser (Middlesex bowler, who made his Test debut in 1989): The Middlesex dressing room was full of it. John Emburey was testing the water and checking whether people would be interested. I was aware something was taking place well before it came out during the Old Trafford Test.

Roland Butcher (Middlesex batsman): I was in the middle of my benefit year and I was coming towards the end of my career. I thought I would not be playing for too much longer and my initial inclination was to take the offer.

After losing the first Test, England were thumped in the second. At Edgbaston the rain saved England, but plans for the rebel tour were well under way.

Fraser: I made my debut at Edgbaston and I sensed there was something being discussed. There were clandestine chats going on and it was a distraction. They were chatting at the back of the dressing room and not at the front so Micky Stewart wouldn't hear them.

Micky Stewart (England coach): I suspected things here and there. I fronted up to a few players and they were not in a position to tell me the facts. I knew there was something not quite right.

David Gower (England captain): I had no idea what was going on. The similarity between 1981 and 1989 was that the England captain didn't know what was going on. The captain of England would never sanction anything that threatened his team so I was not told. People had to make a decision over whether or not they took the offer or stayed loyal to England.

Players were to be paid between £80,000 and £100,000 for tours in 1989–90 and 1990–91. The tours were to be financed through gate receipts in South Africa and television contracts.

Bruce French (Nottinghamshire wicketkeeper): They wanted a wicketkeeper. I had been out of the game for a year through injury and Jack Russell had come into the England side. It looked difficult to get back. I thought I would earn more from the tour than playing international cricket.

It was on the fourth day of the Old Trafford Test that the news of the tour was finally made public. Three players – Tim Robinson, Emburey and Neil Foster – were playing in the match.

Fraser: It gathered momentum and we knew it would come out during the Test. It shattered the dream. I can understand those that wanted one last pay day. Neil Foster's knees had gone and he knew it made sense to take the money but he bowled with tears in his eyes at Old Trafford.

Gower: Ted Dexter [chairman of selectors] and Micky Stewart knew something about it but decided not to tell me. It was another thing on a long list of things they did not tell me that summer. The first thing I knew about it was that weekend in Manchester when it became public knowledge. Finally they [Dexter and Stewart] took me into a room and said there was something they wanted to tell me. I ended up having to go out on to the field knowing the Ashes were almost lost and with some of my players playing their last game.

Butcher: I have always wanted to know how the news leaked out. The meetings were supposed to be confidential and we were told to keep it very quiet. We had our final meeting when we all agreed to the tour and that the news would come out at the end of the season. But the very next day I was approached at Lord's by the chairman of selectors, who asked me what I knew about the rebel tour. A newspaper then named all 16 players and got all 16 right. I would love to know how they got those names.

The implosion of the England team was the final victory for Australia, who easily wrapped up the Ashes at Old Trafford. The rebel party, captained by Mike Gatting, included two black players – Phil DeFreitas and Roland Butcher. Their presence in the squad sparked immediate outcry.

Butcher: There was a furore straightaway. I was put under a lot of pressure by friends and family. My benefit committee resigned and it kind of snowballed. I was surprised. I thought there might be opposition but the depth of feeling was amazing.

Butcher and DeFreitas quickly pulled out of the tour.

Bacher: Initially I thought it would be important to have the two black players in the squad. Now I'm glad they withdrew as they would have been under more pressure than anyone else.

Butcher: I had to do a lot of negotiating to get out of the contract and it cost me a lot of money in legal fees. I know I did the right thing though.

Fraser: To see Paul Jarvis and Matthew Maynard take the money was really why they never fulfilled themselves. If they were looking to take the easy option at that stage of their career it was an indication they were not going to survive at Test level. I felt sorry for Gatt though. He did not want to go but he felt let down by England over the captaincy and he just wanted to stick two fingers up at them.

Times were changing in South Africa. Apartheid was dying. Public demonstrations became legal for the first time and the tour became a political issue.

Bacher: We had lived in a cocoon. The other tours had been played in a serene atmosphere so we thought everyone in the country was happy with the tours. F.W. de Klerk [South African president] then made a big announcement which made demonstrations legal. The blacks came in their thousands to demonstrate against Mike Gatting's side and made clear their hostility to the tour. From the moment the tour was announced and until it was cancelled there were hostile protests.

Demonstrations greeted England's every move on the tour. Gatting was thrust into a political situation he neither understood nor knew how to handle. When Nelson Mandela was released from prison the tour was effectively over.

Bacher: I think the England team were bewildered by it all. Had we known the tour would anger the majority of people we would have thought twice about it.

Fraser: During the last World Cup we had Ali Bacher demanding England go to Zimbabwe for the good of South Africa and his World Cup. But he did not give a damn about English cricket when the rebel tour was going on, which made it difficult for me to feel sympathy for him when his big day did not go according to plan.

Interviews by Nick Hoult

I have a cunning plan ...

Somerset declare after just one over, Benson & Hedges Cup, 1979

By 1979 Somerset were desperate for a trophy. The county had gone 104 years without a single success and in one weekend the previous season Brian Rose's side had lost the Gillette Cup final and missed out on winning the Sunday League. They were determined not to fail again. A Benson & Hedges Cup group game away to Worcestershire was the setting for a remarkable – and controversial – tactical decision.

Vic Marks (Somerset allrounder): It was a rain-affected game. Had it been sunny it wouldn't have happened. The rain encouraged people to muse.

Derek Taylor (Somerset wicketkeeper): The reggae was playing, there was a carefree atmosphere in the dressing room. It was a desperado decision. Instead, we should have backed ourselves to win.

Brian Rose (Somerset captain): My own attitude as captain had changed. Because of what had gone on the year before, I wanted us to be tough in every game that we played. The intensity was there and we were young and hungry. There was a possibility for us to go out if we lost at Worcester. I didn't want that to happen.

The Somerset plan tested the rules of the competition to the limit. To be sure of qualifying for the quarter-finals, the dressing room worked out that if they lost the game without worsening their bowlers' strike rate, they would still finish top of their group. The idea to bat, then declare immediately, was born.

Mike Vockins (Worcestershire secretary): When there is a lot of rain, players often nip off – go and get a haircut, find somewhere quiet to read a book or something. But all the Somerset players stayed in the dressing room. There were lots of discussions going on.

Norman Gifford (Worcestershire captain): Well, it was their way of trying to make sure they'd qualify for the next round. The problem was it wasn't in the best interests of the game. It wasn't cricket.

Rose: There were one or two reluctant voices, but nothing too strong. The opinions reflected people's characters. Derek Taylor didn't like it, because he was instinctively conservative. That was one of his strengths in fact.

Vockins: I think it was a team effort that utilised the brains of Peter Roebuck and the muscle of Ian Botham to push it through.

Taylor: I was the senior pro in the side and Peter Denning and I got the players' views. I was outvoted. Never at any stage was I in favour of doing it. As it turned out, I happened to have the same view as the rest of the country.

Before going out to open the innings, Rose canvassed the opinion of Somerset officials and Donald Carr, the secretary of the Test and County Cricket Board. The phone call with Carr was a crucial ingredient of what was to follow. What was said remains a matter of some dispute.

Vockins: I think Brian must have used my phone in the office. I suspect a general question was asked rather than one that was specific.

Rose: I phoned the TCCB [Test and County Cricket Board] and spoke to Donald Carr and explained what we were planning to do. There are certain things I feel very strongly about regarding that phone call, but I don't want to go into detail. But put it this way. If the TCCB had told us we couldn't go ahead, we wouldn't have done it.

Gifford: There was a rumour going around that something may have been going to happen. We didn't quite know what it was until we saw it.

Rose and Peter Denning strode out to bat, knowing they were about to take part in one of cricket's briefest innings.

Marks: There was still some uncertainty as to whether he'd do it or not. Viv Richards was at No. 3 and he was padded up.

Rose: When we went out, even though I'd made up my mind, I was still thinking about the whole thing, which probably explains why I didn't declare after one ball.

The first and only over of the innings was bowled by Worcestershire's Vanburn Holder. It included a no-ball. Suddenly Somerset had a total to defend. At the end of the over, Rose declared.

Marks: I was slightly bemused because Brian played the first ball and didn't walk off. I think Worcestershire knew something might happen. Dear old Giff – when Brian left the field, Norman did a drama school-qualifying show of horror from backward point. He threw his hands in the air, his face was aghast.

Gifford: That was the first – and thankfully the last – time that I witnessed anything like that on the pitch.

Vockins: I was absolutely, utterly perplexed. My first thought was what the hell has happened here? Everybody was stunned. The umpires were gobsmacked. I went straight to our chairman and simply said: 'Everyone's getting their money back.' There was no discussion about it.

Worcestershire took 10 balls to score the two runs needed for victory. It had all taken 20 minutes from start to finish – including the ten minutes' break between innings.

Rose: We got back into the dressing room and the boys were all pretty much ready to go. I made a wishy-washy statement in the car park and then, to be honest, we legged it.

Vockins: Somerset's dressing-room door was bolted from the inside and the room was clear within minutes. I think that made people angry because they weren't even prepared to hang around and offer an explanation.

Marks: Not many of us showered – there was no need – and we buggered off. Then the fallout began.

Rose: Probably the worst thing was that there were spectators there. I regret that they didn't get to see the game they were expecting.

Vockins: It was very embarrassing. There was a lot of ill feeling at the ground. The members from both counties were the hard-core traditional cricket fans. They were very upset.

Taylor: Other players from across the counties started phoning me up asking: 'What the hell's going on?'

Rose: I do recall that on the drive home we heard the first statement from the TCCB. I think the gist of it was that the declaration hadn't broken the rules, but that they'd look at things for the future.

The rain continued to fall that week and there was little cricket played. Instead, plenty of column inches were written about the controversy.

Marks: Within a day or two we all felt like absolute pariahs and feared that our careers would be blighted for evermore. Rosey had been knocked about a bit and had wondered whether or not to keep going as skipper.

Rose: Because it was a collective decision, it had an extraordinary effect on the side and drew us even closer together. If I'd planned the strategy by myself, I think my head might have rolled.

After a complaint from Glamorgan who had lost out because of Somerset's scheme, the TCCB met with the counties. They decided that Somerset should be disqualified from the competition. The club's own officials voted in favour of the punishment and only Derbyshire supported them.

Taylor: I've no idea why Derby voted in favour of us. It was probably sympathy. They'd never won anything either. But we were kicked out and rightly so. If you're paid to play cricket, that's what you should do – play cricket.

Marks: We didn't play for a while after the disqualification. When it came, our next game was at Taunton – a Sunday League match versus Hampshire and it was packed. Rosey and Denning went out to bat and the crowd gave them an uproarious cheer. Then when Brian was out for 20-odd he got cheered all the way back to the pavilion as if he'd got a century. That helped clear everybody's minds.

Taylor: I remember walking out to field with Peter Roebuck next to me and we got a great reception. Roebuck turned and said: 'Who's right now Derek – you or me?'

Rose: The strange thing was, to this day, I've never had any personal hassle over what happened. It was a bloody oddity for sure but it wasn't an earth-shattering event.

Marks: I think the whole thing was an indication of how desperate we were to win something. It was a jokey piece of lateral thinking that turned into a cast-iron plan. It wasn't cynical.

Despite the furore, 1979 turned out to be Somerset's best season since their formation. They won the Gillette Cup and the Sunday League.

Taylor: If we'd tried to beat Worcestershire in the Benson & Hedges, we might well have won three trophies that year. Our plan only had one flaw. It got us disqualified. We forgot to take that into account.

Rose: Would I do it again? Well, speaking as a 56-year-old, the answer is 'of course not'. But as a young man I was a lot more ruthless and that's why sport is tough. People have always tested the rules – and they'll continue to do that.

Vockins: Obviously the man-of-the-match award wasn't handed out. We kept the trophy and sold it at the club auction. A bloke from London bought it for £300.

Interviews by Simon Lister

CHAPTER 3

Nail-biting Finishes

If we played on Friday the 13th, Shep would strap a matchstick to his wrist with an elastic band. It was supposed to ward off evil or bad luck or in-swinging yorkers or something.

Gloucestershire bowler David Graveney on one of team-mate David Shepherd's many superstitions during the 1977 County Championship

overleaf:
Mike Procter and his Gloucestershire team on the Bristol balcony after their superstitious moustaches came up short against Hampshire in 1977

Third, by a whisker

The 1977 County Championship

With one round of matches remaining, Kent, Gloucestershire and Middlesex all stood a chance of the title. Which of the three would triumph?

Clive Radley (Middlesex batsman): We had a great dressing-room atmosphere in those days. We thought we could beat anybody.

David Shepherd (Gloucestershire batsman): You would have to describe us as unlikely favourites. Question was, could we hang on?

Alastair Hignell (Gloucestershire batsman): We'd been nowhere in July, then won a lot. Suddenly we were in with a shout. We were a bunch of marauders. We played like a runaway bus. No one thought we could do it.

Radley: We had a lot of powerful personalities. Brearley, Edmonds, Wayne Daniel. It was about this time that we got a reputation around the circuit for being a bit cocky and arrogant. I think it's probably stuck to this day.

Derek Underwood (Kent spin bowler): At full strength – Alan Knott, Asif Iqbal, Bob Woolmer, Alan Ealham – we were putting out a pretty good side.

Radley: There were rows, too, of course – no names, no pack drill – but that was inevitable with the sort of talent we had. No one bore grudges, though, as I remember.

On 7 September the three counties started their final games. Gloucestershire led the table by five points and would play Hampshire at Bristol. Kent took on Warwickshire at Edgbaston. Middlesex were at Blackpool, playing Lancashire. Victory was a must but so were precious batting and bowling points. It was the climax of an intriguing season.

Mike Selvey (Middlesex bowler): It had been a strange summer in some ways. We had pleasant surprises but things were taken away from us too.

One of those pleasant surprises was Middlesex's 'home' game against Somerset at the start of September. It had been rearranged from earlier in the season because the two sides were playing in the semi-final of the Gillette Cup.

Selvey: Had it been played when it was supposed to be, it would almost certainly have been rained off like many of the other county games that week. As it was, we drew it and picked up some points. Not often that we played a home game at Chelmsford.

The reason for the unusual location was that Lord's was being prepared for the Gillette final. Middlesex had not played a home game out of the county since 1939. The seven points they gained were a godsend.

Underwood: We were very disappointed by the way their game was postponed, then rearranged. Why Chelmsford? I think the feeling was, if that game meant we finished second, it was going to leave quite a bitter taste in the mouth.

Selvey: It wasn't all good fortune for Middlesex. On the downside we'd played Gloucester in July and the umpire, Bill Alley, stole an over from us. They'd been bowled out in their first innings for a tiny score but batted well, following on. I think we needed 70-odd to win from 13 overs on the last afternoon but Bill got the regulations wrong and gave us only 12.

Middlesex finished on 63 for 7. 'A note from Brearley to the umpires as Middlesex vainly tackled their task proved fruitless. Against Procter at his fastest Middlesex sacrificed wickets recklessly but finished 12 short,' recorded Wisden. It was turning into a season of memorable games for Selvey and his team-mates.

Radley: Wasn't that the year we had that game at Surrey and declared without scoring?

It was. In a game much shortened by two days of rain Middlesex bowled Surrey out in their first innings for 49 on the last morning and immediately declared at 0 for 0 after one ball, thus giving them the chance of 12 extra points for a win. The Surrey No. 3, Monte Lynch, got a pair before lunch and Middlesex won by nine wickets.

Radley: That game was special. For a start it was Surrey, if you know what I mean, but to bowl them out twice was a great effort. That result – that bold tactic – was a demonstration of the sort of confidence that existed in the team.

Selvey: I claim total credit for all this. I thought of the idea while waiting at Wolverton station on the way to the match. 'If we declare, we can win this bloody game,' I thought to myself. When I arrived, I let the skipper know.

Radley: Selve's idea? Oh no, I think he's spun you a yarn there. I came up with it, didn't I? At least I think I did. Anyway, tell you what, let's credit it to Brears. Give him the glory. After all, he was the genius, wasn't he?

So Middlesex had some good luck and bad luck in 1977. Over in the West Country Gloucestershire were trying to manufacture a bit of good fortune for themselves.

Hignell: As our winning run continued, we developed all these superstitions. 'What did we do the night before the last victory? Oh yes, we drank a lot. Let's do that again!'

David Graveney (Gloucestershire spin bowler): And you've heard about the moustache-growing competition, I suppose?

Hignell: We had this thing about people not shaving, because it would ruin the luck. It turned into a moustache-growing competition. I was the judge because I already had a big beard. I can't remember who won it but David Shepherd got the 'artistic merit' prize because he got his sideboards to meet up with his 'tache. I think Jim Foat was given the 'most pathetic effort' award.

Graveney: It must have struck a chord with me; I kept mine for the next 30 years. You shouldn't really be surprised that a side which contained David Shepherd was superstitious. If we played on a Friday the 13th, Shep would strap a matchstick to his wrist with an elastic band. It was supposed to ward off evil or bad luck or in-swinging yorkers or something.

And so to those final games. At Blackpool Middlesex won to get 16 points. But they were bowled out for 148 in the first innings – two runs short of an extra batting point. Would it cost them the title?

Shepherd: Our last game was at Bristol against Hampshire. It was such a slow wicket and we had a poor record at that ground. We used to do much better at Chelmsford.

Kent were playing Warwickshire at Edgbaston and sneaked a win by 27 runs on the last day.

Underwood: We won – that was all we could do. Our captain, Asif Iqbal, was a great leader that season – so adventurous. He often declared early but more often than not it paid off. He believed – as do I – that the secret to good cricket was to have enough time in the field to bowl a side out. I think that's the mentality of a confident side.

Could Gloucestershire win at Bristol?

Hignell: The rumour was that great lumps of Weston-super-Mare had been brought down to the ground to cover the square to make it turn. It did but not with any pace.

Shepherd: In the past we'd always had two offies or two slow left-armers. That year we had one of each. The bowling wasn't the problem, though. Gloucester always struggled a bit for runs.

Hignell: There was a great spirit between us and Hampshire. Our skipper, Mike Procter, was a mate of Barry Richards and I think they wanted us to do well, so they said: 'Look, if you set us a target, we'll chase until last man down.' And they did.

Graveney: As I remember it, Hampshire had a bone to pick with us. Proc had got a hat-trick against them in the Benson & Hedges semi-final, don't forget. They wanted to win this game. There was quite a bit of rivalry between him and Barry Richards.

Hignell: Proc was a piratical, buccaneering captain. He would will us to victory through sheer force of personality. It was derring-do, he never really analysed the game, he just played. He changed the way the side saw itself. I think previously there was a sense that we ought to be hard-working, cap-doffing professionals. Proc just drove us forward like a juggernaut.

He certainly did. Procter won the toss on a damp pitch and batted. From 49 for 5 his county made 223. He made 115, then took 6 for 68 as Hampshire were all out for 229.

Hignell: I made a few in our second innings, 92 I think. I also ran out Zaheer Abbas. He had a leg injury and I called him for a sharp single. All my fault. Twenty more from Zed and we'd have set them a decent target.

The target ended up being 271. Hampshire took on the chase.

Hignell: They opened with Gordon Greenidge and Barry Richards. We needed to get them both out quickly.

On 30 Greenidge skied David Graveney to deep mid-off.

Hignell: Brian Brain put him down. That may have been a decisive moment.

Graveney: I remember it well.

The West Indian opener went on to get 94. By the time he was out Hampshire were well on their way. Gloucestershire's chance had gone. Hampshire won the game by six wickets.

Hignell: We knew if we were to win that last game it would have to be done at a great pace because the Bristol track was so slow. And that, probably, led to our undoing.

Graveney: We got within touching distance of the Championship. It was a late challenge but it's still pretty sad that we failed. It was a fantastic season but I feel the pain of the failure even today.

Hignell: There was a big crowd there. We'd won the B&H earlier in the summer and they were hoping for more. Defeat was a bitter thing but we all knew we'd come from nowhere.

Graveney: I played county cricket for years afterwards and that was as close as I got.

Shepherd: We all went up on to the balcony and Proccy spoke to the crowd. It was both a speech of thanks and one of apologies for not winning.

Graveney: Procter was a champion. 'Give me the ball, the bat and I'll make it happen.' That was what he was like. He could do anything. I mean, they even renamed the county after him. We were known as 'Proctershire'.

Shepherd: That was my greatest disappointment as a cricketer – not winning the title. Of course it had been a long time missing from

Gloucester – and still is. We won the cup but the Championship was the real one.

Hignell: That night it was a wake, of course there was disappointment, but it was an Irish wake, if you like. A celebration of the season's life. What a summer. What a great year. It had been nothing less than full steam ahead.

So what about the Championship? Kent's win in Birmingham had brought them 16 points. Middlesex's victory against Lancashire brought the same. Both sides finished on 227 points. The Championship was shared.

Underwood: I don't expect they'd let two sides tie for the title nowadays. There'd probably be a 10-over game to decide it.

Selvey: I remember I was chosen to collect the trophy from Buckingham Palace. Not from Her, it was the husband who was at home. I guess they must have made two that year because Graham Johnson from Kent came with me, we were both there.

Underwood: Was it a Championship lost? I don't think so. If you end up with equal points, so be it. Ask Gloucestershire. Would they have settled for a half-share? Of course they would.

Interviews by Simon Lister

Cork releases the Fletcher genie

England v West Indies, Lord's, 2000

The 100th Test at Lord's was one of the most tense. West Indies were one up in the five-Test series. Nasser Hussain had cracked a thumb and Alec Stewart led England, who had won only two of their past 11 Tests at Lord's. They looked doomed by the second day but won a nail-biter on the third evening. It set them on the way to a first series victory against West Indies for 31 years. It was also a turning point in Duncan Fletcher's tenure as coach.

Dominic Cork (England bowler): I had been recalled and had some history of playing West Indies at Lord's [7 for 43 on debut in 1995] but I still needed a solid performance.

England dropped several chances and Nick Knight was struggling with a sore back. Either side of tea they hit back to take 5 for 41, and West Indies were 267 for 9 at the close.

Cork: West Indies were going well at 162 for 1, so we desperately needed a breakthrough after lunch and I got it, having Sherwin Campbell caught at long leg for 82. Darren Gough bowled well, we all bowled well, in good areas.

Andrew Caddick (England bowler): It didn't quite click for me in the first innings. I bowled all right, kept things tight, but it was Darren who did most of the damage.

Alec Stewart (England's stand-in captain): Goughie always bowled well at Lord's. He was great friends with Cork – they were joined at the hip. They used to wind each other up.

Courtney Walsh was out quickly the next morning but England managed only 134 in reply, with Curtly Ambrose and Walsh taking four wickets each.

Nasser Hussain (England's injured captain): West Indies needed only about a hundred in their second innings to make the game safe in those conditions. For the first time – but certainly not the last – I wondered how secure my position was as captain.

But astonishingly West Indies were bundled out for 54.

Caddick: Our first innings didn't go great; we were down and out. We needed to bowl them out cheaply and we could hardly have bowled them out more cheaply. Nasser said I decided to wake up and bowl – he was about right. It was electrifying standing down at third man at the Nursery End. It was one of the best days of Test cricket I can remember, one of the best days I've ever had.

Caddick bounced out Campbell with the help of a spectacular over-the-head catch at third man by Gough, who hit his head on the turf as he fell backwards.

Darren Gough: Caddick had struggled in the first innings and he was a little bit down. I took that catch off him and Duncan said that was the turning point in the series for him.

Stewart: We needed that wicket. It was a good catch at third man, in front of our balcony. Gough banged his head and made a fuss.

Gough: After that first wicket Caddick woke up, got that confidence and his performances picked up for the rest of the series and then he was away. My figures were 8–3–17–2 but I didn't get back on because Caddick and Cork cleared them up. That was a strong attack, with Craig White and Matthew Hoggard as well.

Stewart: Caddick's spell was the best I kept to from any bowler for England. He was in his element; good pace, control, swing, and he got it in some great areas for both the left- and right-handers. Andrew had had 18 months out and came back a different person. I'd said to him, 'Just show everyone how good you are.' He did everything I asked.

Hussain: Caddick is at his best when he's bowling from the Nursery End, slightly up the slope with the wind coming from fine leg to the right-hander. He just kept on hitting the pads or getting them to nick off.

Cork: Goughie and Caddick bowled very well – we had to do something. The atmosphere was great. The crowd had expected us just to let West Indies pile up the runs but it improved throughout the day. Once we walked off, though, it was still dispiriting to feel we'd bowled them out for 54 but still needed 188. We knew it was far from over.

England faced seven balls before the close without scoring. It was the only day in Test history which contained a part of all four innings, with 21 wickets falling. England needed 188 to win but a delayed start because of rain added to the anxiety.

Stewart: The ball was darting round, it was overcast, it wasn't typical of Lord's. It made for a low-scoring Test – very exciting. To say it was tense is a polite way of putting it.

Mark Ramprakash went early but the two Michaels, Atherton and Vaughan, put on 92 for the second wicket.

Cork: Vaughan and Atherton batted very well and we were starting to feel a bit more secure. Walsh was still fighting though and it felt like he was bowling all day. Ambrose was also bowling perfect length. Knight had injured his hand [trying to catch Ridley Jacobs on the Friday] so he just tried to hold an end up.

Caddick: I thought I was going to do it. I scored seven.

At 160 for 8, England still needed 28 to win; victory remained a distant spot on the horizon.

Gough: I was disappointed Caddick got in before me as I always believed I was better than him with the bat. It was anyone's game – it looked as if they were going to go 2–0 up.

Cork: When Goughie came in you could see the team on the balcony looking dejected; resigned to defeat. I don't think I've ever been so nervous, but I'd much rather be out in the middle where you can do something about the situation, rather than on the balcony. Goughie didn't say, 'Let's play cautiously'; he said, 'Think how famous we'll be if we score these runs.' It was a good thing to say. It relaxed me.

Gough: Corky and I put on 31. I just played a supporting role – it's the first time I really blocked in a Test [4 not out off 19 balls] – and gave Corky the strike. Hoggy was next in.

Stewart: Hoggy was in his helmet and gloves sitting just inside the door. He got through three pairs of gloves – not through sweat but through chewing them.

Cork: It was the stillest of days – a big crowd, but so tense, clapping every run, willing us over the line. I pulled a short ball from Franklyn Rose for six. It wasn't the biggest of boundaries but we'd had so few loose balls. Then I hit the winning runs through the covers – there was a sense of disbelief in the dressing room.

Hussain: It justified Duncan's preference for picking bowlers who could contribute with the bat.

Caddick: It was a hell of an innings by Cork.

Gough: I love games like that. The two turning points for me were that catch off Caddy – he was such a terrific bowler but lacked confidence and that just set him on his way; he went from strength to strength after that – and then Cork's innings.

Caddick: That game was one of the highlights of my career. It was a great era – myself and Gough. People compared us to Fred Trueman and Brian Statham.

Cork: We had a great spirit in the camp and even when we were up against it we were 100% behind each other; the fact we pulled it round is testimony to that.

Hussain: There have been great Tests since but that was the ultimate Test.

Stewart: It proved we could beat West Indies. It was definitely one of the better wins of my Test career.

Ricky Skerritt (West Indies manager): After we lost, Ambrose and Walsh sat in the corner of the dressing room, quietly sharing their last moment at Lord's in defeat. No words could explain their emotions and I shared their disgust at our performance. But the young fast bowlers, who hadn't bowled very well, were in the bus probably looking forward to their next meal and ready to go and have fun.

Interviews by Huw Turbervill

'Twenty20 cricket 50 years ahead of its time'

Sussex v Yorkshire, Hove, 1959

The County Ground, Hove. Tuesday, September 1, 1959. Yorkshire, seeking their first outright Championship since 1946, know that only victory over Sussex will give them a chance of ending Surrey's record sequence of seven successive titles. And Sussex leave them 215 runs to win in under two hours.

Bryan Stott (Yorkshire opener): It was the last game of a hot, hard summer and all along it had been nip and tuck between four sides: Yorkshire, Surrey, Gloucestershire and Warwickshire. Nobody had expected us to do well. We were re-building after the sacking of Johnny Wardle and [other] retirements. Ronnie Burnet was 40 and in his second season as captain. A lot of us had played for him in the 2nd XI; he pulled us all together.

Hove was the fifth and final game of Yorkshire's end-of-season 'Southern Tour', then they returned home for the Scarborough Festival to play MCC. In 1939, Yorkshire were playing at Hove when war broke out. Now, 20 years later, they had started the tour badly, losing by 16 runs against Somerset and by an innings after Gloucestershire had bowled them out for 35.

Stott: A disaster. We'd started the tour on top; after two defeats we were third. Worcester was real muck or nettles. We won by six wickets and set off for Hove leading Surrey, who had two games left, by four points. [But] the equation was straightforward: win … and hope Surrey didn't.

Sussex would finish the season in 15th place, with six wins in 28 matches. But they were dangerous opponents. Jim Parks, Ted Dexter and Ken Suttle each scored over 1,500 runs and Ian Thomson was one of the most miserly pacemen on the circuit, with 120 wickets at 21.32. And traditionally no one gave Yorkshire anything.

Stott: A lot of counties had head coaches who'd played against the Yorkshire side of the 1930s. They won seven Championships in nine years but didn't win graciously. There was still very much an attitude of 'we're not letting these bloody Yorkshiremen win'. Teams would rather play out a draw than give us a chance.

Jim Parks (Sussex wicketkeeper): It wasn't just because it was Yorkshire. In that situation, with the Championship at stake, we wouldn't have given anybody anything.

Sussex skipper Robin Marlar, who declined to speak about the game to TWC [the Wisden Cricketer], elected to bat. With Yorkshire's pace attack depleted by injuries to Bob Platt and Mel Ryan, Brian Close shared the new ball with Fred Trueman. But it was the medium pace of opening batsman Ken Taylor that made the early breakthrough with the wickets of Alan Oakman, Suttle, Dexter and Parks for figures of 22-9-40-4.

Ken Taylor (Yorkshire batsman and Huddersfield footballer): I suppose I only bowled because everyone else was knackered! I used to do a fair bit of bowling under Ronnie and then Vic Wilson. But I hardly bowled from 1963 onwards under Closey, even though I got Sobers twice against the West Indies at Middlesbrough.

Sussex made 210 but Yorkshire slumped to 81 for 5 when Ray Illingworth was joined by Jackie Birkenshaw, 18, playing only his seventh Championship game. They added 112. First-innings points were secured during Illingworth's sixth-wicket partnership of 66 with Don Wilson.

Brian Bolus (Yorkshire batsman): Raymond played the leading role. He was an absolute master in the middle order, a real craftsman. I don't think people quite appreciated the massive contribution he made with the bat over the years for Yorkshire, Leicestershire and England.

Illingworth's century – he also claimed match figures of 7 for 117 – meant Yorkshire led by 97 but Sussex knocked off the arrears with only two wickets down and began the last day 46 in front.

Stott: At lunch they had a lead of 193. With 140 minutes left, there was no real prospect of anything other than a draw. The dressing rooms at Hove were close and, if you walked down the corridor, it was possible to hear what was going on. So we listened in. They were split about what to do. Some thought Marlar should declare, leaving time to bowl us out. The others wanted to give us nowt.

Alan Oakman (Sussex batsman): I don't recall a declaration being a particularly big issue but knowing Robin, there was no way he would declare in that situation.

Stott: Marlar did not declare and that was absolutely the right decision. Why should he? If we wanted the title we had to go out there and win it. Even so, the last few batsmen struck out and went for quick runs. They could easily have propped and copped, settled for the draw. A target of 215 in 105 minutes gave us an outside chance. As we walked off the field, two Yorkshire fans ran up and said: 'What are we doing? What are we doing?' 'We're going for them. Obviously.'

Bolus: It was a formidable target but Stotty was absolutely convinced we could do it and said so.

As he was putting on his pads, Stott had a word with Yorkshire's stand-in scorer.

Philip Sharpe (Yorkshire batsman): I'd lost my place three weeks earlier but my father had arranged a business trip around the Worcester game so I went along. When Cyril Turner, our scorer, was taken ill I was asked to step in. I kept the job until the end of the season. Brian asked me to work out how many overs we were likely to face and to show the number bowled on the scoreboard.

So the chase was on.

Parks: Of course we expected them to go for it, even though it looked virtually impossible. Surrey were struggling at The Oval but even so, Yorkshire still had to win the match to clinch the title. We thought we had a good enough attack to contain them.

Oakman: Northern sides were usually good at chasing. They had been brought up in league cricket, where winning and losing really mattered, whereas we didn't play for league points.

Stott: Ian Thomson's first ball gave me a chance to play one of my favourite shots, through the covers off the back foot. Four. We took 15 off that over, roughly the same off Ted Dexter's first from the other end and I hit the first delivery of Thomson's second over straight back over his head for six. I can still see his face now. Pure disbelief. In the space of three overs we were ahead of the rate and on our way.

Ian Thomson (Sussex bowler): He just came down the wicket and clouted me back over my head for six. Bryan played really well that day.

Thomson's final figures: 10-0-87-1.

Parks: It was the only time I ever saw Ian taken apart. He was one of the most accurate bowlers around.

Thomson: Not the only time. In 1955 I went for 28 in an over against Glamorgan at Cardiff. Jim McConnon wasn't the greatest batsman in the world so I kept pitching it up and he kept clearing the boundary. At the start of the next over I dug one in and that was that.

Taylor fell with the score on 18 in the second over and, during a brief cameo, Close smote a six out of the ground, causing a five-minute hold-up while another ball was located. Time Yorkshire could ill afford to lose. When Close left with the score on 40, Doug Padgett joined Stott and the match-winning partnership began.

Parks: Stott and Padgett really got them going. They scored a lot of runs very quickly, pushed their luck at times but got away with it. Doug and I toured New Zealand with the MCC in 1960-61 and I got to know him very well.

Stott: I said to Doug: 'Look, we've got to run for everything, try to make every one into a two.' We were a right-hand, left-hand combination and Marlar could easily have packed one side and changed the field after each single. That would have taken up a significant amount of time. That was his real quandary, not the declaration. He kept his fields more or less split and very little time was lost. To my mind that was a very brave thing to do.

Oakman: I was a specialist close fielder and I'd never been so far from the bat in my life. I was at the south end of the ground and Robin was at the north, the field was spread far and wide and I can remember him shouting at the top of his voice to be heard. It was Twenty20 cricket 50 years ahead of its time and we chased some leather that day.

Thomson: Their running between the wickets was magnificent but we had all our fielders spread around the boundary and couldn't bowl to that field. That made it easier for them. I think Robin was in a panic and we should have got together in the middle and said we wanted a different field. But that would have looked like time-wasting.

Stott: We put on 141 in just over an hour and they simply couldn't contain us. It was so thrilling to be involved. Pure exhilaration. We broke the back of the target and from then on it was just a normal game of cricket.

Stott and Padgett were out with victory in sight. Illingworth, inevitably, and Bolus saw Yorkshire home with seven minutes left, Bolus turning Ted Dexter to the fine-leg boundary for the winning runs. They had scored 218 for 5 in 28.3 overs.

Bolus: My memories of that shot are pretty vague. I only had a walk-on role among some wonderful performances. It would have been far more appropriate if Raymond had hit the winning run.

Surrey finished pointless against Middlesex. It was Yorkshire's title. Champagne appeared along with pressmen, radio and TV reporters.

Stott: After our defeats at Bath and Bristol the national papers had more or less decided we weren't going to win it. They went to The Oval instead. The Yorkshire press lads told us later how new faces kept appearing as events unfolded.

Parks: We all went into the Yorkshire dressing room and said well done. I don't think we thought at the time that they would go on to become such a strong team, even though they'd ended Surrey's run of Championships.

It was 7pm before the White Rose convoy headed for Scarborough ... with one notable absentee.

Taylor: Yorkshire and Huddersfield had an agreement that if we were in contention for the Championship, I could play for Yorkshire until the end of the cricket season. But the deal didn't include Festival games so I missed all the celebrations. And over the next few years, Town didn't see a lot of me until early September.

Stott: There were no motorways then so it was quite a journey. It wasn't until two in the morning that we started to arrive in dribs and drabs to discover that none of our supporters had gone to bed. It was a wonderful reception. The following morning thousands of people were milling around outside the ground. I'd never seen as many people at a cricket match. Before we took the field the whole crowd swarmed on to the ground and formed a corridor for us between the pavilion and the square. They gave us a tremendous ovation. People had come to Scarborough just to be there on the day we returned with the Championship. We'd never expected to win the title but I'm convinced the game at Hove was the catalyst for 10 years of Yorkshire success.

And it was. Yorkshire won the Championship six times in the next nine years and the Gillette Cup in 1965 and 1969.

Interviews by Andrew Collomosse

Bears savaged by vegetarian

Anil Kumble's seven-wicket innings, Edgbaston, 1995

It was the hot, dry summer of 1995 and an epic race was under way for the County Championship between the holders Warwickshire, Middlesex and Northamptonshire. At the end of July Warwickshire, now the leaders, met second-placed Northamptonshire at Edgbaston. What followed was, in the words of *Wisden*, 'a nerve-shredding encounter . . . probably one of the best [Championship matches] of all time'.

Alan Fordham (Northamptonshire batsman): There was a hell of a lot riding on the game. The rivalry between the two sides was acute that season – both sides were really going for it.

David Capel (Northamptonshire allrounder): It was a clash of the titans, wasn't it?

After Allan Lamb won the toss things went badly for Northamptonshire – they were skittled for 152, with only Capel's half-century preventing complete humiliation.

Capel: When we came out to bowl, I remember [umpire] Kenny Palmer saying, 'Capel's going to have to get seven-for, Northants have to limit the lead to less than 100, then they can go out there and get some runs.' It was remarkable that it all happened that way but that sort of comment sows the seed in your mind.

As Palmer outlined, Capel took a career-best 7 for 44 as Warwickshire replied with 224, including 140 from Roger Twose. Northamptonshire then forged ahead thanks to a century from Fordham and 70 from Russell Warren at No. 8.

Fordham: It was probably one of the best hundreds of my career in the context of the game and with Allan Donald doing his best to get me out. I was pretty satisfied with myself for getting a century against one of the best bowlers in the world.

Dougie Brown (Warwickshire allrounder): I remember dropping Russell Warren on 0 at third slip off Allan Donald. He went on to get 70 and turn the game round.

Ken Palmer: Allan Donald was having a go at Russell Warren. I said, 'Come on Springbok, let's just get on with it.' He said, 'It's OK, I'm just asking him where he's going for a drink tonight.' There was a bit of aggro throughout the game but, whenever I told them to pack it in, they did. They were a credit to the Championship.

Warwickshire were set 275 to win, but Anil Kumble, Northamptonshire's Indian leg-spinner, was in the middle of a magical season which would eventually bring him 105 Championship wickets.

Brown: We devised a plan to play Kumble off the back foot because he got a lot of bounce and the pitch at the time was quite bouncy. He did me for pace in the first innings and then sent down this Exocet in the second, which I tried to cut. I was caught behind third ball. What we learned is that if there's one thing you don't do against Kumble, it's go back to him. He bowled brilliantly.

Palmer: I said to Lamby – this Anil Kumble, they've got to play forward to him. He said, 'Don't tell them that.' It was crazy to go back to him.

Warwickshire stumbled to 53 for 6 but a fighting partnership between Dermot Reeve and Neil Smith dragged them back into contention. At lunch on the final day they were 222 for 7, still needing 53.

Capel: Anil was the only vegetarian on either side but Dermot, who was batting at the time, came in at lunch and took the only vegetarian meal. It was a really hot day, and when Anil realised there was no food for him, he was pretty pissed off. I asked him if there was anything I could get him and he said, 'Don't worry, I'll just eat two bears after lunch.' And that's exactly what he did.

Kumble removed Keith Piper and Reeve to claim his sixth and seventh wickets of the innings and complete a haul of 10 for the match. That made it 228 for 9, only for the game to take another twist as Donald and the No. 11 Tim Munton got their heads down.

Capel: The ball was getting softer on the brown surface and the seamers were pretty fatigued. We left it a little bit late. I'd been out of the attack for a while and, when they needed 30 or so, I was thinking, 'I've got to get on here.' With 15 or 20 runs to go, I said to Lamby, 'We're leaving this late, aren't we?'

Brown: You could see Northants getting worried. All of a sudden they had eight different captains. Lamby was in charge but everyone was putting in their tuppence worth.

Fordham: I think we always thought we were going to win it. We always believed we could break the partnership.

Lamb finally recalled Capel, who trapped Munton leg-before with the score on 267. Northamptonshire had won by seven runs. According to Peter Deeley in the Daily Telegraph, *'Capel disappeared beneath a scrum of jubilant fielders.'*

Brown: It looked from where we were sitting that it was sliding down the leg side but Kenny Palmer gave it.

Capel: It wasn't plumb and it slanted in a bit but he was hit on the shin and he was back in the crease. Those two factors probably counted in my favour. I wouldn't have been surprised if it had missed leg but there would have been a lot of players on our team who would have been disappointed if it hadn't been given.

Palmer: It wasn't going down the leg side, I can assure you of that. Tell Dougie Brown it was knocking the lot out. As Capel went up for the shout, Allan Donald turned round and started walking to the pavilion. It was plumb. There was no fuss at all.

Deeley described the match as having 'more twists and turns than a mountain pass'. Lamb said, 'It was like a little bit of a war out there.'

Fordham: It was the best Championship game I played in without a shadow of a doubt. It was one of those games where you came off wishing that every game could be played in that type of atmosphere.

Capel: It was the sort of game you don't forget, a real hard-fought battle; there was no quarter given. It was the way the game should be played.

Brown: It was a brilliant game of cricket, one of the best you're ever likely to be involved in. It ebbed and flowed and could have gone either way, right until the end.

Palmer: It was the best game I've umpired. Really super.

Despite the defeat Warwickshire went on to retain their title, winning 14 of their 17 Championship matches. Northamptonshire finished third behind Middlesex and remain one of three sides – along with Somerset and Durham – never to have won the title. There was more heartache for Northamptonshire in September when they lost in the final of the NatWest Trophy . . . to Warwickshire.

Capel: There was an appeal from Kumble against Reeve that was plumb at a crucial stage of the game but Dickie Bird didn't give it. That would have been game, set and soldiers and it left rather a bitter taste. But I suppose both sides can have a whinge now. They can say Munton wasn't out, we can say Reeve was.

Interviews by Lawrence Booth

Breathtaking Bore

The County Championship deciders, 1984

The 1984 Championship was not decided until the second-last ball of the last over of the last game. The contenders were Essex and Nottinghamshire. Essex had won their final game against Lancashire in two days. Now all they could do was wait to see what would happen at Taunton. If Somerset were beaten, the title would be heading to Trent Bridge.

Derek Pringle (Essex allrounder): After our game at Old Trafford we all drove down to Chelmsford and sat in the President's room – a grand name for a terrible place – to listen out for what was happening at Taunton. It poured with rain the next day in Manchester, so if we hadn't won so quickly, the game would almost certainly have been a draw.

Richard Ollis (Somerset substitute fielder): I was often 12th man that season and never minded getting on the pitch because it meant you didn't have to run the baths, make the drinks and help with the lunches.

Ollis's captain was Ian Botham. Nottinghamshire had declared 52 runs short of Somerset's first-innings total of 274. It now looked as if Botham would return the favour.

Pringle: We were all saying, 'Botham won't declare; he won't give Nottinghamshire a chance,' but he set them a very gettable target. He always enjoyed a good joke on his mates at Essex.

Ollis: I fielded in both innings. When Viv Richards and Joel Garner were in the side, you tended to get on quite often.

Vic Marks (Somerset allrounder): Botham made a clever judgement, wanting to keep the game open. I think he also wanted to declare slightly earlier because he couldn't be bothered to have a bat. I was thinking, 'We haven't got enough.'

Clive Rice (Nottinghamshire captain): Botham said, 'I'll give you a chance, I'll set you a target and our spinners will bowl all the way through.' Old Skid Marks bowled from one end and the young left-arm spinner Stephen Booth came on from the other.

Marks: I may be making this up but it's possible there could have been a conversation where I said 'We need more runs' and Both said something like 'Well, you go out there and get them then.'

Marks added a few more and Botham did declare. He set Nottinghamshire a target of 297 for the game and title. The time left meant that 60 overs would be bowled. It was a very different finish from the one Essex had just enjoyed, a 10-wicket victory. The trip had featured a memorable contribution from the Lancashire and England batsman Frank Hayes, who was not even playing.

Pringle: We'd being staying at a pub on Portland Street in Manchester and Frank, who had been forced to retire earlier in the season, was desperate to meet up with his great pal Ray East and have a few drinks.

Rice: We had played Sussex in the previous game and their captain, John Barclay, had decided that, because we had beaten them to the Championship in 1981, he was not even going to give us a game. So it ended in a draw. He gave us a pathetic declaration figure. Clearly he still had a chip on his shoulder.

Pringle: Keith Fletcher was having none of it and Ray was told to stay in his room. 'You're not going out with that madman Hayes,' Fletch kept telling him. Frank did not give up, though, and very late he erected a pile of fire extinguishers outside Ray's door. In the middle of the night they crashed down and sprayed all over the hall.

Marks: Botham was good in those situations because he liked Essex; they were a fun side to play against. But he felt obliged to get the balance right and he did that day. A lot of skippers would have killed the game.

Pringle: The landlord said: 'Right. That's it. You lot aren't ever coming here again.' Fletch pointed out that it was hardly our fault.

Down in Taunton Botham was true to his word. He and Martin Crowe took the shine off the ball before handing it to the spinners Marks and Booth.

Rice: Botham's target was outstanding. How can you judge it so well?

Marks: Everyone got some tap. It was a frenetic run chase because they had to go for it come what may. I've a feeling I got Derek Randall caught and bowled with a horrible full toss he hit straight back to me.

Chris Broad and Tim Robinson put on 70 as Nottinghamshire chased down their target. Paul Johnson, Richard Hadlee and Bruce French weighed in with 20s in the middle order. They were giving themselves a chance.

Rice: Hadlee holed out on the boundary. It was a bit controversial because the guy who caught it fell through the advertising boards and in those days I think that was still out. Even so there was all sorts of hoo-hah over the decision because it was such a tight game.

Rice had scored 98 including three sixes and nine fours from 109 balls when he went for his 13th boundary. Ollis stood between the ball's path and Rice's hundred.

Marks: I got Clive Rice caught for 98, did I? Well, knowing Clive it would not have been a dolly popping up at short leg.

Ollis: I was at long on when I caught Rice. I was just to the left of the old pavilion in front of all the Nottinghamshire fans. They were getting a little bit agitated and Both said to me: 'Look, if you get another catch at the death, I shouldn't hang around but leg it straight over to the dressing rooms.'

Marks: Ollis was a young batsman and a good goalkeeper and fielder, a good athlete, in fact. One other thing I remember: his father ran a transport business in Frome.

Nottinghamshire continued to hit out bravely but wickets fell. The ask became 79 from 10 overs then 36 from the last three. The Nottinghamshire No. 10 was Mike Bore, a specialist bowler who would end his playing days with a first-class batting average of 8.24.

Rice: If you knew Mike, then believe me, every run he made was an unexpected bonus. I wasn't daring even to watch. No one was allowed to move inside the dressing room. Everyone stayed in their seats as we got closer and closer.

Mike Bore: If it was pitched on the off stump, I thought, I'll hit it straight. If it's on my legs, I'll sweep it.

His plan was working. He had made 17 before the last over started. Another 14 would mean he would never have to buy a drink in Nottinghamshire again.

Marks: Mike Bore was a Yorkshireman, not renowned for the power of his batting. If he pulled this off, it would have been the innings of his life.

Booth to Bore. The last over of the season. First ball, four. Second ball, four. Third ball, two.

Bore: They were calculated slogs.

Four needed from three balls. Nine wickets down. Five months of toil and hope compressed into half an over. Bore blocked the next delivery.

Bore: The non-striker and No. 11 Andy Pick came down the track and said, 'What did you do that for?' I replied: 'It wasn't in the right place.'

The next delivery was in the right place. Bore gave it all he had and the ball sailed towards the stands.

Bore: As soon as I hit it, I thought, 'That's it, we've won.'

Rice: He really got hold of it nicely, and if Ollis doesn't grab it, it's six and we win.

Ollis: It came over and I caught it 10 feet in from the boundary, just above my head.

Marks: He took a good catch. Another few feet and the hit would have gone for six.

It was all over. Nottinghamshire had lost by three runs and the title belonged to Essex.

Rice: So we'd gone the whole season and we end up with a one-ball hit to decide the Championship. It was really tough. We'd been fighting for the title and it came down to this. How depressed could you get? Afterwards, well it was shocking. All that hard work and that's how it finishes.

Ollis: Winning the match didn't make a great deal of difference to our position in the Championship, so it was sad for Notts. For me as a young lad it was a chance to pick up a win bonus.

Bore: We were stunned. We got in the car and I don't think we spoke a word until we were well past Gloucester. No matter how many times I lie in bed and replay that ball I never score those four runs.

In the President's room at Chelmsford the cheers rang around.

Pringle: We had a very strong side. Norbert Phillip and Ken McEwan were fine overseas players and everyone in the team knew what their roles were. It was a great dressing room – a lot of fun – but we would turn it on when we went on to the pitch. Keith Fletcher was the best captain I played under.

Rice: Whoever Upstairs mapped this game out hellishly well.

Ollis: The next season I was picked for the game against Essex and John Lever did me for a duck. As I walked off Derek Pringle said with a smile: 'That's no way to treat the man who won us the title.'

Interviews by Simon Lister

Taken to the wire

England win the fourth Test of the Ashes – by 3 runs, Melbourne, 1982

A rebel tour the year before had weakened England and they went to Melbourne for the Boxing Day Test 2–0 down. Australia would regain the Ashes with even a draw. On the fourth day England looked to be heading for a comfortable win until a last-wicket stand between Allan Border and Jeff Thomson. For some of the players the scars have only just healed.

Jeff Thomson (Australia fast bowler): I could not talk about it for years. It was one of the all-time low moments in my life.

Geoff Miller (England spin bowler): It was the best and most exciting Test match I ever played in.

Bob Willis (England captain): It all boiled down to the captain's tactics against the last pair.

Geoff Lawson (Australia bowler): We thought we had lost going into the last day. It was great. You didn't have to take any of your gear to the ground; you just wandered down there.

After winning a key toss Willis opted to bat and England made 284, with Chris Tavaré and Allan Lamb scoring half-centuries.

Miller: It was a strange time because we were 2–0 down but still held the Ashes. We knew we had to win in Melbourne but the pitch was not conducive to scoring runs and all the innings scores were about the same.

Kim Hughes top-scored with 66 and there were half-centuries for David Hookes and Rodney Marsh as Australia took a three-run first-innings lead. But the umpiring throughout the tour had incensed England and Willis was again angry in Melbourne.

Lawson: There was not much between the two teams the whole series and Melbourne was a close game. Norman Cowans bowled fast – Shaun Tait reminds me of him a little, technique all over the place, let it go and bowl it sharp. He got some people out.

England had to set a winning total. They made 294 and Australia needed 292 to win. At 71 for 3, two to Cowans, they were up against it.

Willis: They were a better team than us; there is no doubt about that. They had a better batting side and a better bowling side but we were determined to hang in. In those days Melbourne was low and slow and it was going to be difficult to score that kind of target.

After a century partnership between Kim Hughes and David Hookes Australia collapsed to 202 for 8, when Lawson was out, and were in deep trouble.

Lawson: I got bounced out by Derek Pringle, caught at fine leg. The way they bring the ropes in these days it would have gone for six as it was right on the fence at Melbourne. When I went out there I think we needed about 100 and I thought I'd play some shots and see what happened.

Border was under pressure after a poor series but was determined to stick around. Even when the last man Thomson came in with another 74 needed for victory, the Australians had not given up hope.

Thomson: When I went out to bat there was no pressure on me. Everyone expected me to play a stupid shot and get out. AB [Allan

Border] had not been having the best of times but I played with him for Queensland and we were good mates. I went up to him and said: 'Let's beat these fruits.'

Lawson: I think that was the start of AB being a great player under pressure. He was like Steve Waugh. When the game got into a bad period he played his best. It started with that innings.

Miller: Batting last was always going to be a problem and we thought we had done enough. We had got rid of the quality batters and we thought if we bowled a straight one, it probably wouldn't get up and Thommo would miss it.

England decided to give Border singles to get Thomson on strike. It was a controversial tactic from Willis as Border was able to chip away at the target.

Willis: It was the captain's call. I had given up on my senior players after they persuaded me to bowl first in Adelaide. The captain takes the rap no matter what happens.

Thomson: The rest of the blokes in our dressing room thought I would have a slog and get out. But it didn't happen that way. I can still picture the England side's growing anxiety. They had stupid fields, bowled badly and everything was in the batsmen's favour.

Lawson: There were some strange bowling changes and field placements; they looked a bit rattled out there. Edgbaston this series reminded me of it; there were some poor fields.

Thomson and Border were hardly troubled as they batted out the fourth day. At the close they were 37 short of victory, halfway there.

Thomson: I was never worried while I was batting and it was never much of a drama for me. But all the blokes in the dressing room were drinking while we were batting. When I got back they were all pissed.

Lawson: Thommo fancied himself hanging in there. He is no mug; he can bat OK and it wasn't a case of 'if the ball is straight enough, it is good enough'. When you are nine down with 40-odd to get, you think you have a chance but it will take something unusual. You are resigned to probably losing the game. But AB and Thommo never looked like they were going to get out.

A crowd of 18,000 turned up on the final day. It could have lasted one ball but they got a thrilling session.

Lawson: We didn't do any warm-up, just a few throw-downs to AB and Thommo. It was a very strange morning. Then all these people turned up. Thommo was very relaxed but he's always relaxed. He can't be any other way.

Thomson: All the boys had to be wearing the same gear and sitting in the same positions they had been the day before. It also meant they were drinking again.

Miller: Thommo was riding his luck a bit and they were getting pretty close to the target. We didn't really have much of a team talk. We said that they had got halfway there, so they could do it.

Border was allowed to bat with freedom while Willis and Cowans, despite his six wickets, could not make the breakthrough, even with the new ball. Willis turned to his champion allrounder.

Miller: Ian Botham came on. I was at first slip and I said to Chris Tavaré, who was at second slip, that we had to move forward because it was a low-bouncing pitch. We moved up a couple of yards but we forgot about the new ball.

Lawson: I only thought we had a chance to win when they got it down to about five.

Thomson: They had Norman Cowans, Bob Willis and Ian Botham. Instead of trying to make things happen they just expected them to happen.

With four runs needed Botham had Thomson on strike.

Thomson: I was not worried about getting out. I looked up at the board and we needed only four to win. I thought I would get a single, so AB could hit the winning runs. How stupid is that?! Botham could have bowled a full toss on leg stump.

Botham pitched one outside off stump and Thomson nicked it.

Thomson: It was a half-tracker and a bit of an away-swinger. A bad ball really. I just tried to push it out for a single rather than smash it. All I did was get an edge.

Miller: We were fairly close at slip for a new ball and it just flew straight at Tavaré. He got a hand on it and it hit him and popped up. It was a difficult catch for him but it just looped up for me.

Lawson: I walked downstairs with Rod Marsh. We couldn't watch the game but we could hear what was going on with the crowd noise and radio commentary. We heard: 'He's nicked it, he's been caught, no he's dropped it,' then a couple of seconds later 'No, he has caught it.' We thought we'd at least tied because, if he has dropped it, it's gone for a few runs. Emotions changed very quickly then.

Australia had lost by three runs. It was the closest Ashes Test since 1902.

Thomson: I was spewing. I had lost and I couldn't believe it. I was so angry because I had decided what to do with that ball before seeing it. It really wound me up. I went into the English dressing room and lost it. I gave them a real mouthful and told them they were going to pay for it at Sydney. That was not like me. Beefy was a good mate. I bet they all thought 'what a dickhead'.

Willis: You never give up and you never think it has gone.

Lawson: The Edgbaston Test this summer [2005] was very similar. You think that, if you have a bit of luck and things go your way, you can win those games. When a five-day game goes down to a couple of wickets or runs, there is no telling which way it will go. That is why it is still such a memorable game.

Interviews by Nick Hoult

CHAPTER 4

Bad Behaviour

Aggression is different from passion.
We were passionate. We never had
any inclination to destroy.

Colin Croft on West Indies' 1979–80 tour of New Zealand

Michael Holding kicks down John Parker's stumps after the batsman
is given not out during the first Test at Dunedin

Ding-dong in Dunedin

West Indies tour of New Zealand, 1979–80

At the end of 1979 West Indies were the best cricket side in the world. On a tour of Australia they had beaten the hosts there for the first time. But when they headed to New Zealand the three-Test series was dogged by ill will, accusations of cheating and terrible sportsmanship.

Geoff Howarth (New Zealand captain): The niggle started before they arrived.

Fred Goodall (umpire): There were adverts on the TV of Joel Garner saying 'We've beat the Aussies, man, and now we're gonna beat you.'

Howarth: They were supposed to be unbeatable – there was no contest. They had been through a hard trip of Australia, they were a little blasé, a bit homesick. They were expecting a quick jaunt and a few wins inside three days. We caught them on the hop.

Clive Lloyd (West Indies captain): We were jaded and Viv Richards had gone home with a sore back.

Don Cameron (New Zealand cricket journalist): New Zealand won a one-day international and then, before the first Test at Dunedin, it was like MI5 spy stuff with all the misinformation flying around.

New Zealand picked an extra spinner, trying to kid West Indies that the pitch would turn, but Dunedin was sharp and quick and [Richard] Hadlee was brilliant. He got a lot of lbws.

Hadlee got seven lbws plus another four wickets in the match. There were 12 leg-before decisions in all – a record for any Test at the time.

Goodall: West Indies got very upset. Hadlee had three lbws in the first session. I gave all of them.

Howarth: They couldn't complain. If you walk in front of your stumps at Dunedin, you'll get given out.

Cameron: The umpiring was indifferent. The pitch at Dunedin kept low but West Indies thought they were getting too far forward for the umpires to be sure.

Goodall: I'd umpired county games in England. We weren't professional, though. I was a schoolteacher.

The atmosphere worsened as the Test went on. It became desperate when Michael Holding thought he had John Parker caught behind on the second day. When the umpire John Hastie gave Parker not out, Holding kicked down the batsman's stumps.

Colin Croft (West Indies bowler): The ball didn't brush the glove – it tore the glove off. Deryck Murray took it in front of first slip. Parker was on his way to the pavilion when he was given not out.

Lloyd: Michael Holding is an honest guy. If he was so incensed that he would do that it just shows you how bad these guys were.

Goodall: After Holding kicked down the stumps, I asked Clive Lloyd to control his players. As I was doing so, Lawrence Rowe at second slip said to me: 'You're nothing but a pack of cheats.'

Croft: The photo of Holding is the best sports picture I've seen. He should have been signed up by Manchester United on the strength of it.

Cameron: The photo was taken by a guy from a different town who wasn't working for the local paper, so it didn't appear for a few days. Then it was sold to Fleet Street and everyone saw it. Things really got nasty after that.

Needing 104 to win in the last innings, New Zealand got home with a leg-bye, nine wickets down. In the Wisden Book of Test Cricket *Bill Frindall noted that the result 'precipitated much truculent behaviour from the West Indies team and management'.*

Cameron: Hell, they were really bolshy. By Christchurch and the start of the second Test it was worse. There was a lot of ridiculous nonsense. A local radio station composed a satirical calypso ridiculing West Indies.

Goodall: Things went OK until the third day when Geoff Howarth gloved a catch to Murray. I saw nothing and heard nothing but apparently there was a brush of the glove.

Howarth: I leant back to a short ball and got a thumb on it. It was one of those ones where everyone behind the wicket knew it was out but no one in front could tell. That was the straw that broke the camel's back for West Indies.

Howarth was on 68. He went on to make 147 to help his side to a first-innings lead of 232 and put the game beyond reach. At tea he was 99 not out.

Goodall: The other umpire came up to me and said: 'I've got news for you and it's all bad. West Indies aren't coming out.' They wanted me changed there and then. But the New Zealand board stuck up for me.

West Indies unlocked the dressing-room door and came out 12 minutes overdue. Their arrival on the pitch marked the beginning of an extraordinary passage of play.

Goodall: That final session took the game into disrepute. West Indies let the ball go to the boundary and they dropped catches accidentally on purpose.

There was a rest day after the third day's play. Relations were so poor that West Indies emptied their dressing room and seemed set to abandon the tour.

Cameron: I was in the same hotel as the West Indies players and I got on well with Desmond Haynes. In the evening I went into the players' room and they were all there eating fried chicken. 'Why the party?' I asked Dessie. 'Oh, we're going home,' he said. Straightaway I phoned Jeff Stollmeyer, head of the West Indies board in the Caribbean, and asked him for a comment. 'It won't happen,' he said. 'The manager [Willy Rodriguez] will be told that they'll be carrying on.'

Stollmeyer was right. The teams returned for the fourth day.

Goodall: By this stage I was having a running battle with Colin Croft. He was bowling very wide of the crease and was being no-balled for his front foot but also for being outside the return crease. 'Go back to teaching,' he'd say, 'you don't know the rules.'

Croft: I admit that it wasn't proper international cricket behaviour. Some of our demeanour was not good.

Cameron: It was an awful bloody atmosphere and West Indies gave up playing. Then there were more dodgy decisions.

Goodall: Hadlee slashed at a bouncer from Croft. Everyone appealed and I thought I'd made a good decision giving him not out. Only years later did Hadlee tell me he'd got an edge on it.

Howarth: Fred was a stick-in-the-mud, officious, but he was our top umpire. He wasn't frightened to make a decision; neither was he a cheat. He was just out of his depth.

Goodall: Croft then flicked the bails off with his fingers. Jeremy Coney was the non-striker and he said to me: 'Whatever you do, Fred, don't pick those up. I'll do it.' The next ball Colin Croft carried on straight through his run-up and cannoned into me. I was knocked sideways.

Lloyd: I had a word with Crofty. This had happened once before with his close run-up. He'd knocked Bill Alley during a game for Lancashire. He ran in very straight then broke away.

Croft: In the heat of the moment they thought I did it on purpose. I did not do it purposely. If Fred Goodall was in Hollywood, he'd have picked up an Oscar. I'm six foot six and 230 pounds. If I'd meant to hit him, he wouldn't have got up. It's crap that I barged him deliberately.

Goodall: I had to walk over to Lloyd at slip and I said: 'I've taken verbal abuse as an umpire but I've never been struck before. You sort this out now.' But he let Croft stay on.

Howarth: Croft tried to pretend he'd lost his run-up. It was disgraceful. He should have been banned for life. It was because it was 12,000 miles away in little old New Zealand that the authorities turned a blind eye.

The tour had reached a new low. The second Test ended in a draw, as did the third. On the last day several West Indians had to be dissuaded from taking early flights home. The rancour lasted for years – especially as Fred Goodall was alleged to have made racist remarks about the tourists at an after-dinner speech.

Goodall: They could, I suppose, interpret what I said as a taunt. It was a flippant remark that could have been taken the wrong way and some people decided it was racist. When Vivian Richards captained the side in 1987, he wouldn't speak to me except to say: 'We'll teach you to make fun of our people.' It was very unpleasant.

Cameron: Goodall made several speaking engagements around the country after the Test series and made some biting and racial criticism of the West Indies. Viv Richards was aware of the angst even before he returned to New Zealand as captain of the next touring side.

Lloyd: They were just bad umpires but we should not have behaved in that manner. I think if I'd had my time over again I'd have handled it differently. I regret it even until this day that things went so far.

Goodall: I eventually got a photocopy of an apology that had been sent to the New Zealand board from West Indies. Would I ever meet Colin Croft again? Not on your nelly.

Croft: Aggression is different from passion. We were passionate. We never had any inclination to destroy.

Interviews by Simon Lister

Two tribes go to Waugh

South Africa in Australia, 1997–98

An historic rivalry threatened to ignite when South Africa crossed the southern hemisphere in 1997. Hansie Cronje gouged the ball with his spikes, while Mark Waugh walked into his stumps in the final Test and either got away with it (if you ask South Africans) or was rightfully ruled not out (according to every Aussie). South Africa won five of seven one-day internationals against Australia, but their two losses came in the finals. No wonder Cronje put a stump through a door.

Pat Symcox (South Africa spin bowler): You felt the weight of history, not least because of the presence of people like Ian Chappell, who had been on the South African tour in 1970 and averaged about 11. We were part of that history, and you wanted to make sure you pulled your weight. There was a lot to take out of the '97–98 tour, particularly on the emotional side of things. The technical and physical aspects are part of the game, you can prepare for that. But you didn't know what was going to happen to you at an emotional level.

Ian Healy (Australia wicketkeeper): The feeling between the sides was pretty good I think. Obviously there was bad blood between

Daryll Cullinan and Shane Warne and I think Cullinan might have been in tears in Melbourne. They were at it all the time.

Shaun Pollock (South Africa bowler): Australia is a tough tour, and it does get mentally difficult towards the end. To have the last few breaks not going our way didn't help. The guys tended to get along pretty well off the field. There was obviously a bit of heat between Daryll and Shane, I don't think they chatted much. Quite a few of them kept to themselves. But some of their more outgoing guys always had a beer after the game.

Stuart MacGill (Australia spin bowler): After the warm-up game [against Australia A at Brisbane, which was drawn] they were not dismissive exactly but very, very comfortable and casual about how they would go. I remember thinking, 'God, these guys have judged their whole summer based on an absolute belter in Brisbane and that's not how it's going to be at all.'

Jacques Kallis (South Africa allrounder): It was at the start of my career and it wasn't an easy entry for me. It turned out to be a hell of an eventful tour. In fact, every one since then has been pretty boring by comparison!

South Africa escaped with a draw in the first Test at Melbourne, where Cronje was booed to the crease because of his dirty dancing on the ball during an earlier ODI at Sydney and Kallis announced himself with a maiden century. But there was nowhere to hide at Sydney, where Australia won by an innings.

Symcox: Melbourne was all about survival. Three days later we started the second Test. We were worn down and then they put us back under pressure immediately in Sydney. Hell, we fought hard. I remember leaving Sydney thinking, 'What else can we do?' We played nine days of Test cricket in eleven, and were under the whip for eight of those nine. It was bloody hard.

And so to Adelaide. Injury ruled out Allan Donald so the strike bowler's mantle was passed to the callow Pollock. Australia handed a debut to MacGill.

Pollock: It was all a bit nerve-racking, I was going to lead the attack for the first time. But I was also pretty excited because I felt I had been bowling well throughout the tour.

MacGill: Lance Klusener, who is renowned for being a determined, strong, silent type, before the Test match, off his own bat completely, came up to me and said congratulations on being picked. He was the only one in their team, I might add.

South Africa won the toss, and Adam Bacher and Gary Kirsten took advantage of an Australian attack minus the injured Glenn McGrath and Paul Reiffel and shared 102 runs in the first session. Australia held the visitors to 305 for 7 midway through the second day. South Africa's fate rested in Brian McMillan's hands. He was ably supported by the lower order, and 212 runs were added for the last three wickets. No. 11 Symcox scored 54 off 42 balls.

Symcox: McMillan was saying, 'Block the shit out of it, let's not get out here.' And I thought, 'What the hell is this? What are you talking about?'

Day three, and a hot wind whipped temperatures to 39°C. Pollock bowled 29 overs and took 6 for 62 on his way to a haul of 7 for 87. Australia were dismissed a day later still 167 in the red, with Mark Taylor's 169 not out marking the end of a long drought for the Australian captain. Symcox questioned why he was allowed only 13.5 overs.

Symcox: I'm not adding another twist to it, I'm just saying it was very strange. We scored 517, and they bowled spinners. Then, when we bowled, I remember wondering, 'What the hell's going on here?' It was in 1998, after all.

Kirsten's 108 not out steadied South Africa's second innings and the declaration left Australia a target of 361 from 107 overs. Matthew Elliott and Taylor were gone before the close and Mark Waugh should have been caught.

Symcox: The second ball he faced, he pushed forward and was dropped at short leg by Adam Bacher off my bowling. I've watched it on video many times, it went straight in and straight out. And he got a hundred to save the Test! I took a blinder [in the gully to dismiss Ricky Ponting] and I dropped an easier one [Steve Waugh]. We dropped a lot of catches in that game.

Controversy reigned on the final day as a bouncer from Pollock hit Mark Waugh above the elbow, causing him to wheel away and clip his wicket with his bat. There were eight overs left in the match, Australia were six wickets down and Waugh was on 107.

Pollock: He summed it up when he said his arm went numb and he lost control of the bat. If a batsman loses control and hits the stumps, that's out. That was a crucial blow for us. We weren't sure what had happened at first. The ball looped up to gully. So we were appealing for the catch. We weren't sure whether it had hit his arm only or his glove as well. It went to the third umpire, and the guys in the dressing room were signalling that he was out. Then the verdict came back as not out.

MacGill: When he got hit, knowing the way he carried himself, all of us saw him playing the stroke and then just sort of flopping around and carrying on a bit because it hurt. None of us really thought there was an issue until the South Africans raised it. And then we were a bit nervous because we didn't know how the umpires would respond. I don't believe it was controversial at all.

Healy: It was well after the shot and it wasn't part of the shot when the wicket was broken. I was of the opinion it was the right decision.

Kallis: I was in the covers, and I thought it was, umm, very close to being out. I don't think too many of us were too interested in inviting him out for dinner after that. There were harsh words. But if you're going to play like that, if you're not going to walk in those circumstances, then you must expect the opposition to come hard at you.

Waugh, who batted brilliantly, survived. As did Australia. It was all too much for Cronje, and as he passed the umpires' dressing room he used a souvenir stump to communicate his feelings.

Symcox: We all saw it, and there were no objections because we were all pretty unhappy. It was a game of bad blood between South Africa and Australia. The Mark Waugh incident was really bad. There was no doubt he was out, we all knew. It's water under the bridge now, but at that stage of South Africa's development as a team it was quite critical.

MacGill: We kind of thought it was a bit funny because you love seeing the opposition frustrated. He lost it and denied doing it.

Healy: It came out that Hansie didn't own up at the time. A team management letter from the South Africans was the only apology. We thought at the time that it was a bit soft.

Pollock: We knew we had worked hard and dominated the Test match from day one. We also played good cricket throughout the one-day series, but we didn't manage to win that either. Dave Richardson's retirement was the culmination of a long tour that ended without much having gone our way.

Interviews by Telford Vice and Nabila Ahmed

Reverse discrimination

Old grudges nursed during Pakistan's tour of England, 1992

Relations were already strained. The 1982 tour had been hit by accusations of biased English umpiring. The memory of Mike Gatting's finger-wagging row with Shakoor Rana still lingered five years on. And England had just suffered a bitter defeat to Pakistan in the 1992 World Cup final. When the victors toured England later that year, the old ball swung hugely in their hands and suspicion of tampering spilled into fresh animosity.

Robin Smith (England batsman): Look, it was always going to be a closely fought contest. These days we are focused on people's actions but then there was a lot of talk about tampering with the ball. It got pretty heated.

Aqib Javed (Pakistan bowler): With 80% of teams around the world we would get on pretty well but with the English team, especially after the World Cup win, which really annoyed them I think, relations weren't great.

Moin Khan (Pakistan wicketkeeper): I don't think relations were that bad. The media played it up too much. They were pretty fearsome throughout that tour.

The series started at Edgbaston. A flat pitch led to a dull draw. There were hundreds for Alec Stewart and Smith.

Smith: I was pretty happy with myself after that innings. Mushtaq Ahmed bowled a lot of overs and there was talk about my ability to play spin bowling. I batted against him and proved I would be able to cope with him for the remainder of the series.

The series came to life at Lord's. Wasim Akram and Waqar Younis were fit and would win the match for Pakistan. Waqar took five in the first innings.

Aqib: I guess the most memorable moment must be the Lord's Test. Waqar had already bowled a phenomenal spell in the first innings, where just like that, he finished the innings.

Smith: We felt they were doing something illegal with the ball. Pictures were shown on television and in the *Sun*. From that Test onwards we were up for the fight because we felt they were getting an unfair advantage. But I'm the first one to say it was sour grapes because we were not good enough to cope and that was part of the reason why we were so angry.

England put themselves in a strong position. Set 138 for victory, Pakistan slipped to 95 for 8 in their second innings. Wasim and Waqar were at the crease as England scented victory.

Aqib: Watching Wasim and Waqar with the bat in the second-innings chase was amazing. I was next and last man in and I watched every single ball; I played every ball in the balcony with them.

It was agonising for both sides. England could not call upon the injured Ian Botham and ran out of steam. Wasim and Waqar were unbeaten as Pakistan won by two wickets. A draw at Old Trafford was played out on another flat pitch. But it will always be remembered for an angry exchange between Aqib and the umpire Roy Palmer.

Aqib: This actually started at Lord's. When Waqar and I were batting in the first innings Devon Malcolm had been liberal with the short stuff at both of us. We just retaliated at Old Trafford. In that over I bowled one bouncer to him and then another. On the second one the umpire warned me. I told him I should get a warning if I bowled another one after that because in those days you were allowed two bouncers in an over.

When Palmer handed Aqib his jumper at the end of the over it became stuck in the loops of his jacket. An argument ensued with Aqib claiming Palmer threw the jumper at him.

Aqib: Maybe I shouldn't have said anything back to him but as a fast bowler sometimes you get worked up over these things. The whole sweater thing was regrettable. Had Imran Khan been captain, the whole situation would have probably been better handled.

Moin: We had appealed excessively throughout the match and Roy Palmer didn't like it. We weren't happy as we thought he was giving wrong decisions. Javed Miandad at one point threw his hat down in frustration, so things were boiling over then.

England had to win at Headingley to give themselves a chance of winning the series.

Derek Pringle (England bowler): It was a tense low-scoring affair. We picked Neil Mallender; he did well. It was a horses-for-courses selection with Headingley suiting his seam bowling. I did all right and thought they might pick me for the next Test.

Graham Gooch's 135 gave England the start they needed and they took a first-innings lead.

Pringle: I remember a run-out appeal against Graham Gooch and Merv Kitchen giving him not out. There was a big Pakistani presence there and they went wild. They gave Merv a hard time. [The Prime Minister] John Major was there watching and they gave him a hard time throughout the day and when he left the ground.

Smith: Gooch's innings was one of the great knocks, particularly as it was at Headingley where it was not always easy to score runs.

Pringle: It was a low, slow pitch and he batted well. I also think the reputation of Headingley played on their minds but it did not turn out like that.

England won comfortably and the series was set for a tense decider at The Oval, where tempers frayed. The ball reverse swung as England were bowled out for 207 in the first innings.

Pringle: Reverse swing dominated the game. The pitch got drier and more abrasive, which aided the reverse swing. We did well against the new ball and that was the best time to bat. As the ball got older, it became more difficult and we were blown away in 15 overs.

Smith: It was very difficult to combat. You had to watch them very carefully, so you could see which side of the ball the shine was on. You knew from that which way the ball was going to swing.

Wasim took 6 for 67 in the first innings and England were in serious trouble. Pringle was bowled by Wasim.

Pringle: I remember marvelling at it. I just remember saying 'How do you play balls like that?' Mike Atherton was muttering that I missed a half-volley. In fact the ball started around leg stump but swung 10 feet and hit off. Getting the ball in that condition was a thing of wonder, whether it was legal or not. Wasim Akram used to make the ball talk.

Aqib: We didn't tamper with the ball. In any case everyone reverse swings it now, so is it tampering? No, we just did it better than anyone else and I think we still do.

Pringle: I asked to see the ball at The Oval. I wanted to see it out of interest and not because I was whingeing. The batsmen always whinged. But the bowlers were fascinated to see how it worked.

The ball was two-tone. One side was smooth and the other roughed up. It was a work of art. The ball would go around corners at 90 miles an hour in that condition.

After Pakistan made 380 the Test was over for England. They had no answer to Wasim and Waqar and were bowled out for 174, leaving Pakistan four runs to win.

Aqib: We had a very good group of players, lots of potential match-winners in the team but above all we had this real aggressiveness.

Pringle: I did not feel cheated. It was a special thing they had at that time.

Smith: They really pushed the regulations to the full. But, if we had been good enough to impart the reverse swing with their pace, we would not have said so much.

Interviews by Nick Hoult

One year a messiah, the next mutiny

Derbyshire implode, 1996–97

By the mid-1990s Derbyshire had not seen the County Championship for 60 years. Under Kim Barnett a couple of cups had come their way but there had been no sustained success. Then, in 1996, the Australian Test player Dean Jones arrived to lead the side.

He wanted change – and it came by the barrowload.

Kim Barnett (former captain): When Dean arrived I'd been captain for, well, it must have been 13 seasons. When I first took over we used to get hammered, then we had a bit of glory, then we were crap again.

Gerald Mortimer (*Derby Evening Telegraph*): I'd been watching Derbyshire for 32 years and I think 1996 was the most enjoyable county season I saw. Dean Jones was always likely to be a contentious figure. He was also a bloody good player. He got a very good season out of a lot of players.

Jones had come to Derbyshire after a dispute with his Australian state side, Victoria. The coach, Les Stillman, had resigned. Both men were looking for a new challenge.

Neil Hallam (*Daily Telegraph*): When Dean and Les Stillman first arrived, people were very impressed. They trained with medicine balls; on cold days the slips were given hand-warmers to keep in their pockets. The club started winning matches and the players thought: 'We like this.'

Les Stillman (coach): The county was crying out for some direction and enthusiasm and Dean Jones had plenty of both. I wanted to get the team to enjoy their cricket – but also to learn about what we call the 'one per-centers': fielding, running between wickets, diet, preparation.

Barnett: I remember when they came they were pretty cut-throat. On the part of the players there was a pretty positive reaction. For captain and coach it was a big opportunity to prove themselves to a new team.

Derbyshire finished second in the 1996 season, playing fine cricket.

Stillman: There was a real nucleus of talent at the club: Phil DeFreitas, Devon Malcolm, Chris Adams, Karl Krikken. In 1996 I enjoyed it and the players enjoyed it. The county enjoyed it. At the end of the last home game I did something unusual for me and got on the public address system to thank the crowd for a wonderful year.

Barnett: I actually think second was about right that season. I don't think we were quite good enough to have won the Championship.

Yet all was not well. There had been committee-room rows and some tension in the dressing room. When the title was still within reach, there had been an uncharacteristically conservative declaration by Jones against Somerset – 'an excess of caution' according to Wisden.

Hallam: By the end of the 1996 season there began to be a bit of resistance to Dean Jones's personality. Some thought the record had got stuck in the same groove, others thought the declaration at Somerset to be a captain's error.

Barnett: Jones didn't like the reaction he was getting from some of the players. According to him the mistakes were all down to other people. My thoughts about captaincy are a bit different. If you're in charge you take the praise when it goes well and you accept the flak when things go wrong. The buck stops with the skipper.

Stillman: My memory is that Kim Barnett wasn't a supporter of Jones. He thought that I'd work against Jones and with him. I'd known Dean for years and although he had his faults, his good qualities far outweighed his shortcomings. I never had any problems with him.

Dean Jones: I know some people at the club might have been satisfied to finish second that year but Les and myself were not. We wanted to win something for the club and the supporters. I could not have asked any more out of the boys we had in 1996, but if we were going to win a Championship, I knew we had to make some changes.

Hallam: I don't think the coach and captain were as close as people thought. Les Stillman was a political man.

Mortimer: Dean trod on a few egos – probably for the good of the side. Kim Barnett had been captain for a long time. He was the most successful batsman and captain in Derbyshire's history – guts, resolution, mental strength. But he was not the most flexible man in the world.

Jones: I was warned at the end of the first year to be careful what I said in the dressing room because some of the guys in there could not handle what we were telling them. Cricketers are funny people – you give them a rocket and they take it personally.

After the rockets came more fireworks. In 1997, without the victories of the previous season to dilute the tension, the dressing room – and the club – began to unravel. Chris Adams, the middle-order batsman, had even offered to buy himself out of his contract in an effort to leave.

Jones: I was not going to mess with fools. There were some people on the committee who were not pulling for the team and some players who were not pulling for the team and that had to change.

But there have been troubles at the club since Christ was a boy and I knew it would not be easy.

Mortimer: The club were a bit like Derby County FC. When they were successful they were also at their most vulnerable.

Stillman: I had no idea that Derbyshire had an eternal tradition of eating themselves.

Hallam: Derbyshire have always been a team on the brink. One row away from a huge bust-up.

As the 1997 season went on, divisions in the dressing room hardened. Anti-Jones, anti-Stillman. Pro-Jones, anti-Barnett. Pro-Barnett, anti-Adams. It came to a head against Hampshire.

Hallam: Jones declared and Derbyshire lost. That was at Chesterfield. It all blew up. Dean had his suitcase packed and had virtually pissed off by the end of the day.

Stillman: I warned the club that they'd better support Dean or he'd walk. He didn't really need the money or the crap he was getting but the club didn't believe me. My position was clear. I supported Dean. When he went, I was left without any support.

Jones: Some people will think I took the soft option but I thought: 'Why waste three months of my life playing for a club that doesn't want me?' I am not going to lose any sleep about the players who wanted me out but what was sad was that I really wanted to give every player the chance to grow into a successful cricketer.

Except it was not that simple. In his parting shot Jones made a public statement, sanctioned by the club. 'Over the past month,' he said, 'a few senior players have failed to give me any support in my endeavours to carry on the Derbyshire success from last year. The players have great difficulty in coming to terms with the fundamentals that bring success.'

Barnett: He meant Dominic Cork, Phil DeFreitas and myself. We had always been the ones who'd told him what we thought to his face.

Hallam: Jones poured rubbish on everyone, telling them they weren't a club of winners. The players were enraged because the club had allowed him to do it.

Barnett could not contain himself. He passed on his strong views about the turmoil in an interview with local radio. The club promptly fined him £500, later increased to £1,500.

Barnett: The club told us that we had no right to reply. I think that was appalling. How can you expect to remain silent in a situation like that? I was so upset to get fined £1,500 for speaking my mind.

Barnett claimed at the time most of the players wanted to help pay his fine and that he had the support of nine out of ten players in the dressing room.

Mortimer: Chris Adams became very isolated after Dean Jones left. The atmosphere was poisonous.

Stillman: Chris Adams blossomed under Dean. I came here with that Australian 'one in, all in' attitude. You know, you put the hat on your head and that means you're a mate of the other 10 men wearing it too. The Derby dressing room had a lot of unstable people in it obsessed with contracts and their careers. They weren't interested in success. That was a real shock to me.

Barnett: I didn't want the lads to pay. I'd never expect them to dip their hands in their pocket for me but the principle was nice. I can't really remember if they all said they were going to do it but, yes, it wasn't everyone in the dressing room.

The crisis entangled the whole club. The decision to fine Barnett was a mistake. The ECB and the players' union, the PCA, knew that speaking out was not against the rules. Barnett was vindicated and the committee turned upon itself.

Hallam: It became a typical Derbyshire bugger-up. Factions everywhere.

'During an extraordinary four months,' noted the Almanack, *'Derbyshire contrived to lose their captain, coach, cricket chairman, chairman, secretary and commercial manager . . . It was a horrible summer for the long-suffering membership.'*

Hallam: Les Stillman tried to distance himself from it all but I think the players sent him to Coventry. They cut him adrift because what they'd seen in the dressing room meant they could no longer trust him.

Stillman: It was pretty messy. I ended up being told to go and take the second team to Kent. What a special day that turned out to be. I had no contact with the 1st XI. I didn't leave England straightaway, though. My children were at school here; they had made lots of friends. Our home in Victoria had been rented out and wasn't available. We ended up going on lots of trips.

Jones: We were hoping to use the 1997 season to maybe take a couple of steps back to move forward on the longer term and some people did not like that. That didn't mean we were going to get rid of the older players. I wanted them to be part of the direction we were taking but a lot of guys get pinchy towards the end of their careers.

Barnett: Just look at their record at Victoria, my record at Derby and theirs at Derby. That's the beauty of statistics in cricket. Sometimes they explain a lot. People in charge of cricket teams can't just expect to take the smooth but not the rough. You cannot just choose when you want to be praised.

A season after being a win away from the Championship, Derbyshire finished in the bottom three. It was a horrible summer.

Hallam: The consequences of it all? They were felt for years. Up until very recently in fact. A decade of misery, penury, poor play and bitterness. It was a miserable place to be around. Derbyshire is a very small county.

Stillman: It all fell apart and was very sad. I decided afterwards that I would never coach again because of what happened there. I haven't coached since. It knocked the stuffing out of me.

Barnett: I'd had enough and I left the club. That was very difficult because I thought I'd stay there for my whole career. I'm not a person who likes to move around.

Mortimer: There have been a number of bust-ups at the county ground over the years and one thing I learned is that no dispute is entirely black and white.

Barnett: We always had a tough changing room because we had to go to all parts to get players. So there were often a lot of strong characters in there. Having men like that is both a strength and a weakness. I always accepted that when it went right, it was down to the talent but mavericks aren't always the best people to have around if it's long-term success that you're after.

Interviews by Simon Lister

England in a fix

England in South Africa, 1999–2000

England were booed by the Oval crowd the day they lost the home Test series to New Zealand in the summer of 1999. They had a new skipper, no coach and had slipped to the very bottom of the Test table. What could possibly ease the pain? Ah yes, a winter tour to South Africa …

Nasser Hussain (England captain): We weren't the worst side in the world. It's just that sometimes we played like it.

Mark Butcher (England batsman): We were pretty low.

Shaun Pollock (South Africa allrounder): We were a settled side. The recent series against West Indies, which we'd won 5-0, established a lot of people. We knew where we were moving.

Butcher: After New Zealand I'd be going on the tour regardless. That said, I really didn't want to go. My personal life was pretty complicated at the time.

Hussain: I wasn't especially apprehensive. We knew we had a mix of players either towards the end of their careers or very inexperienced. There were some who wanted to get rid of all the older lot, the Athertons, the Stewarts, the Goughs and Tufnells. Fletcher and I had to battle hard to keep them.

'Fletcher' was Duncan Fletcher. England had eventually appointed a coach – a laconic Zimbabwean.

Butcher: When I met him, I liked him. He was very clever, always thinking and always communicating. He had a clear vision of how a team should work. Before his time England had never seemed like a team to me. It was more like a group of cricketers who were doing all they could just to play in the next Test match.

Chris Adams (England batsman): Duncan said little but observed a lot. He drew conclusions and made judgements.

This was a tour that would separate the sheep from the goats. Not everyone would end up sitting at the coach's right hand ...

Butcher: It was an exercise to see who had the skills and the mental attitude for Test cricket. I mean, let's be honest – we had no chance of winning the series. Some would be kept, others would be discarded.

Hussain: It was a case of having to take drastic measures. I think we were prepared to pick five, just to find one.

Go on ...

Hussain: From the first hour of the tour, from the first net, you could tell whether or not someone was going to be a Test player. Michael Vaughan, for instance, you could tell he was going to be a Test cricketer just from the way he walked through the airport.

Having passed the airport exam, Vaughan would soon be walking to the middle to bat in his first Test at The Wanderers. Adams and Gavin Hamilton also made their debuts.

Adams: There was an eerie feel about the day. It was dark and spooky. Murky.

Butcher: It was raining and the ball was going to go all over the place.

Pollock: The pitch always did a little bit on the first morning in Johannesburg. It was more the overhead conditions that would work to our advantage. There was rain in the air. For Allan Donald and me it really worked out well.

Hussain: I've absolutely no doubt that in all my 96 Tests this was the most important of all lost tosses.

The South African captain, Hansie Cronje, invited England to bat.

Adams: When Atherton and Butcher went out I was sitting back in those soft Wanderers chairs with a cup of tea trying to soak up the atmosphere. What happened next was extraordinary.

Hussain: It was like a league cricket wicket. I remember taking guard, hitting the crease and seeing the moisture coming up through the grass. It was proper wet through. And the light was worse than marginal.

Adams: All the feedback we'd been given was that Donald was completely out of sorts, he'd lost his away swinger, he was falling away horribly. It turned out he was vicious, frighteningly quick and could move the ball anywhere.

He sure could. With the last delivery of his first over, he tore out one of Mike Atherton's stumps. Donald reckoned it was the second-best ball he ever bowled.

Butcher: He was actually a bit perplexed because he couldn't control it. Normally he'll swing it away from the right-hander but even though he was holding it for that, it was shaping in sharply. I think he decided to just go with it.

Shaun Pollock just went with it too. Hussain went and England were 2 for 2. By the end of Donald's next over, two more Englishmen, Mark Butcher and Alec Stewart, had come and gone: 2 for 4.

Adams: I was literally re-enacting the nightmare that all cricketers have, where you've got to bat and you're not ready. I heard the almighty shout for Stewart's lbw, I knew he was out without looking. I was next in and I had one pad on.

Hussain: I turned to Fletcher and said, 'Welcome to the England dressing room.'

Chris Adams was making his Test debut for England at No.6 and was walking out with Allan Donald on a hat-trick after 17 minutes of play.

Adams: The first thing I said to Michael Vaughan was 'What's happening?' and he chuckled and said: 'I've no idea – I've not faced a ball yet.' It was almost a comedy moment.

Pollock: We never thought the game was won but it was the perfect start. We knew that, if we could get our foot on England's throat early in the series, we could keep it there.

Given the circumstances, the two new boys did all right. A cut to the boundary from Adams doubled the score. They made it to a drinks break and added 30 runs between them. Then Adams was out. But only just.

Adams: The ball hit the top of my bat handle. I always walked, and off I went. But it was a muted appeal. I hate to say this but I do regret walking that time because I don't think I'd have been given out. Sometimes I've looked back and thought: 'I was in there, off and running in my first Test innings.' If I'd have gone on in that situation who knows what might have happened.

What did happen was that England kept losing wickets. By tea they had been bowled out for 122. Perhaps now their bowlers would get their revenge on the tacky pitch. But no. The sun came out.

Pollock: Yeah – in South Africa we're pretty well connected you know? We know who to talk to, to get the weather to come on and off! The sun shone and, while it still did a bit, it was certainly better than batting first.

Better to the tune of 281 runs. South Africa made 403, England never recovered and they lost the first Test by an innings and 21 runs.

Pollock: Allan and I got 19 of the wickets. We talked about trying for all 20 – someone said it hadn't been done for a long time – and we were quite determined. But Paul Adams got Andrew Flintoff caught and bowled.

It was a very bad start to the tour for England.

Hussain: We did some silly things, like trying to hook Donald when he already had three men out there for the shot. So we needed to have a team chat to try to tell some of us to be sensible. But we didn't panic. I've been in too many sides where you lose and you have endless mothers' meetings just for the sake of it. I wasn't that cross. Then we went off to Sun City for a day or two.

The rest and recreation did England some good. They played much better in the second Test at Port Elizabeth, which was drawn. The result denied South Africa their 11th successive home victory. The third Test was at Durban. Wisden described it as 'tedious ... the sort of Test match for which the word "attritional" might have been coined'.

Pollock: Nasser got his big hundred but it was very slow. I think that's as kind as I can be.

Butcher: He had a hell of a lot of stamina. It was damn hot. Very sweaty. Tough going. It was exactly the bloody-minded thing you'd expect from him. If it meant he had to bore the crap out of us all for two days, so be it.

Pollock: It wasn't a firecracker.

Hussain: It was worse than that, it was diabolical.

Butcher: Nasser was a man with very little ego as captain. All his thoughts went into making the side better. That was all he cared about.

Hussain: I was in good form, felt comfortable and I enjoyed the responsibility of being captain. And I bored the pants off everyone.

His 146 not out in the first innings took more than 10½ hours but it made sure that England would not lose. For a while it looked as if they might win. Andrew Caddick took seven wickets when South Africa batted and the home side had to follow on for the first time in 73 matches. The game was saved by Gary Kirsten, who equalled the South African Test record.

Pollock: Gary was under serious pressure. There was talk of him losing his spot. I was out there with him at the end. Uncle's [Graeme Pollock] record had been 274 and Daryll Cullinan had got 275 not out just six months before. So Gary needed one more run. Mark Butcher was bowling his off-spinners and it was down the leg side so Gary swept but was bowled. Quite funny really. A strange end.

Butcher was bowling because England's best spinner, Phil Tufnell, was struggling. He ended up with 0 for 117 in the second innings.

Hussain: It was the beginning of the end for poor Cat. I think Fletcher pretty much said afterwards that, if he couldn't bowl a side out on a last-day pitch, then there wasn't much hope. I mean even Butcher got two wickets. I liked Tuffers but that was it for him really.

One of the new boys had been struggling too.

Adams: I'd got in, weathered the new ball, seen off Donald and Pollock, and I got a sense that this was the moment. If I didn't do well here, I could get dropped. Paul Adams came on and to this day I cannot understand why I did what I did. He bowled me a full toss, I knew exactly where I wanted to hit it, I saw the ball coming down, I delivered the bat how I thought I wanted to, then I missed it and got bowled. I thought: 'That will probably be it for a while then.'

It was not but Adams was not the only person who thought his time as a Test cricketer might be coming to an end. During the fourth Test at Cape Town the South African wicketkeeper, Mark Boucher, delivered one of modern cricket's more memorable witticisms when Adams came to the crease in the second innings.

Adams: I was aware that Boucher had come right up to the stumps, even though they had the quicks on. 'Mr Adams, welcome,' he said. 'Welcome to the last day of your Test career.'

Wow.

Adams: I thought it was absolutely brilliant. That is how to sledge. Sensational. And he was more or less right. I had a tough series but I was extremely grateful for the opportunity and very, very proud that I represented England. I wish things had turned out differently but I'm very happy that cricket has brought me all that it has.

Two poor team batting efforts at Newlands saw England lose the Test by an innings. The series was gone.

Pollock: We rolled them out twice and the wicket wasn't really untoward. They were tired and maybe mentally drained. We really fancied ourselves and were playing some really good cricket. They'd come on tour and given debuts to so many players and others were young. We weren't really surprised about how it all went.

Butcher: I begged Nasser to let me go home. My personal life was in ruins. But he wanted me to stay. He said we had so many inexperienced lads that, if I went, it would seem even worse.

There was still one more Test to play – at Centurion Park. For a while it was a memorable game, then infamous.

Pollock: There wasn't much on the game and we were thinking about the one-dayers, as the rain went on and on.

There was play on the first day and then nothing for a further three. The rain kept falling.

Pollock: Then on the last morning Hansie came to us and said: 'Maybe we could set something up.'

The captain's plan was for both teams to forfeit an innings and for England to chase a contrived target. No such thing had happened in a Test match before.

Hussain: Alec Stewart came up to me and he said: 'I've just passed Hansie on the stairs. He wants a word with you about making a game of it.'

Pollock: In our changing room some of us were saying: 'We've won it 2-0. Why are we even giving them a chance of winning a game?' Others thought 3-0 would be even more impressive. There was even talk that, if we won, we'd go up the rankings. I remember thinking: 'Ach, it's the end of the series, we've bowled enough overs already. Let's bat for as long as we can and bowl as little as possible.'

Hussain: Fletcher and myself are both cautious souls and our first thought was to leave it. We even wondered if it was the right thing to do. It was a Test match after all.

Hussain declined Cronje's offer and South Africa resumed their innings. Then he had a change of heart.

Hussain: After 10 minutes or so it was obvious that the pitch was doing nothing and I thought, 'This could be so boring.' So I pretended to the umpires that I needed a toilet trip and I went to see Cronje, fully expecting him to say, 'Sorry mate, you've missed your chance.'

But the offer was still on. The two men haggled over runs to be scored and overs to be bowled.

Hussain: Tufnell was my chief negotiator – he knew what he was doing having played with Mike Gatting for so long at Middlesex – and the three of us made a deal in the showers.

Pollock: On the county circuit in England there was a tradition of captains getting a finish on the last day. I think if we had been playing against any other side it wouldn't have happened.

Hussain: Don't forget I'd grown up at Essex under Keith Fletcher, who was a legendary 'let's get a game out of it' captain. Also there was a sense of frustration for the supporters, the Barmy Army, who'd come a long way to watch it rain.

Out of the showers and on to the pitch. South Africa would bat on to give England a target. 249 to win in 76 overs.

Hussain: The first thing I did was run Darren Gough ragged. He'd had one too many rum and cokes the night before and had a significant hangover, so I bowled him into the ground to get the rum out of his system.

Cronje was as good as his word. He declared on time. Then England batted.

Hussain: There's no doubt he was trying to win the game and for a while he looked as if he would. But even at the time I did think, 'Why is he putting himself on to bowl?'

England were huffing and puffing towards their target. Wickets fell but mini-partnerships took them closer. At eight down they needed nine from the Test's final 13 balls. Chris Silverwood and Darren Gough did the necessary. England had won an unusual game.

Pollock: We weren't as depressed as if we'd lost a normal Test. We had given them the opportunity by creating the game. I remember seeing the England players celebrating in the dressing room and a couple of the guys were saying: 'Wow – they get excited over this?'

Butcher: Afterwards, on the team bus, I felt really flat. I was chatting to Atherton and I said I felt uneasy – I mean none of us for a second knew what had really happened, but something wasn't right.

Hussain: Well, at the time I think a few people were quite proud – 'what a good day for cricket' and all that. And if South Africa had won, and taken the series 3-0, everyone would have said what a masterful captain Cronje was.

Except he was not masterful, he was a cheat. Months later it was revealed that the South Africa captain had spent a lot of time trying to fix matches with bookmakers. This had been one of them. Cronje had been given £5,000 and a woman's leather jacket to try to engineer a win for one side or the other.

Pollock: Afterwards a lot of people came up to me and said, 'I told you we shouldn't have done it' and 'I knew something was on the go', but I don't think any of them did. Of course, looking back, that was one of the occasions where we were let down but there and then no one thought anything of it.

Hussain: I was well chuffed at the time but of course it was tainted. Now I don't view it as one of my Test wins. How naïve we all were. We fell victim to a horrible virus.

Interviews by Simon Lister

Men behaving badly

England's 'sex, drugs and rock 'n' roll tour' of New Zealand, 1983–84

England's trip to New Zealand was mired in allegations of improper behaviour off the field and poor performances on it. Tabloid headlines dogged the team throughout, culminating in Ian Botham's later admission that he had smoked dope during the tour 'as a way out'.

Stephen Boock (New Zealand spin bowler): If they made a television programme about it now it would be called Cricketers Behaving Badly.

Nick Cook (England spin bowler): Players were left to do their own thing during the trip and there were perhaps one or two big names on the tour who, shall we say, might have done things differently.

England began their trip with a short jaunt to Fiji, where they warmed up with two matches before flying to New Zealand.

Cook: Before leaving England I did some training at Leicester City with players like Gary Lineker, Alan Smith and Mark Wallington – all Leicester legends. I did a lot of short sprint work which was supposed to make me quicker. It never worked.

The first Test at Wellington set the scene for the tour. England threw away a winning position with Jeremy Coney scoring a match-saving century for New Zealand.

Cook: I bowled 67 overs in the second innings and every single one was into the wind. For a normal person the Wellington wind is more than a normal breeze. Lance Cairns came in and I had him lbw first ball but the umpire said no. He and Coney put on a record stand and that was the end of my series. My dad travelled all the way out for the last two Tests and never saw me bowl a ball.

England picked up a couple of injuries in a warm-up game against Otago. With Graham Dilley and Neil Foster struggling, the England management called up Sussex's 25-year-old Tony Pigott, who was playing state cricket for Wellington.

Boock: Tony Pigott was a real shock for us as Neil Mallender was head and shoulders above him as a bowler. Mallender had bowled well for years for Otago and in our camp we thought he would have had far more impact than Pigott.

Tony Pigott (England bowler): I had been injured for a month and was just coming back. I was playing my first game at Central Districts' Palmerston North and my shins were sore. I was sat in the pavilion feeling sorry for myself when someone said there was a call for me. This guy said he was Alan Smith, the England tour manager. I said 'right ho'. But he was serious and said they had some injuries and were going to fly me down to Christchurch.

There was a slight complication. Pigott was due to get married on the third morning of the match.

Pigott: Alan Smith asked me if I was fit and I said 'yes, absolutely', but I said there might be a problem as I was getting married on Sunday and the Test was due to start on the Friday. He asked me if that was an issue. I rang my girlfriend and explained the situation and she told me to get down there and play. I wasn't about to throw away the chance of a lifetime.

New Zealand also made a surprise choice. They brought back Boock after four years out of the Test side.

Boock: I thought I'd never play again but the selectors brought me back to bowl at David Gower. I never enjoyed bowling to left-handers and it would have frightened the living daylights out of me to find out that the selectors thought this was a good tactical idea. Knowing my record, Gower would probably have agreed with our selectors and thought it a good idea for me to bowl to him.

The pitch at Christchurch was awful and England felt they could blow New Zealand away with a four-man pace attack. Pigott made his debut.

Pigott: When I got to the ground I went for a warm-up and saw the injured lads having a fitness test. It was soon after that I learned I would play. Within 24 hours I'd gone from sitting in that pavilion at Palmerston North to bowling for England.

Richard Hadlee (New Zealand allrounder): The pitch was two-paced but you can't blame the pitch for the way England played.

Boock: It was not a good pitch. The fourth ball was bowled by Bob Willis and it hit a big crack and flew over Bob Taylor's head, one bounce and into the sightscreen.

England captain Willis won a crucial toss and New Zealand were in trouble at 87 for 4. Pigott started with seven maidens and two wickets in his first 11 overs.

Pigott: I can't remember being nervous. The only problem I had was that there was a big slope at Christchurch and I was a downhill bowler. Here, though, I had to bowl uphill and into a stiff breeze, but to be honest, if there had been a brick wall I would have run through it.

New Zealand were saved by Hadlee and England's tactics. The Botham v Hadlee rivalry was an intriguing sub-plot, and as England grew increasingly desperate, it was clear who was going to be the winner. Hadlee made 99.

Hadlee: I didn't find it too difficult to score runs. England gave me a lot of room to play shots and they bowled too short. People ask me if I was disappointed to get 99 but I know that it was worth 300 in the context of that match.

Pigott: We thought they couldn't play the short ball. Hadlee changed the whole way they thought, though. They were nervous but he came in and slapped them out of trouble. He changed the innings by slogging.

Boock: England played bully-boy cricket. There was no finesse about their bowling and the way they approached the games. Hadlee making 99 was frustrating for Botham. The shorter Botham pitched the ball, the further Hadlee stepped away and smashed it through the off side.

Cook: We just played badly and Botham got carried away trying to outdo Hadlee.

Hadlee eventually fell when he thick-edged an attempted slog and was caught behind. New Zealand made 307. It was 100 more runs than they would need.

Pigott: I didn't get any advice from anyone. Richard Hadlee was smashing me everywhere and I kept thinking I would not get another bowl but they kept giving me the ball. I wasn't offered any advice or help.

England started their innings poorly. Boock dismissed Graeme Fowler with his first ball.

Boock: It was at the end of the day. I just rolled my arm over and got it down the other end. Like many of the other batsmen I bowled in my career Graeme Fowler played for turn and it went outside his bat and hit his off stump. It was a pretty remarkable comeback and began the second half of my career.

England lurched to disaster. They were bowled out for 82 in the first innings and were forced to follow on.

Hadlee: Blokes were out caught on the boundary and Gower shouldered arms. It was not all down to the pitch. We bowled line and length and let the conditions do the rest.

Boock: England batted the way they bowled. Brainless. They were incredibly dim.

In the second innings England fared little better. Boock dismissed Botham first ball and England were bowled out for 93. The match lasted 12 hours, as did Pigott's Test career. He never played for England again.

Boock: Botham's attitude was an eye-opener. He was a remarkable player but he let himself down badly. When he walked off after I got him out, he was laughing. It was quite remarkable.

Pigott: Looking at the amount of preparation I had had I thought I had done pretty well. I thought I would get another opportunity. When I look back it was only a small part of my life but it was a huge three days. Running in to bowl for England was a fantastic experience.

After the Test, newspapers in New Zealand reported that cannabis had been smoked in the England dressing room. The sex, drugs and rock 'n' roll moniker for the tour was born.

Cook: People said there were wet towels put over the doors of the dressing room to stop the smell of cannabis coming out but that was a load of rubbish. I can categorically say that never happened. I suppose it was a good old-fashioned tour. The nickname was a bit unfair because it tarred everyone with the same brush. I'm not saying everyone was pure as driven snow but I never saw anyone take drugs.

Ian Botham (from *My Autobiography: Don't Tell Kath*): I found my escape in an occasional joint. Dope was merely a way out of the pressures; it is not something I condone, it just happened. I can't justify my actions but there were times when I hid in my room, had a joint and totally switched off, otherwise I think I might have gone round the bend.

A flat pitch in Auckland allowed New Zealand to draw and win their first Test series against England. England fared little better in Pakistan. Botham's remark that it was the kind of place to send your mother-in-law was a suitably ill-conceived epitaph for England's winter.

Interviews by Nick Hoult

CHAPTER 5

Great Performances

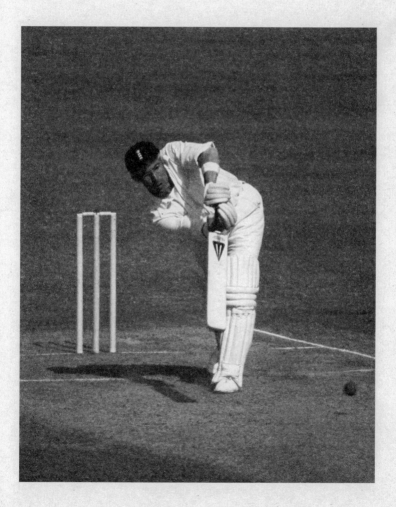

… bowlers felt as if they were trying to knock down a tank with a pea-shooter …

Somerset captain Peter Roebuck on Graeme Hick's 405 not out for Worcestershire at Taunton in 1988

overleaf:
David Steele batting for England at Lord's during the second Test of Australia's 1975 tour

At the mercy of Percy

Pat Pocock's magnificent seven in 11 balls, 1972

A county match between Sussex and Surrey at Eastbourne. Unremarkable? Far from it! Those who played that day witnessed 'Percy' Pocock bowl one of the most memorable spells ever seen.

Pat Pocock (Surrey spin bowler): The Saffrons was a nice ground. Small though, and a good wicket. The ball didn't turn an awful lot.

Robin Jackman (Surrey bowler): That's right. Good track. Not much there for the bowler.

John Spencer (Sussex bowler): It had been a nice wicket but by 1972 my view is that it had changed. It took a bit more spin as I remember.

Micky Stewart (Surrey captain): When I was a kid, I played for the West Surrey club and we used to tour Sussex and have a game at Eastbourne. Some of my old pals from West Surrey had come along to watch this one.

They were enjoying a relatively inconsequential three-day Championship match in August and Surrey were the defending champions. Rain had taken away most of the first day's play, so after three declarations, Sussex had been asked to chase 205 in two and a quarter hours on the last afternoon. It was becoming a cruise.

Jackman: We were completely dead and buried. We were going to lose quite comfortably.

Stewart: A few times I had to fetch the ball from the boundary in front of my mates and they said: 'You'll never win this one, Micky.' I said: 'Tell you what. If we do, you give me a fiver and if it's a draw I'll take two pounds and ten shillings off you . . .'

With nine wickets in hand, Sussex had made 187 with three overs of the game left. They needed 18 runs from 18 balls when Pocock stepped up to bowl his penultimate over of off-spin.

Paul Phillipson (Sussex No. 11 batsman): We'd finished our bowling and the feeling at the time was: 'That's our bit done, boys. Now it's over to you to knock the runs off.' And that's what was happening.

With his first ball, Pocock bowled Geoff Greenidge for 68. That brought Mike Buss to the wicket. His brother Tony was also in the side.

Pocock: Ah, of course. The two Busses. Their nicknames were 'Omni' and 'Trolley'.

Mike Buss (Sussex allrounder): Strange to say it for such a remarkable match, but I have no memory of it whatsoever. Have you tried my brother, Tony?

Tony Buss (Sussex bowler): Was I playing in that game? I was? I'm terribly sorry, but I don't remember a thing about it.

The first Buss lasted two balls then departed. Bowled by one that went straight through. Sussex were 187 for 3 with 16 balls left.

Jackman: 'Percy' had a good arm ball which he'd bowl as a little swinger. It was his other ball because no one bowled a doosra in those days. He'd set it off wicket to wicket and it got a few people out, especially those playing the sweep shot.

The former England wicketkeeper Jim Parks had now come in at five and took two from his first ball. He blocked the fifth ball but was caught by the bowler off the last delivery.

Pocock: Poor old Jim. Caught and bowled, Pocock. A rare way to go. He doesn't know how unlucky he was.

Pocock's over had cost two runs and he'd removed three Sussex batsmen. Sixteen were needed from 12 balls. Robin Jackman ran in to bowl his last over of the match. It went for 11. Five to win from the final over and six wickets still in hand.

Jackman: Thanks for reminding me. I'd conveniently forgotten that part of the day. Couldn't we say I bowled a maiden?

Phillipson: We'd had a wobble, but by this stage we were confident we'd get the runs.

Stewart: However well you're batting, especially in a limited-overs game – which this had now become – the last 20 runs are the hardest to get.

Pocock began his last over. Roger Prideaux, three short of his second century of the match, was on strike. He tried to end the game in one blow.

Pocock: He smashed it to the deep and Robin Jackman was under it. Deep square leg or midwicket, I think. Anyway, it was another wicket down and meant I was on the hat-trick.

It was at about this time that the phone rang outside the Surrey dressing room. Arthur McIntyre, the county coach, was calling from London for a progress report.

Pocock: The 12th man, Ian Payne, answered. 'What's happening?' asked the coach. 'Well, they need five off the last over but Pat's just got a couple of wickets. His hat-trick ball's coming up.' 'I'll hold on then,' said Arthur.

The man facing was the Sussex captain Mike Griffith.

Spencer: He went for a big swipe and edged it. Another catch.

Pocock had his hat-trick. His coach was still on the line getting commentary from the dressing room. Jerry Morley was the next man in and he too tried to end the game as quickly as possible.

Pocock: Jerry charged at me and missed. Arnold Long didn't take it cleanly and the ball ended up on the floor but Jerry kept walking towards the pavilion, thinking he was stumped. Then he tried to make a desperate leap back to his crease while I was shouting at Arnold: 'Well take the bloody bails off then!'

Pocock now had four wickets in four balls. The Sussex chase was falling apart and in the dressing room, panic was rising.

Pocock: I would have loved to have been in there when it was all happening. 'What the hell's going on? How could we have messed this up?'

Spencer: We just tried to slog it. Our brains went. I'm a schoolmaster nowadays and whenever I see the boys chasing a target and getting overexcited and losing the plot, I remember Pat Pocock's game. We were professionals and yet it was like watching the school house side.

Stewart: As a skipper you do a few things in these situations, but a lot of it is just to put a bit of doubt in the batsman's mind. Take your time, make sure he can hear you when you say 'Just a bit squarer Jackers, in case he plays for the turn.' Things like that. It's all kidding though.

Phillipson: I don't think I had a pint in my hands, but I had been pretty relaxed. Then all of a sudden – terror! A huge hurry. I was sitting there in absolute disbelief, quickly buckling them on.

Spencer: We had a few fellows in the side who could biff it. And so I think we always thought we'd get the runs. We often changed the lower order to suit the match conditions. Mind you, these collapses were not unheard of at Sussex so it would be unusual for the lower-order lads to be changed and packed. Just in case.

Spencer now made his way to the wicket. There were three balls of the match left. Outside the Surrey dressing room an increasingly irate Arthur McIntyre was still on the phone.

Pocock: Now Arthur could be a bit of a tyrant, and Payney was talking him through the over, saying: 'Oh, there's another wicket . . . blimey and another one!' By this stage Arthur was convinced that he was having the piss taken out of him and he was shouting down the phone: 'I'll get you for this Payne. Just wait till I see you back at The Oval!' All Payney could say was 'Actually coach, Percy's just bagged another!'

Phillipson: Total confusion reigned. I was up and down like a yo-yo. 'Will I bat? No, it's OK. Oh, I will be needed . . .' The pavilion there was very small and the windows were at the back. The spectators were right on top of us and we were in the dressing room and just kept hearing these shouts and another batsman would return.

Spencer: The ground had a couple of shortish boundaries on both sides of the square. And I think that actually counted against us because if it had been at The Oval, say, a much bigger ground, there would have been plenty of twos and places to knock the ball around.

Stewart: By this stage they were seven down and I was thinking: 'We could nick this . . .'

John Spencer was now taking guard. There were three balls of the match left, Sussex had three wickets remaining and still needed five to win. Spencer defied Pocock and scored a first-ball single, but with Tony Buss now taking strike, normal service was resumed. Another wicket fell as Buss was clean bowled.

Spencer: What did Pat do? He bowled it full and straight. Everyone just kept missing it. I was up the other end staring in disbelief.

Pocock's over had taken nearly a quarter of an hour to bowl. Four wickets had fallen and there was still one ball left. A four would still win it for Sussex. The club's overseas player, Uday Joshi, took strike. He scored a single but then tried for two. The match ended with a run-out. Sussex were still three runs short and had thrown away a great opportunity.

Spencer: We really messed that up because we enjoyed beating Surrey. It didn't happen too often and when it did, we liked it as they got pretty miserable when they lost.

Stewart: I always think of this game when I'm listening to a match and the commentator says 'and they're coasting it now'. We got out of jail all right. And I took home an extra couple of quid courtesy of the chaps from West Surrey.

An extraordinary match had ended in a draw. Sussex had lost eight wickets for 15 runs. Their collective failure was brought about by a single man. Pat Pocock had equalled or broken several bowling records. Five wickets in six balls. Six wickets in nine balls. Seven wickets in 11 balls. His last two overs read: W•W2•W then WWW1WW(run out).

Pocock: Many's the time I bowled a damn sight better for nothing.

Jackman: Percy was a fine off-spinner. If he had played in a different era he'd have played many more Test matches. You know Ray Illingworth was the England captain at this time, so that meant there was one less spinner needed. Then Tony Greig came along with his spinners and cutters . . .

Pocock: It was my publicity day, I think that's how I remember it. Most people remember me as an England nightwatchman getting bounced by West Indies, but there was this too. And you know what? It wasn't even my favourite bowling memory. I'll tell you what that was: nought for 152 from 57 overs against West Indies, Sabina Park, 1973–74. With a 55-yard straight boundary.

Kallicharran, Lloyd, Kanhai, Sobers. Best I bowled in my life.
When I tell people that they say, 'Pat you're talking double Dutch,
mate.'

Interviews by Simon Lister

Look who's grovelling now

Michael Holding bowls fast and full,
The Oval, 1976

England captain Tony Greig started the series with the greatest motivational speech of his life. Unfortunately for England, Greig's promise to make West Indies 'grovel' only inspired the opposition and their formidable pace attack. By the time the series reached its conclusion at The Oval, England had lost the Wisden Trophy and a generation of British West Indians were about to celebrate a great triumph. Viv Richards was king and Michael Holding was a hero . . .

Having lost the series at Headingley, England made changes for the final Test. In came Middlesex's Mike Selvey to open the bowling and Dennis Amiss, returning to Test cricket after a 14-month absence, to open the batting.

Mike Selvey (England bowler): At the start of the season Dennis had been hit on the head by Michael Holding while playing for the MCC at Lord's. It knocked his confidence quite a bit. I turned up to nets on the Wednesday and was told to bowl off 15 yards to Dennis. I was supposed to be opening the bowling for England the next day but I was preparing by bowling off 15 yards. You can imagine what that does for your line and length, not to mention your self-esteem, especially when you know the guys in the other side are 15% quicker.

1976 was a long hot summer. By the time of the fifth Test, The Oval was parched. The outfield was patchy and the pitch baked hard. West Indies won a vital toss and batted first. Gordon Greenidge was out for a duck but Viv Richards took England apart.

Michael Holding (West Indies bowler): I remember Viv batted with a Stuart Surridge Jumbo bat in those days. It was huge. He had a good partnership with Lawrence Rowe who made a brilliant 80-odd but because of Viv nobody remembers Lawrence's innings. Viv just blasted it. He was batting brilliantly the whole summer and it carried on at The Oval.

Selvey: Knotty dropped a catch off me. It was my first over and he needed one catch to break the world record. Roy Fredericks nicked it straight to first slip and Knotty tried to pinch it but missed. It's probably the only catch he ever dropped. By the end of the first day Viv was 200 not out. It's probably the only time in a Test match that a No. 3 batsman has scored 200 in a day.

At the start of the second day talk was of the 24-year-old Richards breaking Garry Sobers' Test record of 365.

Selvey: Even to this day I can't work out why he got out. Tony Greig got him out somehow through a combination of bowled, caught and stumped. He had never looked like getting out and he was on course to beat Sobers' record. It was not a question of if but when.

Dickie Bird (umpire): Richards' innings was one of the best I've ever seen. It was just awesome. His range of shots was magnificent all around the wicket.

An excited West Indian crowd invaded the pitch when Richards reached 200. It happened several times throughout the match.

Bird: There were discarded rum bottles and Coke cans all over the pitch. The West Indies supporters were all good-natured though.

One big West Indian chap came up to me and put his arm around me and called me Professor Dickie Bird: the professor of cricket.

West Indies made 687 – their highest total in England. Derek Underwood toiled through 60 overs for England.

Selvey: On the evening before the match Tony Greig said at the team dinner that we may not be able to outbat or outbowl them but we can at least outfield them. I remember looking around while Derek Underwood was bowling. Derek looked terrible by that point and in the field he had the likes of David Steele, Bob Woolmer, Peter Willey and me. I don't think a bigger set of stiffs have fielded for England in a Test. I thought: 'Well said, Greigy.'

On such a good batting strip England were confident of avoiding the follow-on and their reply was led by Amiss. He had devised a new tactic against fast bowling. He moved back and across and hit into the leg side.

Selvey: Dennis played a fantastic innings. They say he had been playing that innings in the nets for three months. Bob Willis told me he had spent months in the nets with the fast bowlers firing it in at him. He was a tremendous player off his legs and all he did was step right across his stumps and flick the ball away through the on side. It was brilliant.

Dennis Amiss (England batsman): Everybody had written me off against fast bowling. I'd had some problems and I was determined to try and put the record straight. My confidence had been low but I came back. It was an important innings for the team and myself.

Holding: We were trying to hit his leg stump. He had this awkward stance and I kept bowling at leg stump but he would just glance it away. The only chances he gave were through the leg gully area but I didn't have a fielder there.

Amiss made 203 but apart from a fifty by Alan Knott England were destroyed by Holding. Despite the conditions he took 8 for 92, his best bowling figures.

Selvey: I don't remember them bowling any bouncers because of the pitch. Holding just bowled fast from the Vauxhall End and he bowled straight. It proved his rank as one of the greatest bowlers in Test cricket. It is hard to overestimate how well he bowled. It was fast. It was straight. It was accurate. It was awesome.

Bird: I nicknamed him Whispering Death because I couldn't hear him when he was running in. It was the most fantastic piece of fast bowling I had ever seen.

Amiss: The worst part was when Tony Greig came in. He got them going after the grovel remark. Before he came in they were bowling at a nice pace of about 85 mph but when Tony came to the wicket it went up to about 90 and three bouncers an over. I've never been as pleased to see an England captain bowled.

Clive Lloyd decided against enforcing the follow-on. Fredericks and Greenidge made 182, allowing West Indies to declare. England had to bat out six hours to save the match.

Amiss: As it was such a good strip we were confident of saving the match. Michael bowled very quickly and he was the Rolls-Royce of fast bowlers when he was purring.

Holding took 6 for 57 to finish the match with 14 for 149, the best-ever figures by a West Indian.

Holding: I was 22 years old and just ran in and bowled. I didn't even think about the conditions – you don't at that age. I tried to bowl as accurately as possible because there was no way I could bowl a bouncer. I was getting good in-swing and I kept the ball full. It was my best Test as far as figures are concerned but I bowled better than that in different circumstances. At The Oval it was simple: bowl fast and bowl full.

Interviews by Nick Hoult and Howard Sanders

Gooch's Indian Summer

Graham Gooch's triple century against India, Lord's, 1990

Graham Gooch had taken on the England captaincy late in his career but rarely can anyone have led from the front so effectively. England beat New Zealand 1–0 in the summer's first three-Test series, winning the final Test at Edgbaston, with Gooch hitting his ninth Test century. He then made 177 for Essex against Lancashire at Colchester. He had turned 37 yet was in the form of his life and it was about to get even better.

India won the toss and put England in, to the annoyance of their coach, Bishan Bedi.

Graham Gooch (England captain): I would have batted first. Normally at Lord's it's slowish on the first day, then hardens up a bit. I was feeling good after Colchester and my 154 against New Zealand at Edgbaston. I'd been having a fantastic season, working hard on the technical side, playing nice and straight, strong mentally. I was 37 but my body was still in tip-top condition. When I coach now I tell youngsters they must work just as hard when they're in form as when they're out of it.

Angus Fraser (England bowler): It was my first Test back after a rib injury. We were put in and it didn't appear such a horrendous decision at the time; the pitch wasn't damp but it wasn't bone-hard.

Mike Atherton (England batsman): It seemed a pretty good pitch but there was no great uproar when they shoved us in.

When Gooch had 35 he reached 30,000 career first-class runs. One run later he was dropped by the Indian keeper.

Kiran More (India wicketkeeper): I clearly remember it was a straightforward catch, except in England the ball wobbles a bit in the air after it passes the bat and that's a test for a keeper. I failed the test on that occasion. I'm often ribbed about it. But it just shows you how tough cricket can be.

Gooch: Sometimes you get luck. You don't get too many chanceless innings.

Changing his left glove as a superstition after each 50, he then went on to record his 13th hundred that summer.

Atherton: It was pretty inevitable he was going to score a big hundred. He was in fantastic form – right at the top of his game. He was absolutely set, never gave his wicket away. He was remorseless.

Fraser: As a bowler, watching a team-mate bat like that gives you a joyful feeling, knowing you can put your feet up. It wouldn't happen now but it gave me the chance to catch up with mates in the corporate boxes.

Gooch ended the first day on 194.

Gooch: That night I had dinner with Doug Insole, a friend and wise counsellor. I was really tired, because in those days you didn't get much more than a day off between matches. Doug told me not to drink too much red wine.

Gooch took an early net on day two with coach Micky Stewart, then carried on where he left off. A four off Manoj Prabhakar took him past his previous Test best of 196. Then he overhauled Wally Hammond's 240, the highest Test score by an Englishman at Lord's, and Geoff Boycott's 246, the best for England against India. He then beat Don Bradman's 254, the highest by anyone in a Lord's Test. He survived a 'flutter of nerves' in the 290s, particularly as he went to tea on 299, before becoming the 12th Test triple centurion.

Fraser: I bowled to Brian Lara during his 375 in 1994 and the relentless nature of Gooch's innings was similar. They went on and on and on . . . and on. There wasn't any noticeable upsurge in tempo in any particular session, no moment when the innings took off; just Gooch, with that hangdog expression, demonstrating his insatiable desire for runs. The only thing that changed was his partners.

Gooch: I knew of Sobers' 365 record but I can honestly say the only target I had was 300 because I'd scored 275 against Kent at Chelmsford, got myself out and kicked myself. I just wanted to get my 300, for Robin to get 100, then declare. When I got out – to a lazy airy sort of drive off Prabhakar – I got a mild ticking-off from Micky; he said I should have got the record. Afterwards, I have to say, I did wish I'd gone on – but it's not keeping me awake at night now!

More: Gooch kept building on and on in little blocks. Being on the receiving end of an innings like that makes you a better cricketer.

Sanjeev Sharma (India seamer): It was difficult even to beat the bat, or get a number of dot balls in once Gooch was set. He was great against the medium-pacers and played adventurous shots against the spinners Narendra Hirwani and Ravi Shastri. The sweep was his strength, and he used a heavy bat, but he lifted the ball over square leg regularly.

Ravi Shastri (India spinner): The match was great entertainment. You had six hundreds, a good track for batting but I remember it for the amount of fielding. Graham Gooch's bat just got wider and wider. I was sick of bowling at him after the World Cup semi-final in 1987 [where he made 115]. He had taken the game from us when I thought we were going to win back-to-back World Cups. That was the most disappointing game in my entire career. We would have beaten Australia in the final for sure. Lord's was rubbing salt into the wound.

Narendra Hirwani (India spin bowler): It's almost wrong to go back to that knock. How can you even ask me to remember? I've been trying to forget how badly we got hit. The way he massacred us is painful. Unlike some of the other English batsmen in history, Gooch really knew how to play spin. He had three types of sweep – on the ground and in the air, in front of square and behind. He hit us to every part of the ground.

Sanjay Manjrekar (India batsman): Our attack was made to look mediocre. In the 1990s outside India we didn't have the aggression – our fast bowlers rarely bowled bouncers. Even when he was on 200 Gooch was still hitting the ball with lots of energy. I was at forward short leg – we were obsessed with that position no matter what the score was – and from close quarters I remember his heavy bat punching balls all over the park.

Dickie Bird (umpire): It was magnificent batting by Graham and I had the best seat in the house. I really thought he'd go past Garry Sobers' record, but it was still a tremendous feat. I kept having a natter with him, geeing him up a bit, keeping him going. The best knock I saw him play was his 154 not out against West Indies at Headingley in 1991 but this was nearly as good.

Gooch finished with 333, from 485 balls with 43 fours and three sixes, and declared soon after he was out with England on 653 for 4. India struck back with 454. Shastri scored a hundred and Mohammad Azharuddin's innings was particularly special.

Shastri: We fielded a heck of a lot and we then had 70 minutes to survive before close of play. It started beautifully and I was 20-odd not out at stumps. The next day I played really well to reach a hundred, then, when it was the best part of the day to bat, when the sun came out on a packed house on the Saturday, I threw it away trying to hit Eddie Hemmings over the top. I got carried away with the occasion. I should have got a big one and it stayed in my mind, so when I got runs at The Oval later in the series I made sure it was a big hundred [he made 187].

Fraser: Azharuddin's innings was superb; it's why I rate him the second-best batsman I bowled to after Lara. If you bowled two inches outside off stump, he'd clip you through midwicket. Six inches outside and that magnificent cover drive would send the ball flashing through backward point. It was a brilliant innings by a brilliant player.

Atherton: Azhar was blessed with genius. Fantastic, wristy strokeplay, he had a wafer-thin bat but he hit it as hard as anyone.

Fraser: The pitch was slowly getting harder. Things were happening a bit quicker. I bowled well. I'm not bitter but some of my best performances have been overshadowed; I took an eight-for at Barbados in 1994, only for Alec Stewart to hit back-to-back centuries, and I bowled pretty well in this Test [match figures of 8 for 143]; but at least people were starting to see I could take wickets on flat surfaces.

Gooch: Gus bowled beautifully, with real snap, it was such a shame he had his hip injury a year later. He was a captain's dream.

Fraser: I had Kapil Dev caught by Goochie at second slip but my follow-through took me in front of the umpire Nigel Plews. He turned to Dickie Bird at square leg for help but he told him he was on his own.

Gooch: I caught it cleanly but I don't really blame Kapil for staying. I remember Dickie's exact words: 'Nigel, I can't help you.'

At 430 for 9 India were still 24 runs away from saving the follow-on. Kapil Dev blocked the first two balls of Eddie Hemmings's 20th over, then hit four sixes in four balls to make England bat again.

Fraser: Eddie started his career as a medium-pacer but his mentality changed and if someone slogged him, he'd toss it up a bit further. He'd say: 'Come on, go for it.' He'd lay down the challenge.

Atherton: I was at long on but they all sailed over my head. There was never any danger of me having to catch one.

Shastri: Those four sixes were typical Kaps, as instinctive as you can get. That was brilliant, 24 to save the follow-on and then boom, boom, boom, boom.

Gooch: I was annoyed, as we got Hirwani lbw straight after. It was the most astonishing assault by Kapil that I'd seen under pressure.

England then made 272 for 4 in their second innings. The first-wicket stand of 204 between Atherton and Gooch was England's best against India for all of a fortnight until they made 225 in the next Test at Old Trafford.

Gooch: We did what we'd set out to do pretty quickly.

Fraser: Athers was determined not to miss out a second time.

Gooch's aggregate of 456 was the highest ever in Tests and second-highest in first-class cricket. Sachin Tendulkar took a stunning one-handed catch to dismiss Allan Lamb.

Gooch: That was the first time we really sat up and took notice of this little curly-haired lad.

Atherton: His 119 not out at Old Trafford in the next Test really made me take notice!

Set 472 to win, India were all out for 224.

Gooch: Angus and Devon really complemented each other. Gus bowled a good line and length while Dev was quick but erratic, dynamic at times but a bit of a wild card. They made a good pair.

Fraser: Gooch's run-out [of Sanjeev Sharma] in the last session knocked out the middle stump – a fitting finale.

Gooch: That didn't happen too often in my career!

Wisden *called the Test 'as brilliant a match as the players could hope to take part in'.*

Shastri: We thought we had played well enough not to be losers in that game. After England scored over 600, we scored 400 in double-quick time. It left too much time to save the game on the last day.

Atherton: A fine balance between bat and ball makes for a great Test but this was dominated by bat, so I'd call it good, not great. There were plenty of talking points, though, and I'm certainly glad I played in it.

Gooch: It was a good tactical game – great for the public.

Interviews by Huw Turbervill and Anand Vasu

Kim's game of his life

Kim Hughes v the West Indies pace quartet, Melbourne, 1981

When West Indies went to Australia in 1981 they had not lost in 15 Tests. Australia had just lost against Pakistan, albeit a dead rubber, by an innings. On an MCG pitch so lively it was deadly West Indies had Holding, Garner, Roberts and Croft. Australia had Kim Hughes.

Terry Alderman (Australia bowler): It was a shocking wicket. If you get a bouncer halfway down the wicket, on a normal wicket you duck under it but on that MCG wicket you weren't sure whether it was going to fly over your head or cannon into you. I ducked into a Joel Garner bouncer and copped it on the back of my head.

Andy Roberts (West Indies bowler): It was not a very good pitch and it stayed that way till the end.

Kim Hughes (Australia batsman): It hadn't been a good wicket for a number of years because it had very dangerous bounce. It was variable and when you are facing fast bowlers of that stature, it is the worst surface to bat on because you're not too sure if it's going to be up or down. Add to that the wetness on the first day and it was quite a task.

When Hughes came in, Australia were 8 for 3. Greg Chappell was out first ball, his fourth successive duck since the Test defeat by Pakistan.

Roberts: Kim batted very well and played a lot of shots, unlike the other batsmen. He played all of them – he hooked, he cut, he pulled and never gave up. He took up the challenge and it paid off for him. It was a great innings. You don't find one batsman playing that sort of innings on more than one occasion. That was just his day. The nature of the pitch demanded an innings where he had to counter-attack.

Hughes: I realised pretty quickly that to hang around and defend was going to be a waste of time because the wicket was such that sooner or later something was going to happen. So, I thought what I could do was try to play as many shots as possible. Hopefully that way the bowlers would forget about bowling at the stumps and try and bowl a bit more at me. Running down the wicket and hitting Joel past cover, hooking Roberts for a boundary, hitting a few square drives off Holding – those were some of the special shots that gave me a lot of pleasure. Sometimes I got carried away. For instance, after that hook shot, I tried hooking another. The ball just came in a couple of yards quicker and Roberts gave me a look that seemed to say, 'Don't get too clever.' I was lucky not to get hit in the head.

Alderman: He went after them. He was ruthless and devastating and at his flamboyant best. We really needed somebody to take on the West Indies. That was the secret: if you fought fire with fire against them, they could crumble just like any other bowling attack.

Gus Logie (West Indies 12th man): Kim Hughes' innings was a magnificent one. He was cutting, driving and pulling against one of the best bowling attacks. It was a lesson in courage and self-belief. I was 21 and that was my first Test series, though I didn't play; I was a substitute in the match. It was a very competitive series. It was the first time I saw, up close and personal, the likes of Dennis Lillee and Jeff Thomson.

There were no restrictions on bouncers, protective helmets were in their infancy and West Indies' attack consisted of nothing but pace, brilliantly intimidating pace.

Hughes: Bodyline was never four quick bowlers all day, it was Larwood from one end for a period of time. The West Indies pace quartet was relentless. You couldn't even get into double figures without respite. They bowled in such a way as to create fear and the best way to do that was to bowl at the head. That was the greatest fear: not losing your wicket but getting hit in the head. That was the greatest bowling attack that has ever been. Michael Holding was a Rolls-Royce – genuinely quick and such a nice action. Then you had big Joel, who was six foot nine, and he had that lethal yorker. And then there was Andy Roberts, who was as close as I've seen to Dennis Lillee with his mental attitude – a quality bowler with a very well-disguised bouncer, and he could vary his pace, bowl cutters. To me, though, Colin Croft was the hardest to face, with his awkward action where he would come from a wide angle and make the ball come in or go away. I found I could get to Joel a bit as his medium pace was easy for me to handle, so I could step out and hit him at times.

Roberts: I didn't look at our bowling as bodyline. Since the wicket wasn't well prepared, a lot of balls that bounced weren't necessarily bouncers. And look at the height of our bowlers – when you've these tall bowlers coming at you, the ball is obviously going to bounce more. For them to say there was a barrage of bouncers was actually fear.

While Hughes fought fire with fire at one end wickets tumbled at the other. The next top score in Australia's first innings was 21. At 155 for 9, Hughes was joined by Alderman, who had a Test batting average of 6.

Alderman: When I went out, Kim was on 70 or so and looking for his hundred. So I told him, 'I might not be hanging around too long with the way this wicket is and the way they're bowling, so you better get after them.'

Hughes: When he walked in, I wished Terry good luck. I almost said to myself that he was gonna need it, because he wasn't the greatest batsman. But he gutsed it out – got in behind them, missed some, hit some and had his share of luck. He didn't flinch, even if he took a few on the body. We were 150-odd when Terry came in and we put on about 40. That lifted everybody's confidence and we finished on a good note. My father-in-law was very ill at the time and he died within about a week of that innings. I knew he was watching. So, the hundred was a special one. Joel bowled one wide of the off stump and I cut it to the point boundary to get to the three-figure mark. It was Boxing Day and the crowds were emotionally involved – a couple of hundred jumped the fence to storm the ground. Immediately after my hundred Terry got out. Croft came running towards me and I thought, 'He's not gonna hit me now, is he?' He said, 'Well played, maan, well played.' In all the years I played against West Indies they never said a word. On that day they appreciated how difficult it was to bat against the four of them and they respected my courage. It was not only my best innings but the greatest day of Test cricket seen at the MCG. Most importantly, we won the Test.

Alderman: When you think of the pressure that Kim was under, batting with the tail, and with his father-in-law in bad shape – taking all those factors into account, it was just one of those outstanding individual efforts.

Hughes had made exactly 100 not out off 200 balls out of 198 all out. Could Australia's own speed merchant Dennis Lillee make use of the dodgy track?

Hughes: We had an hour or thereabouts to go on that first day after we were all out. Our bowlers were all fired up with our fight-back. The crowd were really involved and were chanting and the occasion was ripe for Dennis to do what only he could. Terry got the breakthrough. Then Dennis got Desmond Haynes caught and the nightwatchman Croft lbw. The crowd went ballistic. Viv Richards walked out but he got an inside edge on to the stumps off the last ball of the day. Fifty thousand hands went up in unison. That was probably the only time they were beaten in a match where the conditions suited their bowlers.

Logie: When Richards walked in late in the day, after Hughes' heroic innings, there was this reverberating chant of 'Lillee, Lillee, Lillee,' and the next three words were 'Kill, kill, kill.' Lillee bowled his heart out and had us against the ropes. We were stranded at 10 for 4, from which we never recovered.

West Indies actually secured a tiny first-innings lead but it was a personal triumph for Lillee, who became the leading Test wicket-taker of all time, passing Lance Gibbs' total of 309. West Indies were set 220 to win and fell 58 short, Lillee completing a 10-wicket haul. During the match the Melbourne club announced the relaying of the square over the next three years.

Roberts: We lost the Test match mainly because of umpiring errors – Allan Border got caught at short leg [in the second innings] and it wasn't given. He went on to make 60-odd and that played a crucial part in Australia taking the Test away.

Logie: One interesting thing was, we had not brought the Frank Worrell Trophy to Australia with us, since we couldn't find it. We were wondering what we would hand over if we lost the series. But after the fantastic Test in Melbourne we managed to draw the second and win in Adelaide to draw the series.

Interviews by Nagraj Gollapudi

The Deadly battle of Hastings

Derek Underwood's only first-class century

The Kent and England bowler 'Deadly' Derek Underwood loved the seaside Central Recreation Ground at Hastings. Since the 1960s he had taken wickets there against Sussex for fun. In 1984 he arrived to play in a three-day County Championship game. It turned out that he would be the centre of attention once more.

Derek Underwood (Kent): It was the first proper ground I had played on for Kent schools. So it was already special for that reason. Then I just kept getting wickets whenever I went there.

John Barclay (Sussex captain): It was a lovely ground. A famous ground. In a sort of bowl and they say the playing area was below sea level. When the tide was in there was certainly a lot of moisture around the square.

Underwood: Yes, that's right. If the tide was in, there was seam. If it was out, you batted.

Chris Cowdrey (Kent allrounder): Beautiful ground. In the town, seagulls, the smell of the sea close by. I would say just a decent three-iron into the water. And you know, the thing about Hastings was that it had a ridge. Not a big one – it wasn't a ramp or anything like that but it was there. It was enough.

Barclay: Was there? A ridge? I didn't know that. There could have been I suppose … in fact, let's say there was. Then we have a reason for being bowled out so swiftly.

On a damp and green Saturday at the end of June the Kent captain, Chris Tavaré, won the toss, ignored the tide and batted.

Tavaré: Don't know why I did that, actually.

Barclay: Chris batted and I suppose that could have been viewed as a surprise decision seeing as we bowled them out by lunchtime.

For 92. But Sussex didn't have much fun in their first innings either. Late in the day they were dismissed for 143. Underwood, surprisingly, had seen his two wicketless overs go for 14. But he was soon back in the middle – as nightwatchman. He came in first wicket down as Kent made another fragile start.

Barclay: Twenty-one wickets in the day. That would send the pitch inspectors scurrying nowadays.

On the Monday the game resumed. Apart from Underwood, the break had done nothing for the concentration of the Kent middle order. When the Australian Test bowler Terry Alderman came in at No.10, Underwood was still there but Kent were 155 for 8 with a lead of less than a hundred.

Alderman: I spent half the 1980s bowling in England. 1981, '84, '86, '88 and 1989. Oh yeah – and before all that I played in Scotland. Club cricket for Watsonians. Your wickets were good for me.

Barclay: Derek was brave with the bat. Not blessed with enormous technique or finesse but worthy of a good score in the teens. He certainly wasn't hopeless. Derek, you see, had a very mild face but my word he was a tough cricketer.

Alderman: He was a barnacle. He cherished his wicket but was not always an attacking batsman. Not the prettiest. But he was gutsy.

Cowdrey: It would be fair to say that Derek's natural batting style was ungainly. He always used to bat in his great long bowling boots for a start. But he was the bravest of nightwatchmen. He never gave his wicket away. It was like with his bowling; every ball he bowled he tried his best. His favourite shot – or most used shot – was 'the shovel'. He would shovel it around the corner. In fact, it was his only shot.

Tavaré: Always solid. Very brave. We all recall that photo of him fending off Michael Holding in 1976 below. When he wasn't a nightwatchman, he liked to drive but his shot I remember most was a sort of paddle through the leg side.

Paddle or shovel, it was working well. Underwood made 50 and then stayed for some more.

Underwood: My plan was to race to 30, which I did. Then I thought, 'Bloody hell – I'm all right here.'

Barclay: We bowled badly at him, too full or too short. Derek skilfully chopped the short ones to third man. 30, 40, 50, on he went.

Tavaré: Garth le Roux was bowling faster and shorter and Derek kept swatting him over mid-off, a sort of tennis shot. He just kept going.

Much to the frustration of Sussex. After more than three hours' batting the thought occurred to Underwood that he was nearing a hundred.

Underwood: I was very nervous. I'd had a fifty at the beginning of my career, then much later an eighty – two innings very far apart. But we didn't have many wickets left. I suppose I considered I'd be left short of the ton and not out. Lord knows what Kevin Jarvis, our No.11, was going through. He was next in and he really couldn't bat.

At the other end Alderman was in support.

Cowdrey: Now Terry. That was a different innings. He did bat like a No.10, a No.10 who did very well.

Tavaré: I remember Terry getting hit several times, particularly by Garth le Roux.

Alderman: I hit Garth le Roux for a six. Must have closed my eyes and swung through. It wasn't the biggest of grounds.

Barclay: Terry looked ill at ease, it's true. A very nice man by the way. We were charging in bowling quicker and quicker. I was taking men off at one end and trying them at the other but something was amiss in my captaincy, I have to say. It was awful.

More runs came as both batsmen entered previously uncharted territory. Then for Underwood, a moment of glory.

Underwood: Mercifully it came swiftly. I was lucky. I remember the shot well. Ian Greig was bowling, I was on 98 and he put it on my legs and I flicked it for four.

Aged 39, after 22 seasons and over 600 innings, Derek Underwood had scored his maiden first-class hundred.

Alderman: Mate, that's a long time to wait for anything.

Underwood: It was very special. I always regret I didn't make more first-class runs. But I couldn't get in the first six at Kent. So usually I just tried to hang in there, often batting for the fellow at the other end.

Soon afterwards Underwood was out. He had saved his team. As he walked off he was looking forward to his team-mates' acclaim in the dressing room – except it was empty.

Underwood: I looked around. 'Where are you, you ungrateful buggers?' I thought to myself. The dressing room was deathly silent.

Cowdrey: It was Graham Johnson's idea. He and Bob Woolmer were our practical jokers. Derek came off after all his hard work and we thought it would be fun if we all hid in the showers. Several of us were weeping with suppressed laughter. Then, when he sat down and started taking his pads off, we jumped out and congratulated him.

The prank was so rewarding it was repeated when Alderman returned. He had made 52 not out. It was to be his highest first-class score. The bowlers' batting meant Kent had a target to defend on the last day.

Barclay: We needed less than 200, modest on an improving pitch.

Modest it may have been but, as the afternoon went on, it was beginning to look elusive.

Barclay: Still nervous, I pottered off and bought a cup of tea from the Ladies' Pavilion. This old boy sat down next to me and I just knew he'd strike up a conversation but I have always been quite interested in these sorts of characters and I will never forget this chap.

He had some advice for the captain.

Barclay: 'I used to coach the high jump,' he said. And I thought, 'Oh dear, where are we going with this?' 'Do you know what I used to say to the boys?' he told me. 'I used to say, "Throw your heart over the bar." You'll be fine if you throw your heart over the bar.'

Sussex were trying just that. They had been 89 for 5 chasing 193. Then Ian Greig and Colin Wells had rescued them. At 186 for 6 they were almost home.

Barclay: 'Come on, boys,' I was saying, 'hearts over the bar.'

But with the end in sight, bowling full and fast, Richard Ellison and Terry Alderman both took a wicket. Then Ellison got another.

Barclay: Disaster. Three to win, two to tie. Our last man in was David Smith, the reserve wicketkeeper. David was not exactly the sort of chap you'd plan to have in a crisis, but one must never be critical.

Tavaré: When Terry was bowling, there was always a possibility of something happening.

Something happened. The batsmen managed two runs to level the scores. Then Smith faced Alderman. One to win.

Barclay: As I say, one must never be critical. It was by no means a disgraceful dismissal. He had tried to throw his heart over the bar.

Tavaré: It was a slow, loopy catch at slip. Terry had got him.

The game had ended in a tie.

Barclay: It felt like a defeat. How could we throw it away? It was a very quiet dressing room.

For Kent, and for Underwood and Alderman, it felt more like a victory.

Underwood: A memorable match. Hastings was a very special place for me and I suspect for many Sussex supporters. Very special.

Alderman: Deadly's right. How could I ever forget it? But you know, what's sad is that I can't even go back, get misty-eyed and re-live the moment. You know what I heard? They concreted it all over and built a bloody shopping mall there.

Interviews by Simon Lister

Ilford Seconds 1, England 0

Hadlee bowls New Zealand to historic victory on English soil, 1986

In 1986 New Zealand came to England for their 10th Test tour. None of the other nine had been victorious. But their hosts had already lost to India that summer and Richard Hadlee was in fine form . . .

Mike Gatting (England captain): It was a difficult time. The defeat to India had hit us hard, David Gower had lost the captaincy and we had no Ian Botham. Something had ended up in his bedside dresser that was of the wrong persuasion, shall we say. Bad time to lose your allrounder.

Jeremy Coney (New Zealand captain): Ah yes, the business with the reefer . . .

At the end of May Ian Botham had been banned from Test and county cricket. The Test and County Cricket Board had found him guilty on three charges relating to smoking cannabis and one of publishing an article about it in a Sunday newspaper without the permission of his county, Somerset. The ban meant he missed the three Tests against India and the first against New Zealand.

John Wright (New Zealand batsman): We knew we had a chance. We'd beaten Australia at home and their place. We rated ourselves.

Coney: It looked like everything in the garden was rosy. But it wasn't. As the tour went on, we lost a bowler, a keeper, a manager, then finally all our kit was stolen from the bus. It wasn't plain sailing.

The bowler who was lost was Ewen Chatfield, the undemonstrative farmer's son from New Zealand's North Island. He had been the perfect foil for Richard Hadlee.

Coney: He'd run into the wind for you all day. If there was something in the wicket, he wouldn't get excited, but his moustache would quiver slightly. I knew I could get through a day if I had Chatfield.

That reassurance disappeared when Chatfield broke a thumb early in the tour. New Zealand had to choose between three inexperienced replacements. Willie Watson, aged 20, won the place. England, too, had a debutant for the first Test.

Martyn Moxon (England batsman): Was I nervous? Anyone making their Test debut at Lord's would be nervous.

Gatting: There was a new captain and the players were still getting used to me. There were no hard feelings from David but it would take a bit of time to get things together.

Moxon: As I remember, there was not a lot of talk about the New Zealand team.

The game was drawn. This was the Test when England used four wicketkeepers. Bruce French was hit on the head and was replaced by Bill Athey, then Bob Taylor, who happened to be at the ground with his gloves and did a stint. Finally Bobby Parks of Hampshire was brought in. Moxon, opening the innings, got over his nerves.

Moxon: I think I got 74, didn't I? I was disappointed not to get a hundred but because I had scored some runs, I could at least settle down and enjoy the rest of the game a bit sooner.

The second Test was at Trent Bridge, Hadlee's county ground. New Zealand's star bowler had already taken seven wickets at Lord's and was looking for more.

Gatting: The groundsman must have forgotten he had an England fixture on the calendar. He prepared the wicket as if Nottinghamshire were playing. There was a lot of grass on it.

Richard Hadlee (New Zealand allrounder): I'd played a lot of county cricket at Trent Bridge – and of course had done well there. They were bowler-friendly tracks in those days.

Gatting: New Zealand knew Hadlee was their trump card. They protected him – and it worked.

It was Hadlee's county benefit in 1986 and he was excused playing for his country in their county games, saving himself for the international matches.

Moxon: It was nipping around a bit. I vividly remember it was green and overcast on the first day and when they batted it was beautifully sunny. Then on the Saturday night, when we went back in, it was murky and dark.

Coney: Hadlee knew the pitches, the opposition and his own body. Of course he had that bowler's elephantine mind – remembered every dismissal – and he had the control to exploit it.

Wright: Richard was really on top of his game. Was it Gatting who said it was like facing the World XI at one end and Ilford Seconds at the other?

It was. At least that is now the legend. New Zealand used the put-down to their advantage.

Coney: What happened next was that we had T-shirts made. Ilford Seconds, they said on the front and World XI on the back with a picture of everyone in the squad. I insisted we warm up in them.

Moxon: By Monday morning after the rest day I just couldn't pick Hadlee up. Trent Bridge had these dark windows at one end and it was the only time in my career that I really had trouble seeing the ball. If I'd been more experienced, I'd have said something to the umpires. As it was, I got out and soon after they came off for bad light.

Hadlee: If you played a Test match at Trent Bridge the colour of the wicket would go very white and it was far harder to get Test wickets than on county pitches but on that occasion I got 10 in the match, which was amazing.

Coney: Hadlee. The Prince. The Prince of Professionals.

Wright: All of us who played at the same time as him count ourselves lucky. Actually I think he's still a little bit underrated.

New Zealand won the match by eight wickets to go 1–0 up with one to play.

Hadlee: I think Gower chucked the last ball to be no-balled to give us the run we needed for victory.

He did and so became the first England player to be called for throwing in a Test in England. Wisden recorded that the match was a triumph for Hadlee's exceptional qualities and the whole team's professionalism. 'For England it was another dismal game, the eighth defeat in ten Tests.'

Moxon: I think in those days England were often chopping and changing. I never played more than two Tests in a row in England. That happened to a lot of people. I think the mood was to get your head down and do well for yourself. The concern was to keep your place. Winning was a bonus. That was at home. On tour it was completely different – a much better, closer atmosphere.

Coney: We were even winning the pre-match warm-up sessions. We were meeting in the hotel at 7.30 in the morning and running around the city together – quite a change from our old habits. Before the day's play we were there, tight, controlled, focused, able to enjoy our cup of tea afterwards. England walked out like Brown's cows.

England could have selected Ian Botham for the Trent Bridge Test but declined. That policy changed for the final Test at The Oval.

Gatting: I said to David Gower, 'What shall I do to pick the guys up?' 'Something might happen,' he said. It did too. Botham came back. He stormed in and someone had got changed in his favourite corner. He roared: 'Which **** is using my bench?!' and threw all the kit across the room. Suddenly there was a bit more bubble around the place.

It was a memorable return for England's allrounder. With his first ball back after suspension he had Bruce Edgar caught at slip.

Gatting: It was a tame long hop. I think Edgar was so surprised it was so slow and wide he just left his bat there. Goochie couldn't believe it was coming so slowly and he nearly dropped it. Anyway Beefy was back.

With his 12th ball Botham passed Dennis Lillee's world record of 355 Test wickets. New Zealand were bowled out for 287 and when England took a first-innings lead, there was a chance the series could be drawn.

Gatting: Ian kept hooking Hadlee out of the ground. We were looking for a great position, something like 300 in front. Then it chucked it down for two days.

There was barely an hour's play on the last two days.

Wright: We weren't sad to see the rain. That Test could have gone either way.

The game ended in a draw. New Zealand had won a series in England for the first time.

Coney: We knew that for many of us this would be our last opportunity in England, so we had determination and confidence. We had been building throughout the 1980s and developed a culture of winning at home. And we had begun to dip our toes in winning waters overseas. In a sense this success went against the grain. A little hard to explain but most New Zealanders are diffident, humble and modest.

Wright: We had become tougher. It started under Geoff Howarth, when he was captain. Then we had Glenn Turner as coach. He was a very tough professional. We were getting more experienced and were growing together. That was our good era. We were good in the '80s.

Coney: England may have believed they were unfortunate but we did enough in the first two Tests to suggest that, at the very least, these were two equal sides.

Moxon: It was a disappointing summer. Not a very stable environment. There was a hard core of five or six players, then you could pick the rest from a dozen others. That makes it very difficult to create a winning team.

Coney: We did believe that England would self-destruct. They had too many selectors, a tendency to amputate vital organs, in this case Ian Botham, and they were tinkerers, particularly at home. We knew if we got things right, we could take the tour.

Interviews by Simon Lister

In days of awe

Brian Lara's record-breaking first season with Warwickshire, 1994

Brian Lara was not supposed to be Warwickshire's overseas player in 1994 but his signing proved inspired. When the Indian seamer Manoj Prabhakar failed a medical on an ankle injury Warwickshire moved quickly to recruit Lara, who was then an emerging talent.

Within a week he was a household name across the globe after he hit a Test-record 375 against England in Antigua. Lara's arrival at Edgbaston sparked unprecedented media interest which continued through a summer in which he scored 501 in one innings, equalled Warwickshire's record of nine centuries in a season and helped them become the first county to win three domestic trophies in one campaign.

Lara arrived at Edgbaston the day before the start of the season to be greeted by a phalanx of reporters and photographers, and his county cap from captain Dermot Reeve.

Andy Moles (Warwickshire batsman): It was the sort of reception you would expect a film or pop star to receive and we lived in his reflected glory. We were run-of-the-mill county cricketers, good players but not superstars, and we were not used to that sort of attention. Initially we were in awe of the big crowds Brian attracted but we grew to enjoy it.

Tim Munton (Warwickshire bowler): The media frenzy that greeted his arrival made us all realise what an awesome signing the club had made. All the adulation and interest meant that we played to much bigger crowds than we were used to in county cricket.

The media returned in force for Warwickshire's opening Championship game against Glamorgan at Edgbaston, Lara's first match since his 375. He did not disappoint with a brilliant 147 from 160 balls.

Munton: When Brian arrived he found a note pinned to his locker from Roger Twose welcoming 'the second-best left-hander in the world'. Twosey got a double century against Glamorgan but everyone had come to see Brian. He had pretty much come straight off the plane but he stroked the ball around so effortlessly and that had an awesome impact.

Lara made five centuries in six innings including two in the match against Leicestershire at Edgbaston, which helped to secure an important draw.

Paul Smith (Warwickshire allrounder): Brian played a lot of match-winning innings that season but his second century against Leicestershire was completely selfless. We had identified Leicestershire as a threat early on and we knew it was important to avoid defeat. He was batting with Neil Smith towards the end, who was no mug with the bat, but Brian kept turning down long singles when he was 99 to keep the strike.

Barely two months after he made his Test record score Lara became the first man to score 501 in a first-class innings against Durham at Edgbaston.

Neil Smith (Warwickshire spin bowler): It was a dead game and we were going to have a second bowl to try to improve our over rate but Brian said quite early on that he wanted to go for the world record. Dermot Reeve said that as long as Brian was at the crease we would bat on and you knew he wasn't going to get out. You could go off during the day for a bit of physiotherapy or to the gym and come back knowing he would still be there.

Gladstone Small (Warwickshire seamer): After he got that record it went crazy. Brian did the round of media interviews, his agent had all sorts of commercial things lined up but we had a Benson & Hedges Cup semi-final against Surrey at The Oval the next day.

I know that Brian didn't sleep a wink that night and he looked absolutely shattered when he got to The Oval next day. We put him in the field instead of at slip to give him a rest but he was so tired he had to come off early in the Surrey innings.

When we got back into the dressing room he was fast asleep. Brian was supposed to bat at three but Bob Woolmer sensibly decided it was better to let him sleep. When he did come in we were in trouble and Brian was still not with it but he made 70 off 73 balls and, given the 24 hours he had just had, that was an incredible effort.

Lara's relationship with Dermot Reeve, Warwickshire's captain, was always uneasy and matters came to a head when the pair were involved in an on-field spat at Northampton in late June when Lara asked to leave the field.

Neil Smith: Brian was allowed more freedom than the rest of us when it came to nets and warm-ups and we accepted that as long as things were going well. But, when things didn't go smoothly, there was some resentment. There was always likely to be a clash of personalities between Dermot and Brian because they both wanted to be top dog and matters came to a head at Northampton.

It was sorted out behind closed doors and from what I understand, Tim Munton has to take a lot of credit for the way that he smoothed things over between Brian and Dermot and the club.

Moles: It was a clash of egos and it was an accident that was waiting to happen. We weren't really aware what was happening when we were on the field but there were a lot of behind-closed-doors meetings when we came off. It was a difficult situation because Brian was a superstar and we didn't know how long he was going to be with us. But we didn't want anything to upset our team spirit and the senior players got together and we felt that we ought to support Dermot as captain.

Lara missed Warwickshire's next two matches with a knee injury but he returned to form a month later with a century before lunch against Derbyshire and a pumped-up Devon Malcolm at Chesterfield.

Moles: Devon had us in trouble early on but he bowled at a completely different pace when Brian came in. He had Brian dropped at slip, then hit him on the helmet and for two hours it was what I imagine Test cricket must be like. It was intense, competitive cricket between two high-quality performers.

Devon Malcolm (Derbyshire bowler): Brian was a nightmare to bowl at because he was such an attacking player, always looking to take at least one four an over off you. He was the best batsman in the world at the time and so I put that bit extra in to try to match him. He always gave you a chance early on and I had him dropped at slip. After that he played extremely well and he slapped us all over the ground.

Lara signed off his record-breaking season with 191 against Hampshire at Edgbaston, the game in which Warwickshire secured the Championship and the second trophy of their treble.

Paul Smith: He was the catalyst for what we achieved that season. It's difficult to appreciate the enormous pressure he was under and I think he handled it better than most people.

Munton: I look back on that season with nothing but fond memories. I was captain for a lot of the Championship games and I had no problems with Brian. He was a fantastic guy to have in the side and a superb batsman to watch.

Small: I always enjoyed catching up on my sleep when we were batting and I used to use the physiotherapist's couch to have 40 winks. But I couldn't during that season because Brian was in a league of his own when it came to sleeping. Not only did he steal my bed but he also brought his own duvet in to make himself even more comfortable.

Interviews by Paul Bolton

'Pure magic'

Warne v Dravid, Portsmouth, 2000

A county game between two ordinary sides in 2000. Hampshire versus Kent at the United Services ground in Portsmouth. Except that each team had one superstar. Shane Warne, the world's best leg-spinner, was at the end of his run-up and facing him was Rahul Dravid, the princely Indian batsman. Few people who saw what followed would forget it.

Matthew Fleming (Kent captain): This wasn't a good season for us. We had several young batsmen who were under-performing spectacularly. They all had shockers. For our coach, John Wright, it proved to be his nadir. We usually started batting from about four or five wickets down.

Rahul Dravid (Kent batsman): I almost didn't play. My little pinky on the right hand was dislocated in the previous game against Derbyshire. I did not field in the slips for a month and a half but on the morning of the game I knocked a few balls and, although it was sore, I decided it was fine to bat. If the game had been a day earlier, I probably wouldn't have played.

Fleming: The US ground was a really big thing for me because of my Army career, my Combined Services games. I really wanted to do well there.

Min Patel (Kent spinner): Rahul was a class act. What you learned about him pretty quickly is that whether it was a Test match, a county game or a knock-about in the back garden, he absolutely loved batting for hours and hours and hated giving his wicket away.

Shane Warne (Hampshire spinner): Even in my final year at the club, members would still ask me about this game at Portsmouth.

Adrian Aymes (Hampshire wicketkeeper): There was a great excitement around the place when people knew Shane was coming. And when you were out there with him, face to face, you appreciated him even more. He always tried and you could see especially on flat pitches he'd work even harder.

This pitch was not flat. It was a turner from day one.

Dravid: It was a bit drier than you would normally expect in a county game but it wasn't a vicious turner. If anything it was two-paced. You could play the shots if you got settled down, yet there was purchase for spinners.

Hampshire won the toss and decided to bat. That meant Warne would be bowling last. First, though, he helped his side get to 320 with the second highest score.

Fleming: He slapped it, carved it, a very difficult man to bowl to. Certainly he was not a man who was ever troubled by self-doubt. I got him out [in the second innings], I definitely remember that. He certainly wasn't caught at slip, but I'll claim it as a master-plan.

Late in the day Kent began their innings. Within four overs Warne was given the ball. He took a wicket with his second delivery.

Aymes: The funniest thing was the look in the batsman's eyes. Warne was a spinner but it was exactly the same look I remember when teams played Hampshire and they'd see Malcolm Marshall polishing the ball at the top of his run.

Warne: Sometimes batsmen play the man rather than the ball. In other words, they might treat a shortish delivery as a flipper when really it's a rank long-hop that deserves to be planted over midwicket.

When the nightwatchman, four balls later, treated a shortish delivery as a flipper and was lbw, Dravid came to the wicket. Kent were 15 for 2.

Patel: It was spinning already but it was slow spin, so Warney wasn't ripping it past Rahul's outside edge. He could get forward or back very quickly and play it off the pitch.

John Hampshire (umpire): Dravid mostly played Warney with a straight bat. That's the first thing to say. In other words, he was playing against the spin.

Warne: I thought I was bowling pretty well but Dravid just picked up the length quicker than anybody else in the match and used his footwork to go all the way forward or all the way back.

No more wickets fell that evening. Dravid and David Fulton scored 16 runs between them to leave Kent on 31 for 2 at the end of the first day. After a night's sleep the contest between spinner and batsman would get under way for real.

Aymes: Warne had the slow legger, the quicker one, the flipper and less often the googly because he'd had his shoulder operated on. The problems came when he went around the wicket into the rough. Then, he could bowl a legbreak which would go the other way if it hit the down-part of a crater. That was difficult.

Dravid: I was looking to play him as I would in India: wait for the bad balls and probably play a few more shots than I would do normally.

Aymes: I could see it out of the hand and keepers will always tell you that the best bowlers put it in the right place. It's the lesser bowlers who have you throwing yourself down the leg side. Mind you, the first ball he ever bowled me was a flipper, against Leicestershire. For whatever reason it came out wrong and squirted down the leg side. The batsman fell out of the crease and I managed to get the bails off. A leg side stumping first ball. Well, I felt like retiring there and then. 'What's all this fuss about Ian Healy taking a year to read you?' I said to Warney in the middle.

Hampshire: As an umpire, you always have to be switched on but this was like umpiring a Test match. It was that good. You had to keep your wits about you and at the same time a small part of your mind was simply admiring the skill.

Warne: Most Indian batsmen pick the length very quickly, even when it is flighted above the eyeline. Dravid moved into position very early but Tendulkar moved quicker.

The Australian spinner began his day's work. Some runs came and some wickets fell. Warne was in for a long spell but Dravid wouldn't be beaten. Tanya Aldred was reporting on the game for The Guardian.

'*White wristband, gold necklace, white Adam Ant sun cream stripes and a surprisingly slight figure. Twirl, turn – step, step, step, step, step, step – skip, skip – unfurl. Then it was hands on hips or a squat down on his haunches, first finger and thumb drawn to his nose in anguish. At times he spun it two inches, sometimes two feet, sometimes it went straight on … but he could not faze the Indian batsman.*'

As Dravid batted on, Warne even tried to bounce him.

Aymes: He never gave me the signal but of course, if you saw two fingers across the seam, you were pretty certain it wasn't gonna be the leggie. Actually, I remember Warney beat the bat time after time but Rahul was a class player. He played everything he had to and, when he miscalculated, he was clever enough to miss it. He played it ever so late but, when he did connect, it was with such quick hands.

Others were less skilful. 98 for 4, 99 for 5, 153 for 6. But Dravid stayed.

Fleming: He did this thing that no one else in the game at the time did. He played Warne by getting his front leg out of the way, towards the off side. So he played with his bat only. Certainly in England, everyone else played Warne by leading with bat and pad together, and that of course got them into trouble.

Patel: Yeah. He'd get his bat a good yard in front of his leg. You see Pietersen do it nowadays but we didn't back then. So what it did of course was rule out the bat-pad catch which is a massive mode of dismissal for the leggy.

Hampshire: I should imagine if there was a wagon-wheel of the innings, it would show that many of his scoring shots went between the bowler and straight midwicket.

Warne: His shot selection and timing were brilliant. He is not a stocky man and when you see him display that kind of lightness on his feet, you wonder whether he could have been a ballroom dancer.

Fleming: It was a spectacular lesson to us all. He never swept and had staggering powers of patience.

Patel: It's not often a world-class leg spinner gives a right-hander a long on, a deep midwicket and a deep backward square leg.

When Dravid reached his hundred, even Warne's toddler son applauded.

Warne: I remember my little lad Jackson being there – he was only a year old but even he managed to totter up and clap when Dravid got to his century. It was about the only thing that made me smile that day.

Warne would not even have the satisfaction of Dravid's wicket when he was out for 137 to a part-time spinner.

Aymes: Giles White got him. Dravid got a full bat on it but it spun back. 'Should have brought him on ages ago instead of Warney,' we all joked as we watched Dravid walk away.

Dravid was ninth man out. Soon the Kent innings was over for 252. But for their overseas player, the match would have been over too.

Fleming: It was a batting master-class and I think even Shane was pleased to be there. Of course we were all mesmerised by Warne. To us he was a magician. To Dravid, he was just another slow bowler.

Hampshire had the advantage but soon lost it in their second innings. The possibility that the pitch had been prepared for spin was working against them. Kent's slow left-armer, Patel, was bowling well.

Fleming: He had the extremely annoying habit of trying to bowl an unplayable ball six times an over. The other thing was that he never knew who he got out, had no idea who he was playing against. He just bowled and took wickets. That said, Min was easily the best left-arm spinner in the country. He really was excellent.

Patel: Well, I wouldn't disagree. At the time I would back myself to out-bowl any English finger spinner. I felt in pretty good rhythm that season. And the way I looked at it I was in a no-lose situation: I was the opposition spinner on a turning deck against the best spin bowler in the world. Everyone expected me to be out-bowled.

Patel had taken four Hampshire wickets in the first innings. Now he was on his way to another five. One of them was special.

Patel: Now, I didn't have a doosra but I had been working pretty fiendishly on a chinaman in the nets, you know a left-armer's leg break. It wasn't a thing of beauty and when I bowled it my action was like: 'Beware! This man is about to bowl a leg spinner!' But this one landed right in the business area.

Dimitri Mascarenhas was facing and was delaying Kent's progress.

Patel: Whether or not Dimi knew it was coming, he couldn't stop it. That was the breakthrough wicket. My only chinaman dismissal in first-class cricket!

Thanks to Patel, Kent had bowled out Hampshire for 136. They needed 205 to win, batting last on a worn pitch against the world's best spinner.

Hampshire: It was a spiteful pitch by now. Shane was bowling at my end round the wicket into the rough and, as I recall, I don't think he had a shout.

That's because Dravid was batting again. The wickets that did fall went to Shaun Udal. But not Dravid's, even though Warne was trying hard.

Fleming: It could never be just another game when Shane Warne was on one side and Rahul Dravid was on the other and they were playing on a wearing wicket. We were watching something special.

Patel: This was one of the great innings against a spin bowler on a dry wicket. But it wasn't at Eden Gardens or the MCG, it was at an old ground in Portsmouth and I was watching it happen.

For every problem that Warne set, Dravid worked out the answer. He was not out on 73 when the winning run was scored. Kent had beaten Hampshire by 6 wickets.

Fleming: He was the sort of man who, when he came in at the end of a long innings, would talk you through the five occasions that he had played and missed.

Patel: Warney had played enough and was bright enough to know when he'd been beaten by a better man.

Warne: Spectators told me afterwards it was the most captivating game they had seen in county cricket.

Hampshire: That's right. It was the finest exhibition of county cricket that I saw. Pure magic. Cricket at its best. An intriguing match.

Dravid: Obviously there is a huge amount of personal satisfaction when you score runs against one of the greats. This was the biggest contribution I made for Kent. The batting revolved around me and you enjoy that sort of thing, especially when you come in as a pro and you want to do well.

Fleming: You could not imagine a greater ambassador for cricket or India. He was a sensational man.

Patel: I drove a lot with Rahul, or rather he was my passenger, so immediately I was impressed by his bravery. Not many people shared a lift, so I put him down as a legend and of course he already was back home in India. It was his humility, I remember, and he just loved talking cricket.

Fleming: Shane was well known for being a good loser but then he could afford to be. He didn't lose that often. He said we all played well but really his congratulations were 75 per cent for Rahul and 25 per cent for the rest of us.

Patel: The difference between Kent and Hampshire this time? We had Dravid and they didn't.

Interviews by Simon Lister

The bank clerk who went to war

David Steele's summer of 1975

It had been a disastrous start to the summer for England. Mike Denness was sacked as captain after Australia won the opening Test by an innings. With Lillee and Thomson scenting English blood, Tony Greig had been appointed captain for the second Test at Lord's and his first act was to call for David Steele, a 33-year-old batsman from Northamptonshire.

David Steele: I thought I had a great chance of playing for England in 1972 when I scored 1,600 runs but I was overlooked. My time was running out but then Tony Greig was appointed captain.

Tony Greig: When I was appointed the first thing I did was speak to county bowlers such as Bob Cottam. I asked them who was the hardest batsman to get out. Two names continually popped up. One was Geoff Boycott; the other was David Steele. At my first selection meeting we had a bit of an argument but I had the casting vote and David came in.

Rod Marsh (Australia wicketkeeper): I didn't know David Steele. I used to have county matches off. Did he play for Northants?

Steele: I was travelling to Dudley to play a Sunday League match when I heard on the radio that I'd been picked. I went into the Test a bit unsettled as my kit had been taken from my car at a benefit match and I was worried about trying to get used to a new bat. I put an appeal in the paper and a guy called me to say he'd got drunk and taken the wrong bag. Getting my kit back helped me relax.

The selection caused a stir. The bespectacled, grey-haired Steele was labelled the 'bank clerk who went to war' but the jibes turned to praise after his debut. He scored 50 and 45 in a drawn Test.

Steele: I had played at Lord's for 12 years but always changed in the away dressing room. We used the Middlesex one for England matches but when I went out to bat I got confused, took one staircase too many and ended up going out the back door of the pavilion. I was a bit late getting to the wicket.

Greig: When you pick someone a bit left-field the Aussies love to target them but David's great strength was he had wonderful focus. He was one of a rare breed of batsmen such as Boycott who could shut it all out.

Steele: After my first Test the press asked Ian Chappell if they had sledged me much. He said they didn't bother after a while because they realised I was in my own world.

Marsh: He showed a lot of guts but I have seen much better players. He annoyed the hell out of Lillee and Thomson and I remember Dennis saying he couldn't wait to get him on the pitches in Australia.

Steele was a hero after scores of 73 and 92 at Headingley helped England draw again. He ended the series top of the England batting averages and was named BBC Sports Personality of the Year.

Steele: It was my benefit year and a local abattoir had sponsored me one lamb chop for every Test run and a steak for every one over 50. I got 600 Test runs in all and didn't have to buy meat for a few years.

Marsh: He played to his strengths. He was a front-foot player and found a method that worked. He is a good lesson to younger players. Sometimes guts and determination can make up for not having all the shots.

Interviews by Nick Hoult

The death of English cricket

Chris Cairns rebuffs the critics to bury England, The Oval, 1999

Alec Stewart had been sacked as England captain after a disastrous World Cup campaign but his replacement Nasser Hussain was faring little better. With the series level at 1–1 a buoyant New Zealand team sensed they were on the verge of something big. Victory at The Oval would give New Zealand their second series win in England. It was a significant match for both sides . . .

Steve Rixon (New Zealand coach): We felt we were playing the better cricket, so psychologically we felt quite confident. My biggest point at that stage was to make sure we didn't get overexcited, just keep a balance on the way we go about things, keep people down instead of jumping around with their eyes bulging out of their heads. I wanted them to be nicely relaxed when they went out to bat.

Hussain missed the previous Test with a finger injury. His replacement as captain, Mark Butcher, was then left out at The Oval in favour of Leicestershire's Darren Maddy, who made his Test debut alongside Warwickshire seamer Ed Giddins.

Ed Giddins (England bowler): There was a bit of an air of resignation. New Zealand had done well in the World Cup but for us to lose to them in a Test series would have been a real low.

Whereas they were desperate to win we were waiting for the backlash before we had even lost.

Roger Twose (New Zealand batsman): I remember the night before the match Dion Nash said a few words. He had this steel in his eyes that I can still picture today. He was a phenomenal competitor and he was able to lift the team single-handedly.

On the first morning of the match Cornhill, the long-standing sponsors of English Test cricket, announced they were reviewing their deal. The implication was clear. Results had to improve. England opted to bowl first in helpful conditions but the first wicket took 26 overs to arrive.

Rixon: We had a lot of youngsters and yes, I think there were probably a few jitters on the first day. There was a little bit of movement in the wicket and they bowled quite well.

After lunch Giddins struck to make it 62 for 4, combining with Maddy in the slips to make Twose his first Test wicket. At stumps New Zealand were 170 for 8.

Darren Maddy (England batsman): I had only started fielding at slip that year. I was expecting to be put under the lid in my first Test but I was asked to go in the slips and took a great catch off Ed. It was pure reaction but I'll never forget the rush of adrenalin after the ball stuck in my hands.

Giddins: I was more nervous than I thought I would be. My first delivery missed the cut strip and hit second slip. If I'm honest, I had rehearsed my first delivery in Test cricket since I was four. Obviously I had not rehearsed it often enough.

England needed to finish New Zealand off on the second morning but Daniel Vettori scored a fifty and they posted a respectable score. It was then the turn of Maddy, as Mike Atherton's 11th opening partner in Tests, to take his big chance.

Maddy: I remember thinking I was going to be his 11th and final partner. I wanted us to build up a good relationship and for the first hour I played quite nicely. My footwork was good and I was hitting the ball well. I got to 14 and then made a big misjudgement. I left Vettori's arm ball. It's a decision I have replayed in my mind for the past four years.

England rallied thanks to Hussain. Enter Chris Cairns. Previously maligned as injury-plagued and lacking in attitude, Cairns finally fulfilled his potential at The Oval. His five wickets gave New Zealand a healthy lead.

Rixon: If I hadn't taken over Cairns would have been dropped and never seen again, along with Adam Parore, because both of them had poor attitudes and the former coach didn't want a bar of them. I saw something different. It was a case of working with him, not telling him what to do but getting him to buy in. The more I got his advice on things the more he thought he was telling me what to do. It was reverse psychology, but it was what was needed. That was the key ingredient to Chris Cairns: make him feel good about himself.

England hit back. Giddins and Caddick shared six wickets and New Zealand were in trouble at 79 for 7. Enter Cairns . . . again. He batted with what Wisden *described as 'Bothamesque belligerence'. From 93 balls he scored 80 including four sixes off Phil Tufnell. New Zealand had the upper hand.*

Giddins: If we had got Cairns it would have been different. I don't think the right bowlers were used at the right time. I didn't captain England in 50-odd Tests so what do I know? But I felt we let Cairns get away.

Twose: I remember thinking, as he hit Tufnell for another six, that 'this is just X-factor stuff'. We knew it was turning in our favour. I kept thinking the next ball could end up in the hands of long on but he continued to hit it in the stand.

New Zealand set England 246, the highest score of the match. Maddy and Hussain were out by the close.

Maddy: I walked out thinking that I would build on the first innings. But I nicked an away-swinger from Nash. I walked off with this terrible feeling inside. It felt like something had been taken away from me.

England needed a big hundred to win but once Atherton was out, having scored his 50th Test half-century, it was all over as England's tail was exposed.

Giddins: Tufnell, Mullally and I were vying for the No. 11 spot. As a bowler I loved to see a tail because you knew you were always in the game. Five wickets down and you had a chance. That was probably how they felt.

Mullally was the last man out, with Twose taking a catch at mid-on. Moments later New Zealand fans were performing the haka on the outfield and Hussain was being booed by the home crowd.

Twose: As I held on to the catch my instinct was to throw it up in the air. But I held on to it and gave it to Cairnsy. He had been the difference.

Maddy: I remember the criticism in the papers. I could not believe that I had been involved in something that had had such a dramatic impact. I wanted to make sure I was never involved in such a low again. Next time it would be better.

The result left England bottom of the Wisden *World Championship and the* Sun *turned its front page into an obituary for English cricket. A year later, though, at the same ground England were hailed as heroes after West Indies had finally been beaten.*

Interviews by Nick Hoult and Emma John

A tank against pea-shooters

Graeme Hick's 405 not out, Somerset v Worcestershire, 1988

Graeme Hick, born in Zimbabwe, was embarking on his fourth full season in English county cricket. He was 21, still three years of residential qualification away from a Test debut that was taken for granted. In his first three summers he had scored 5,148 first-class runs at 56.57. And then he went to Taunton . . .

At Old Trafford in April Graeme Hick had made 212 in a 10-wicket victory. The next best score in the match was 68. At Taunton, where he made 405 off 469 balls, it was 56. He became the eighth man to score 1,000 runs by the end of May and finished the season with 2,713 runs at 77.51.

Damian D'Oliveira (Worcestershire batsman): I asked Graeme, 'What's it doing?' He replied: 'Absolutely nothing.' Graham Rose bowled one on off stump, it moved away and I nicked it. 'That's the only ball that's done anything,' he said. I told him where to go.

Worcestershire were in trouble at 132 for 5 when Steve Rhodes joined Hick. The wicketkeeper made 56 in a stand of 265.

Vic Marks (Somerset spin bowler): The Worcestershire innings was slow going and the ball was doing a bit. At 132 for 5 you were thinking 300 all out at worst.

Graeme Hick (Worcestershire batsman): I just had a go at the ball if it was in the right area and the boundaries are fairly short at Taunton.

Peter Roebuck (Somerset captain, writing in *Wisden* 1989): One mistake from Hick and they'd have been all out for a poor score. He took guard and began hitting the ball in order to score runs. He did not say much and yet he was neither distant nor aloof. I never saw Walter Hammond bat but I imagine he was something like this – authoritative, commanding, civil and durable. Once or twice his leg shots were lifted but they were hit with a power that was efficient rather than savage and they thundered through or over the field.

Neil Burns (Somerset wicketkeeper): They were the longest two days of my life but I had the best seat in the house and I didn't have to pay for it. It was like two games were going on. The ball was nipping about and people were nicking it in one but he was batting immaculately and hitting everything for four in the other. Anything just a little too full he drove straight, anything too straight he clipped through the leg side clinically. He sits back for a period of time but then sits on bowlers in a way they can't come back from. It was exceptional.

Marks: It was utterly mechanical and I don't mean that dismissively. He clinically scored 70 a session. He was more orthodox than Kevin Pietersen. If you bowled a good-length ball he would play it back respectfully, although he was clinical on anything off-line. There were few big shots and he didn't take too many liberties until the late 200s. He popped me over mid-on a couple of times, so I put a long on back. Then he would pop it down there for one. This was before he was tarnished by Test cricket and I was acknowledging he was in charge, cutting my losses and trying to get the other batsmen out, but they were giving him amazingly obdurate support.

Steve Rhodes (Worcestershire wicketkeeper): It was a marvellous innings. He puts the bad ball away more efficiently than anyone. I just tried to blunt the attack. It was a pleasure to run his runs for him. I played only one shot in anger and it got me out.

Phil Neale (Worcestershire captain): Taunton suited Graeme because straight hitting is his forte but he didn't seem to be blasting it. It was sensible batting.

Hick was dropped in the gully on 148 – then there were no more chances until he went past 300. He reached 179 at stumps on the first day.

Rhodes: Hicky's not a big drinker but a group of us went for a Chinese meal and he had a pint of lager. Peter Roebuck came in with Graham Rose and joked the booze could make him succumb early next day.

Neale: The overnight break at halfway in his innings suited him as he could start again refreshed.

Burns: He worked very hard to get back in as there was still freshness in the pitch; his batsmanship from 200 to 300 was exceptional and showed what a magnificent player he is.

Roebuck: Watching him, you cannot tell if he is on 10 or 210. He simply carries on. His game is as pure as a punched hole. It is this that frightens bowlers.

Rhodes: He went from 288 to 300 with straight sixes off Colin Dredge – phenomenal shots.

Hick: I asked Phil what the plan was on day two and he just told me to see how it went. Once I reached 300 I just kept on having a go. I was pleased to pass Worcestershire's record score [Glenn Turner's 311 v Warwickshire in 1982] but I didn't know about Hanif Mohammad's record of 499.

Neale: The game plan was always to get as many as we could, as fast as we could. We were going to declare earlier but I delayed it until Graeme reached 300 – he then got to 400 so quickly we still had time to bowl on that second evening. I think he always knew I'd call it a day at 400. I was aware of various records but the team objective was always the most important thing.

Burns: After Hick reached 300 we had one or two guys carrying niggles and one or two had been overbowled. He was looking to hit everything for four and it was a bit like a benefit match.

Marks: Reaching 300 gave him the licence to cut loose. The ball was flying everywhere. Watching him running between the wickets was superb – not just for his runs but scampering the third for his partner. He was fit and utterly selfless.

D'Oliveira: He received great support from Rhodes, Phil Newport [27] and Richard Illingworth [31 not out]. It was brilliant batting with Graeme.

Marks: I knew Worcestershire weren't particularly aware of Archie MacLaren's record [his 424 for Lancashire at Taunton in 1895 was then the highest Championship score]. I rather grumpily pointed out, 'Someone has got 400 here before you know.' It would have taken him next to no time to reach 425, and the match barely got to day four as it was . . .

Neale: I was also skipper when Glenn Turner scored 311 not out – he didn't mind me declaring because he had blisters!

Hick: Obviously I had more technically difficult innings but it was just great to have such a long time at the crease; you don't normally get that long.

Roebuck: He used a bat so broad that bowlers felt as if they were trying to knock down a tank with a pea-shooter.

Neale: I followed the old adage to chuck the ball to the man who had also scored all the runs.

Hick removed Nigel Felton and Richard Harden that evening and took three in the match as Worcestershire won by an innings.

Burns: It's very sad that the great player he was becoming in the late 1980s didn't go on to dominate in Tests. West Indies came hard at him in 1991 and maybe that was a difficult experience to come back from. One irony was that we played Worcestershire in the return a few weeks later and he scored 8 and 11.

Neale: That was obviously Graeme's highest score in my time at Worcestershire but it probably wasn't his best innings. He was dropped a few times. The best I saw him bat was that 212 at Old Trafford; Lancashire had prepared a turner in April and Graeme was the only batsman who hit the ball in front of square.

Hick: At that stage it was my biggest achievement. Maybe it still is.

Interviews by Huw Turbervill

Rock 'n' rolled for 46

England blown away in Trinidad 1993–94

'It was the worst experience of my cricketing life,' said Mike Atherton. The England captain was talking about the final session of the fourth day at Port-of-Spain against West Indies. It was the third Test of the 1993-94 tour. An English victory was peeping over the horizon but, with the harbour in sight, the skipper and his crew were hit by Hurricane Curtly. All hands were lost.

Keith Fletcher (England coach): I know it sounds a bit stupid now but we were going to win that game.

Jimmy Adams (West Indies): We were an expectant young side. A lot of us were coming in, determined to make it count against England. A big series for all of us. Me, Keith Arthurton, Shivnarine Chanderpaul, Brian Lara. Brian was determined to be known as a world-class batsman by the time England left. We had personal issues to prove.

England had lost the first two Tests in Jamaica and Guyana. A defeat in Trinidad would give the series to West Indies.

Alec Stewart (England): We went on tour expecting and hoping to win. But it was tough. They were still hot. They were a fine, fine side. A long way from decline.

Andy Caddick (England): They were pretty strong. Several world-class players and a world-class opening partnership with the ball.

Fletcher: They had fine bowlers all right. And some decent young batters. Adams, Chanderpaul. Then there was Lara. Well, Lara's Lara, isn't he?

Adams: We thought we'd take some beating. We would remain Kings of the Forest for a little while yet. The point is, we still had the ammunition to get 20 wickets …

Fletcher: Not everyone playing for England was a Test player, let's be honest. You pick from the best you've got. That's all we could do. A pretty average side.

Adams: … as for England, their bowling attack wasn't really going to give us too many nightmares.

Fletcher: He's right. I expect any Test batter of the time would fancy a chance of getting a few runs against our bowlers. We had Angus Fraser – well, he'd had a hip done and wasn't quite the same – Devon Malcolm – he blew hot and cold. Caddick was just starting and Chris Lewis was there. You never knew if he would run in for you or just bowl donkey drops all day.

England, despite their limitations, had played well for the first three days. They bowled West Indies out for 252 and then took a first-innings lead of 76. Graham Thorpe made 86.

Thorpe: I grew up pretty quickly. I'd never experienced that sort of pace before. Curtly Ambrose and Courtney Walsh. That tour changed the way I batted. I learned what Test cricket was about.

Adams: It was a typical Trinidad wicket. Slower, giving a bit of grip, a bit of swing. But it wasn't a devil of a track. What the pitch needed was patience. It wasn't like Jamaica or Antigua where you could shut one eye, swing through the line and watch it come back off the boundary boards.

By the end of the third day's play West Indies were batting for a second time. At stumps they led by 67 runs but had only five wickets left. England spent the rest day thinking of a win.

Thorpe: We were in a great position and were maybe looking for a last-innings chase of about 100.

The fourth day came. The lower order lingered and England could not get Shivnarine Chanderpaul out. Not that they were given no chances.

Fletcher: Didn't we drop him?

Stewart: Twice. Graeme Hick, wasn't it?

Fletcher: If you wanted anyone there to catch at slip, it would have been Hicky. He was the best in the side.

Caddick: It was astonishing. I've spoken to him about it and he still can't believe it. He was the original Bucket Hands.

Stewart: Graeme Hick was possibly the best England slip fielder of my era. Then suddenly he started to drop the ball from left-handers, when it was coming to him from right to left. He shelled Chanderpaul both times.

A fourth-innings target that might have been 100 or so, was now 194. It was after tea when England went out to chase. In the dressing room the need for a good start was made clear and Atherton and Stewart made it, getting on to the field and taking guard. So far so good. Curtly Ambrose bowled the first ball.

Adams: All of us thought England were in a better position. We told ourselves: 'We have to get in there early.' Then there was a moment. A decisive moment.

That's right. Atherton lbw by Ambrose, first ball of the innings.

Adams: Hold on. That wasn't the moment.

Oh. Sorry.

Adams: It was the run-out later in the over.

Of course. After the captain's golden duck Mark Ramprakash came to the wicket. From the fifth ball he fouled up a second run to fine-leg. England were 1 for 2.

Thorpe: Now the target looked more like 490, not 190. We'd been talking about getting a good start and before we knew it we were up against it.

Adams: That was when we smelled it. Watching Ramprakash, we saw that England were more nervous than we were. They panicked too early in the day. One thing you learn from playing games is that when one side knows the other team believes it isn't going to win, then it's over.

Stewart: 190 in Trinidad is a huge total. I'd say 350 on any other ground. We knew we would need skill and a fair bit of luck. The crowd was making a lot of noise. And Curtly was bowling rapid with a lot of control.

Fletcher: I reckon that, if the target was 50 or 60, we'd probably have got there.

Robin Smith was next out. Done for a duck by Curtly through the gate.

Thorpe: It wasn't a massive crowd but they were loud. When Robin got his middle [sic] pole knocked out they became a whole lot louder. It was a nice confidence booster to come in to.

'This was cricket-theatre at its most riveting,' reported Wisden Cricket Monthly. 'Stumps flew, English jaws sagged and pandemonium reigned in the stands ...'

Stewart: The other thing that killed us was the rain. It had fallen in the afternoon and they only had to get through 15 overs before the close. It was one spell from Curtly and one from Courtney. We knew they'd be running in at us hard – and non-stop.

Thorpe: So then it was my turn. It was 5 for 3 and all I could see were Curtly's knees pumping as he ran in down the mountain.

Caddick: We looked like rabbits in the headlights.

Hick was next, then Stewart, then Ian Salisbury. 27 for 6.

Caddick: We'd worked so damned hard to get into a great position, and now this. With my six-for in the second innings I thought I'd done enough to get man of the match – then Curtly came along.

Thorpe: I'd not seen too many bowlers of his quality. I'd faced him lolloping in for Northants at about half pace but he had the badge on his shirt now. It was a bit different. And I have to admit it, there was an element of fear. It ran through your mind that one of these balls could hurt you.

Adams: Curtly was stingy. No runs.

Fletcher: He never gave you anything. I've seen quicker spells of bowling but it was always right there. Then a short one to let you know he was still around.

Adams: What was he like to bat against? Well, you'll have to ask someone else. I always played him OK, no dramas. But I was patient, you see.

Thorpe: All I tried to do was my best. Back then it was still a case of playing for your place each match. That hardened you up a bit.

Thorpe played the longest knock of the innings – 28 balls for three runs. He watched Ambrose get rid of Jack Russell, then, in Curtly's last over of the day, he himself was bowled. England finished on 40 for 8.

Fletcher: It wasn't the most pleasant hour of cricket I've ever seen.

Stewart: We weren't cracking any champagne open, put it that way. Half a day and it had all changed on its head.

'Watching from the top of the media centre,' wrote Vic Marks, 'it was a stunning, stomach-churning experience as the cream of English

batsmanship was ruthlessly whipped. Goodness knows what it felt like in the England dressing room.'

Thorpe: The dressing room was distraught. We'd come up against a great bowler, who bowled a great spell. There was such a lot of disappointment, we'd won the first three and a half days, then lost it all in two hours.

Fletcher: There's not a lot to say is there? 'Well done lads, we've still got a chance in the morning'? People tend to forget that they were doing their best out there. Well, apart from the run-out. That was stupid.

On the last morning wickets nine and 10 fell in 17 minutes. Walsh got them both but it was Ambrose who was carried from the ground on his team-mates' shoulders. England were all out for 46. They had beaten by one run, their lowest score in Test cricket. Underneath their dressing-room window, Lord Kitchener, the famed calypso composer and performer, strummed a new song.

Stewart: Terrible. Rock 'n' rolled for 46.

Thorpe: Soon afterwards Nasser Hussain, who wasn't playing in this match, got this T-shirt printed and started wearing it. It read: 'It's nothing to do with me.'

Fletcher: Yeah. I remember. That's funny. I never lost my sense of humour, despite what happened. To tell you the truth, it was just about all I had left after those five days. In fact, it was a difficult tour. A lot of the time it felt like trying to push a pebble uphill.

Interviews by Simon Lister

One-day one-day wonders

Adam Hollioake leads England to victory in Sharjah, 1997–98

When England went to Sharjah for the four-team Akai Singer Champions Trophy in December 1997, they had played no one-day cricket in six months. They had a new look, built on allrounders, a new captain, Adam Hollioake, and a new experience, winning. For the best part of a decade, it remained the last significant overseas triumph by England's one-day side.

David Lloyd (England coach): Being realistic, we just meant to develop the side. But we were embarking on a one-day specialist team, full of allrounders, and there was an excellent spirit. Adam Hollioake was an exceptional leader and we had lots of fun too, especially with Matthew Fleming out there. It's amazing how far that togetherness got them.

Matthew Fleming (Kent allrounder): I particularly admired Hollioake's captaincy because he encouraged individuals to take responsibility. If he chucked you the ball with six overs to go, he made it clear you were the only man capable of doing the job. It gave you great confidence. I also think David Lloyd was at his best when he had a strong leader.

Nick Knight (Warwickshire batsman): Hollioake seemed to have a good mixture between being the captain and being a good bloke, one of the team. It was like the beginning of a new era.

Dougie Brown (Warwickshire allrounder): He had the knack of making people do things for him.

England's first game was against India, who were on course for victory until Fleming had Sachin Tendulkar stumped by Alec Stewart for 91. Fleming, who ended as the tournament's joint leading wicket-taker, then finished India off to secure a seven-run win.

Fleming: The likes of Geoff Boycott were saying what a clever piece of cricket it was because I had seen Tendulkar coming at me and slipped him a wider and fuller one. In fact, all the credit for that dismissal has to go to Alec Stewart, because it was a bloody difficult take. I didn't see him coming. And I didn't deliberately bowl wider and fuller. It was meant to be a yorker. It was a great result for us but I do sometimes wonder how hard India were trying to win.

Brown: Stewart had hit a great hundred earlier. Then he whipped off the bails to get rid of Tendulkar when it was nip and tuck. We probably shouldn't have won. It was incredible.

Lloyd: It was real gung-ho stuff. We decided to get stuck right into them, like a football match – sort of getting in your retaliation first. We were very aggressive.

Knight: There were a lot of allrounders, and the surface in Sharjah is normally benign and doesn't do much, so we had the right men to take the pace off the ball. It was a real team effort.

In their next game against Courtney Walsh's West Indies, they exploited a sensational start by Brown.

Brown: I shouldn't have been opening the bowling but there was no one else. I knew that Philo Wallace would come after us but with my first ball he got caught on the crease and it nipped back a touch to bowl him. Out came Brian Lara, whom I had played with at Warwickshire in 1994 and had had breakfast with that morning. He played and missed at his first ball, then the second hit him in front. It might have pitched outside leg if I'm honest but we weren't complaining. Later on I clipped Walsh for four to win the game, which was nice.

An eight-run win over Pakistan set up a surprise final against West Indies, the other outsiders.

Fleming: We had absolute clarity of thought – we knew we were going to win. West Indies were a very fragile team at the time. Walsh was their only true pro and he was carrying that weight on his shoulders. They knew they'd overachieved by getting to the finals. India and Pakistan were meant to romp their way to victory.

Lloyd: In England we had beaten Australia 3–0 and now we had beaten India, Pakistan and West Indies. We knew we had the ability to beat anyone.

Brown: I got smashed up front by Stuart Williams, who kept walking across his stumps and flicking me to leg. We were totally out of the game. Then Jazz [Fleming] hit 33 off not many balls and played brilliantly with Thorpey. But he got run out with the scores level but I came in and steered Walsh to third man for four.

Fleming: When the tide turned against West Indies, you could see them thinking, 'Ah well, we got to the final, so that wasn't bad.'

Brown: It was one of those tournaments where, when we needed someone to do something, they did it. Our roles were very clearly defined. You knew what was expected of you. There was no fear of failure because we were just a bunch of bits-and-pieces cricketers who had been thrown together. It gave us a lot of depth.

But things quickly went wrong. Hollioake's side went down 4–1 in the Caribbean, then lost to South Africa in the Texaco Trophy the following summer. Ten games after leading England to success in Sharjah, and with the 1999 World Cup looming, Hollioake was replaced as captain by Stewart.

Brown: In West Indies we needed specialist batters and bowlers but we had more or less the same team as we did in Sharjah. We really needed a strike bowler, especially on those smaller grounds, but Dean Headley was the only one who bowled at any pace.

Fleming: England lost any chance of winning the World Cup as soon as they dropped Adam Hollioake as captain. The selectors had no understanding of what made the team in Sharjah so good. I hold that entirely culpable for England not doing better. I'm stunned that Hollioake was sacked, because he was the best captain of one-day cricket in the country. It was down to a fundamental lack of clarity of thought.

Lloyd: Maybe we made a conscious decision to get back towards a side that resembled the Test team. The experiment with Hollioake had run its course. But I think one thing that maybe doesn't work is to have different captains leading the Test and the one-day teams. It just causes problems subconsciously.

Brown: I never played again after that West Indies series and Matthew Fleming followed soon after. I would have loved to have played an international match in England or to have bowled in a position which suited me. It just wasn't to be.

Knight: You're talking to someone who really believed in Hollioake as captain. He knew how to win games. He was probably pretty unlucky.

Fleming: Had the selectors and the management been able to recreate the spirit of Sharjah in the World Cup squad and in English conditions, they would probably have harnessed the crowds and the support and done better than they did. But they were shit and they lost. When England came to Kent for a warm-up game, I have never seen a more miserable, disjointed bunch. At that time you would have had to be insane not to base your one-day team around Nick Knight, Alec Stewart, Adam Hollioake and Darren Gough. Insane!

England failed to reach the knockout stages of their own World Cup and remain the only major team never to have won a truly global competition.

Knight: It's a really frustrating thing to talk about. I've always felt we had the players but we just haven't done it consistently. I also felt we were always short of experience.

Lloyd: I know that the form in the one-day team is a massive frustration to [Duncan] Fletcher: win a great game, lose two, win one, lose one. You need that confidence and arrogance to win a one-day tournament. They still look hesitant and disjointed.

Brown: I just don't think we really appreciated how important that Sharjah win was at the time.

Interviews by Lawrence Booth

Who got Boycott biffing?

Geoffrey Boycott's mysterious change of form, Gillette Cup final, 1965

One-day cricket was still new and the Gillette Cup in its third year when Yorkshire met Surrey in the 1965 final. It proved one of the competition's more memorable games. Geoff Boycott, without a hundred all season, hit 146 with three sixes and 15 fours. Everyone wanted the credit, even Micky Stewart for putting Yorkshire in.

Brian Close (Yorkshire captain): We were a fine county side in those days. Illy, myself, Boycs and Fred Trueman. Jimmy Binks behind the stumps. I tell you, we'd take on this England side and beat them inside four days.

Ray Illingworth (Yorkshire allrounder): It was a wet morning and a late start but the wicket was OK. There was dampness in the air and the game was delayed for more than an hour.

Close: In 1965 the Championship was out of reach. It was a very wet summer and we hardly finished a game until June. So we applied ourselves to this new competition. We were a good attacking side. We knew how to get people out. But I always felt that one-day cricket reversed the principles of first-class cricket where the bowlers and fielders ask the questions of the batsman and he tries to answer them. In one-day cricket the bowler's running up wondering what's going to happen to the next ball.

Micky Stewart (Surrey captain): I won the toss and put them in. It turned out to be the sort of decision that earns you the freedom of Bradford and Leeds. If you looked at the two sides, I think nearly all of theirs had played for England. We were much more inexperienced and some of our lads were a bit nervous, so I thought we may as well get out there and field first.

It seemed to be a good decision. The Yorkshire openers Boycott and Ken Taylor made a slow start and when Taylor was out, the score was 22 from 12 overs.

Ken Taylor (Yorkshire batsman): It was a slow wicket and I tried to cut. All I ended up doing was giving an easy catch to Ken Barrington in the gully. It was like an underarm throw.

Taylor's dismissal brought Close to the wicket. Some remember it as a spontaneous tactical decision to accelerate the scoring. Others disagree.

Illingworth: There's been a lot of talk about Closey going in early to tell Boycott to get on with it but it wasn't to give Boycs a bollocking or owt like that. It was all about the Surrey left-armer, David Sydenham.

Close: Boycott didn't like the left-arm over bowlers so much.

Illingworth: We'd recently played Surrey in the County Championship and Sydenham had bowled very well to the right-handers. So Jimmy Binks had said to me: 'In the final why don't you tell Closey [a left-hander] to go in up the order?'

Close: Doug Padgett was due to go in three but he looked at the score and said to me: 'Look, skip, you better go in next. It's suited to you is this. Anyway, if I bat with Boycs, he always ends up bloody well running me out.'

Geoffrey Boycott (from *Boycott: The Autobiography*): The suggestion is, of course, that I was piddling along until Close arrived and told me to get on with it or else, thus forcing me to play a memorable innings, which would not have been possible without his rugged intervention. It makes for good reading but it is not the way I remember it at all.

Close: I joined Geoffrey in the middle and said to him: 'Listen, if I call, you bloody well run.'

Boycott: At no time did Close tell me to get on with it or anything remotely similar. Those who believe otherwise are mistaken.

Illingworth: The players used to use me to get messages through to Brian. If you told the skipper 'you're the man for the job', it would appeal to him.

Boycott: It was no last-minute inspiration. We had struggled before against Sydenham. It was obvious that he would be a real nuisance in a limited-overs game, especially to the right-handed batsmen – and Close was the only recognised batsman in the team who was left-handed . . . the plan was formulated at least a fortnight before the final.

Close: We ran a few quick singles and turned the scoreboard over and I went back down and said: 'If it pitches up, give it a bloody belt.' Geoff Arnold bowled the next ball a fraction full and Boycs thrashed him through extra cover. He'd never played a shot like it.

Stewart: Boycs was great. We knew he played well square off the back foot and front foot, so I said: 'Look, don't bowl him any Father Christmas deliveries there.' But instead of getting it in the blockhole we gave him plenty of half-volleys, then adjusted to long hops. He dealt with them very well.

Close: Then the off-spinner came on. Usually Boycs was frightened of hitting the slower lads in the air for fear of getting caught but I told him: 'Just hit it anywhere from square leg to mid-off.'

Taylor: He batted beautifully. It just proved what he could do. So there was no reason why he couldn't have continued like that. But it must have frightened him to death thinking that he had to play like that every innings.

Boycott: I still remember moving down the pitch to Geoff Arnold and lifting him straight for six with the Yorkshire players trying to catch the ball on the pavilion balcony.

Close and Boycott added 194 for the second wicket. John Woodcock wrote in The Times*: 'I shall never again make it an excuse for Boycott that he is unfortunately not endowed with strokes. His magnificent innings contained every stroke in the book.'*

Close: It was a great innings – chanceless. And I think it was the highest one-day score at the time.

With some late hitting from Fred Trueman and Jackie Hampshire, Yorkshire ended up with 317 from their 60 overs, then the competition's highest total.

Stewart: In those days it was an absolutely huge total. I mean in a first-class game if you declared and asked a side to chase anything over four an over, it was thought of as unrealistic.

Illingworth: We got a massive score, even by today's standards, and of course there were no restrictions, so they could put the fielders where they liked.

Stewart: When I walked out to bat, with us needing five an over from the off, Kenny Barrington said to me with a smile: 'What are the tactics skip?' As it happened Fred Trueman ended the match in one over, taking three wickets.

In four balls Trueman had John Edrich caught, Bill Smith leg-before and Ken Barrington caught behind. 'The writing was on the wall,' noted Wisden. *Illingworth also bowled well.*

Illingworth: Five for 20-odd in 12 overs and still not man of the match? That showed that Boycs had batted well. I remember I got two or three with the arm ball. No one could read it and it was swinging like a banana.

Close: Illy was a wise old sod. They tried to have a dip at him and he mixed up his off-breaks with the arm ball.

Yorkshire had beaten Surrey by 175 runs and won the Cup. Doug Insole, the chairman of the England selectors, who had dropped Boycott from the Test side, presented him with the man-of-the-match award.

Boycott: It was one of the best innings I ever played, different in character from many that people choose to remember, but with a context and a significance all of its own.

Illingworth: Boycott always had lots of talent but I think he was frightened of failure. He didn't usually want to take chances. I think he may well say that the best he ever batted was on the Ashes tour of 1970–71 when I was captain because I gave him a lot of encouragement.

Stewart: Boycott played magnificently. There was a lot to hit but he did it very well.

Close: It was a thrill to be there. We enjoyed the day because when we won Championship matches they were always hard-fought. No one ever declared and gave us anything to chase. Each match presents its own way of challenging you.

Illingworth: Boycott had the opposite mentality to batsmen such as Ted Dexter and Peter May. If he had thought like them, he would have played more innings like the one we saw that day.

Close: We were all thrilled for Boycs. It was one hell of an innings, no messing.

Interviews by Simon Lister

CHAPTER 6

Oddities and Innovations

... the next time he went in for his balance, the teller put the book in the machine, the machine went crazy and out it came with a print-off of all this money. 'It's the first time I've ever seen a comma in that book,' said Michael ...

World XI captain Tony Greig on West Indies bowler Michael Holding
signing up for Kerry Packer's World Series Cricket

overleaf:
Dennis Lillee menaces Allan Border with his aluminium bat during
England's 1979–80 tour of Australia

When cricket changed for ever

The Packer revolution

Kerry Packer. Meddler or magician? Iconoclast or inventor? In 1977 he took more than fifty of the best players in the world from under the noses of the game's traditional guardians. The result was two seasons of World Series Cricket (WSC). Those who played said it was the hardest sport they knew. Critics hated it. Whatever the view, no one could disagree that Packer helped change cricket for ever.

Ian Chappell (captain of the WSC Australian side): It was all about TV rights. Kerry, who owned Channel 9, had offered several times more than ABC had to cover Test cricket, yet he was knocked back by the Australian Cricket Board. That made him angry.

Richie Benaud (commentator and WSC consultant): During the early 1970s there was considerable disquiet in the Australian team over conditions and playing fees and a great divide between players and administrators. By 1976 that disquiet had turned to annoyance.

Chappell: There'd been a big fight with the Australian board on the '69–70 tour to India and South Africa about pay and conditions. Before that, in England in 1968 at the final team dinner, one of our players, Bob Cowper, who was a mild man, had really laid into the board over the same issues. That's when player agitation started.

Kerry Packer's anger at not being able to televise cricket coincided with the irritations of the Australian players. Dennis Lillee made more money from his window-cleaning business than he did from playing cricket. It would not be hard to convince the Australians, and then other players around the world, that they deserved more.

Clive Lloyd (captain of the WSC West Indies side): Something had to happen. At the time the risk was that we would destroy our careers but we felt that we had to make a stand. You can't have athletes from other sports being paid properly and cricketers playing for the love of it.

Chappell: I'd been at board meetings talking about how the players were paid when I was captain in the early 1970s. It was Bradman who wouldn't listen. When his hand went up, all the others watched and put theirs up. Because of his attitude he was as responsible for WSC happening as anyone. I thought he'd be a friendly ear but it was exactly the opposite. It was as if we were asking for the money from his own wallet.

Lloyd: We were getting a pittance. And there was very little prize money either. For instance, when West Indies played in Australia in '75–76, the prize money and the money we got from doing adverts was more than the tour fee. Kerry was right when he said we didn't know our worth.

Chappell: We were so stupid. During the England series in '74–75 I was in the dressing room at the MCG and they announced that the gate money was $250,000. 'Hang on,' I thought. 'We're getting $200 each – that's $2,200 – where the hell is the rest of it going?'

Packer came up with an extraordinary scheme. If he was not allowed to buy the TV coverage, why not buy the cricketers and pay them to play in matches that he could televise? His original plan was to find a team of world stars to take on an Australian XI.

Tony Greig (captain of the World XI): Packer said to me: 'You can have 16, Ian Chappell's going to have 16. Make a list and go and get 'em.' There were no restrictions and everybody was to be paid the same – except the captains. They got a few extra bucks.

Plenty of secret meetings followed in 1976 and 1977. It soon became clear that there would be enough players for a World team, an Australian team and a West Indies XI. Greig, who was captain of England at the time, even recruited during the Centenary Test at Melbourne in March 1977.

Chappell: Fifty-odd players kept a huge secret for three to five months. That's unheard of for cricketers. It also gives you some idea of the extent to which cricketers around the world were pissed off with their lot.

Benaud: It certainly was a well-kept secret. We hadn't heard about WSC in late March 1977. In April my wife Daphne and I were having lunch with cricketing friends in Sydney when Kerry phoned and asked me to come into his office. That was the first I had heard about the venture. By that time Kerry's colleagues were already signing players from different countries.

The prospect of the money the players could earn may also have helped to keep them quiet.

Joel Garner (West Indies bowler): When I saw what Packer was offering, it was a no-brainer. The difference was so vast it was unbelievable. When I started playing you earned a few hundred dollars of the local currency. Now we were talking US$20,000 for three months' work.

Greig: Michael Holding tells the story of never having more than a few hundred dollars in his post office account in Jamaica. Then he signed up and the next time he went in for his balance, the teller put the book in the machine, the machine went crazy and out it came with a print-off of all this money. 'It's the first time I've ever seen a comma in that book,' said Michael.

Players who already had commercial contracts were encouraged to get out of them. One such man was the Australian fast bowler Jeff Thomson.

Greig: Thommo? Oh yeah, that took a bit of time but we got him eventually. I think we delivered a speedboat to his front door or something. That probably did it.

Dennis Amiss (England and World XI batsman): I'd done well in a couple of one-day internationals for England and I was encouraged to have a meeting with Richie Benaud. They wanted me in the World XI and I was quite flattered as I'd had some ups and downs and I thought my international career was coming to its end. It was an opportunity to earn some real money. But it was also the thought of being asked to play with the best players in the world.

By May 1977 the news of the competition broke. Tony Greig was hosting a party for the touring Australian side at his home in Brighton, where he dictated a statement to the press:

'There is a massive cricket project involving most of the world's top players due to commence in Australia this winter. I am part of it along with a number of English players. Full details and implications of the scheme will be officially announced in Australia later this week.'

The decision to play for Packer cost Greig the England captaincy. For a time it would cost Lloyd his job too.

Chappell: When it all came out, the Australian board claimed they'd been 'stabbed in the back' by the players. That made me mad as hell. They'd been given fair warning. As far as I know there had been three earlier attempts to stage rival cricket competitions.

It was talked about at the 1975 World Cup, so it wasn't as if all these blokes were suddenly taken by surprise.

The cricket establishment, especially in England and Australia, was flabbergasted by the extent of the project. Arguments raged for and against Packer. Many were appalled by what they saw as crass behaviour by the Australian businessman. Traditionalists took him on in televised debates. In one the former Sussex captain Robin Marlar tried to argue that 'our life, of which cricket is a part, is entirely about behaviour'. Packer's logic and humour won the day. The Sunday Times *TV critic, Dennis Potter, wrote that Marlar was left 'trying to play a straight bat to a raspberry'.*

Chappell: What was Kerry like? When I first met him I was meant to be flying to Melbourne to play grade cricket but was told to go on to Sydney. I was wearing a denim jacket, jeans and a country and western shirt. When Kerry saw me his first words were: 'What are you? Some sort of f***ing cowboy?' His next question was: 'Who do you want in this f***ing side?'

Lloyd: I admired him because when he said things, he meant it. He went the full distance. I had dinner with him once and there was a contract discrepancy for the West Indies players which would have cost him well over $500,000. 'Pay them,' he said to his advisor and that was the end of the conversation. He was not a fellow that you would call stingy.

Benaud: Kerry Packer was intensely loyal, not just to those who worked for him in business but in private life as well. The additional aspect was that, in turn, he expected the loyalty to be returned.

Amiss: He was a big chap and when he spoke, you listened. But he always made us feel very special.

Chappell: He was a businessman and used to getting his way. If you had your argument sorted out, he would respect you. He might shout but he'd respect you. If he found out you'd been bullshitting him, though, you were in deep trouble.

Yet even a personality such as Packer could not guarantee that people would come to watch WSC. The first 'SuperTest' in December 1977 was played between the Australians and West Indies in an Australian rules football stadium outside Melbourne. Fewer than 500 people were there when the first ball was bowled. WSC had not immediately caught the public's imagination.

Lloyd: Of course I was concerned that no one watched the first few games but underneath we were fairly certain that people would be happy to be getting something fresh from this cricket.

Lloyd's prediction proved right. As the first season progressed, more people came to watch. They saw some top-quality cricket.

Chappell: Day in, day out, it was better than Test cricket. Why? Because if you struggled in a Test, you could go to a county game and get some runs. In WSC you faced Andy, Mikey, Joel and Crofty, then the next game you got Imran, Garth Le Roux and John Snow. Then, guess what, it was Andy, Mikey, Joel and Crofty again. If you were struggling, it was a nightmare to try to get in some touch. Nowhere to hide.

Lloyd: It was against the cream. The catching was good, the bowling and the batting was good. During that time most teams took on a more professional attitude. Some of the fielding was fantastic. It was good hard stuff. We won pretty much everything. It was a defining moment for us because for the first time we played with real discipline and that's what saw us through in future years.

Greig: It was damned hard. The fast bowlers in all sides were good and the pitches weren't that good.

Amiss: It was fearsome.

Dennis Amiss became one of the first players to try on a motorcycle helmet with a grille to protect himself against the bowlers' short-pitched deliveries.

Amiss: People did laugh. They were calling out: 'Hey Amiss – where's yer skateboard?' The point is, though, that bowlers were becoming more aggressive. It wasn't 'bodyline', it was 'headline'. I chatted to a few of the boys and they agreed, especially when David Hookes got his jaw broken by Andy Roberts and was eating through a straw for five weeks.

If regular short-pitched bowling became one of the legacies of Packer cricket, so did the white ball, day–night games and coloured clothing. It was decided for a time that the West Indies should wear pink.

Lloyd: It was a maroon that was not as dark as it should have been! Some of the players did feel they had dressed up as fairies rather than cricketers. I've seen a few things in dressing rooms but the sight of Joel Garner's enormous boots painted pink will always come pretty high up on the list.

WSC was taking off and critics had been silenced; Packer had won a case at the High Court where the cricket authorities had failed to get his players banned by their clubs and countries. 'We were stuffed,' admitted the establishment later. In WSC's second season, 1978–79, some of the games were even played in Australia's best-known cricket grounds.

Benaud: I have never forgotten the excitement of the opening of the gates at the SCG to allow in 52,000 spectators for the first day–night match at the ground. It was the 28th of November, 1978.

If he hadn't been accepted, Packer was at least being tolerated. But for some of his players it had not been an easy road.

Greig: It was very hostile in England and I don't think the country's ever come to terms with what WSC was about. I don't think those responsible understood they were doing nothing short of abusing Test cricketers. At Warwickshire in particular it was tough.

Amiss: Oh yes, it was very difficult. Rather than being in the Warwickshire dressing room, I stayed in the middle and scored a lot of runs. I found it easier to stay on the field. The people running Warwickshire in those days were against us. They thought the traditional game was suffering. The club took a hard line and that went right down to the team. It was a tough dressing room to be in. I was a threat, I think. WSC was a threat to their future and I was a part of WSC.

Greig: There were a couple of England players in particular that spoke out strongly against Packer. Well, one of them, I virtually had to pull the pen and the contract out of his hand. I pushed them back because once the England Test pay increased, we did our numbers and I said to them 'You're young – it's just not worth it for you. Stay where you are.' But then I read some of their comments. It was absolute garbage.

Then, after just two seasons and before plans could be carried out to export WSC to more countries, the competition ended. Kerry Packer had got what he wanted. By the spring of 1979 the exclusive television rights to Test matches which he had coveted in the first place were now his and under the terms of the peace settlement, his organisation would control the future marketing of Australian cricket.

Lloyd: Packer realised this wasn't destroying cricket, it was just a different type of cricket. Look at Twenty20. Twenty-odd thousand people at Lord's are enjoying it. The game has evolved and moved on. It's just that for a lot of people Packer did too much, too early. Nowadays people realise what Packer did was great for all sorts of reasons. Is cricket dead? Of course not.

Chappell: Day–night cricket is the most obvious legacy. The way the game is filmed is another. When I first played Test cricket it looked like 11 ants on the TV dressed in white. No one knew what you looked like. With Packer, it was all close-ups and head-and-shoulder shots. Players became marketable.

Benaud: Cricketers these days are able to play the game without financial hardship and television sport-watchers have benefited greatly from some remarkable innovations. Do I have any regrets about getting involved? No. No regrets.

Amiss: I made a decision for my family, to secure their future. Looking back now, a lot of good things came out of it. Would I do it again? Who knows? Perhaps not.

Interviews by Simon Lister

Floodlit flop

English cricket's first night shift, the Lambert & Butler Cup, 1981

The first-ever competition under lights to be entered by all 17 first-class counties was tacked on to the end of that momentous summer of 1981. The Ashes series had gripped the public and the Twenty20 Cup wasn't even a twinkle in a marketing man's eye.

The Lambert & Butler Cup followed in the wake of the success of floodlit cricket in Australia. It was a seven-a-side thrash, using white balls, played on matted wickets and was held at football grounds around the country. Each side had 10 overs and bowlers were allowed to bowl two each.

Despite the presence of Ian Botham, David Gower and Clive Lloyd, the competition was a flop. Crowds were small, even for the finals night at Stamford Bridge, and it was dropped after one year. Coverage in the press was cursory at best and it was afforded only six lines in the 1982 *Wisden*.

Peter Lush (then Test and County Cricket Board marketing manager): It was all very experimental. It was a toe in the water to see whether night cricket would be attractive to spectators in this country.

Graeme Fowler (Lancashire batsman): I had just been capped by Lancashire and we had finished in the bottom four of the

Championship so we thought if we were going to play in this competition we might as well try and win it.

Clive Lloyd (Lancashire captain): It was my first year as Lancashire captain. We had lost in the semi-final of the NatWest when we should have won and I hoped the Lambert & Butler would give us a bit more of a cricketing profile.

The first-round matches were split into regions with the Home Counties playing at Crystal Palace's Selhurst Park, the South-West at Bristol City's Ashton Gate, Midlands at West Brom's Hawthorns Ground and the North section at Manchester United's Old Trafford.

Alan Butcher (Surrey batsman): It was a bit of a novelty to us and we were quite looking forward to it. We just saw it as a bit of fun and treated it like that. I remember Robin Jackman arriving in a helicopter and landing on the pitch. It was his benefit year and he made an entrance.

Fowler: Playing on a football pitch made a lot of difference. The grass was longer for a start so if you hit it along the ground it would go very slowly so the best thing to do was try and hit it in the air. The bowlers knew they were going to take a pounding and their run-ups were bumpy.

With matting pitches and short square boundaries, runs were plentiful and one of the stars of the first night was Butcher. He hit 21 sixes and scored 239 runs in three innings during the competition.

Butcher: It was a bit of a giggle at the end of the season but then it got more serious the further we got in the competition. I must have been seeing it well that night to score runs so quickly at Selhurst Park. All you could do as a batsman was throw your hands through the ball. It was a bit of fun but you soon realised that the boundaries were so small that the ball was disappearing into the stands almost every delivery. It got quite boring because regardless of the quality of the shot, it went for four or six. It was pretty obvious that night that it didn't have a very long shelf life.

While Butcher was the star at Selhurst Park, the Roses match at Old Trafford was being settled single-handedly by the Lancashire captain Clive Lloyd. He hit 12 sixes against Yorkshire and Nottinghamshire, and the ball was lost on three occasions.

Fowler: There was a young lad in the crowd that night called Neil Fairbrother. We didn't know him at the time, but he paid to come and watch us at Old Trafford. They only opened one stand and there wasn't much of a crowd there. I remember Paul Allott and myself were the young guys in the team. We wanted to get to the final because we knew it would mean a couple of nights out in London. It rained but we just carried on anyway. They only opened the main stand and they charged football prices which made it a bit expensive for cricket fans. That's probably why the crowds were so small.

Lloyd: It was marvellous to play at Old Trafford. When I first came to Britain I went to Old Trafford every weekend that I wasn't playing club cricket. To play on the same ground as heroes such as Best, Charlton and Law was very special.

Lancashire made it through to the finals day at Stamford Bridge along with Leicestershire, Surrey and Somerset.

Fowler: We quickly realised by playing at Old Trafford that 10 runs an over was the par score. I kept wicket, which was pretty boring because the ball hardly ever came to me. We were also using a proper cricket ball, which travels a long way on a football field especially when someone like Clive Lloyd hit it.

Butcher: The idea was pretty good but because every ball was either four or six it became a circus. The difference with Twenty20 now is that a six is still pretty rare so there is something special about it.

For the final a crowd of only 2,564 turned out to see Lancashire beat Somerset to reach the final against Leicestershire.

Lloyd: I vividly remember playing at Stamford Bridge. I batted pretty well there and we had a few supporters watching us.

Fowler: I opened with Clive Lloyd in the semi-final against Somerset and he got 80-odd and I think I made about nine or ten as we won by ten wickets. He absolutely destroyed the bowling. He hit one six that would have been out the ground at any cricket venue. It hit the roof of the third tier of the main stand.

In the final Lancashire made 151 from their 10 overs, which proved beyond Leicestershire and their star David Gower.

Lloyd: The floodlights were not too bad for cricket because they were close to the ground. We got the hang of the game pretty quickly and by the time we were in the final we had got in a good rhythm.

Fowler: We sat on the bench by the side of the pitch because at football grounds the dressing rooms don't have windows and were too far away from the middle anyway. We played well on the finals night and the score we got in the final was just too much for Leicestershire. I remember we ended up celebrating in a punk-rock nightclub in Covent Garden that night.

The competition was quietly dropped by the time the 1982 season started and floodlit cricket was not held in England again until 1997.

Lush: We had to pay pretty considerable fees to the football grounds but the biggest problem was that you could not replicate cricket on a football ground.

Fowler: It was good fun and it was a shame we didn't repeat it. I've still got the medal in a shoebox somewhere. At least Lancashire are reigning champions.

Interviews by Nick Hoult

New strap for old jock

Bob Taylor comes out of retirement, England v New Zealand, Lord's, 1986

England were 259 for 6 against New Zealand when wicketkeeper Bruce French was struck on the head by Richard Hadlee. With French in hospital Bob Taylor, aged 45 and working for sponsors Cornhill, was enjoying a glass of wine in the sponsor's tent, when the phone rang …

Bruce French: I remember Hadlee only bowled three bouncers in the match and two of them were at me. The second one was a quicker one and took me by surprise. I remember all of a sudden seeing it about a foot from my face. At that stage you are supposed to keep your eye on it but I didn't fancy watching it into my eye so I turned my head. I don't remember much after that apart from walking through the Long Room.

New Zealand bowled England out and in the period before lunch opener Bill Athey deputised for French but captain Mike Gatting had an idea.

Mike Gatting: We really needed someone and I knew Bob was in the sponsors' tent. He was a brilliant wicketkeeper and I knew he would still be good enough to do the job and it was better than me doing it. We had to clear it with Jeremy Coney [New Zealand captain] and Bob was a bit reticent at first.

Bob Taylor: I was sitting with some guests when the curator of the indoor school said he had Mike Gatting on the phone.

Jeremy Coney (New Zealand captain): Poor old Bob was in the tent drinking a glass of wine when he got the call. I've always taken the view that cricket is about sportsmanship and with that in mind I couldn't say no for the sake of gaining a few byes or a dropped catch.

Taylor: I made my way around to the dressing room but I didn't have much kit. Luckily I had my gloves in the boot but I borrowed Bruce French's spare flannels and a jockstrap from Graham Gooch. Thankfully it was a new jockstrap straight out of the box. I then ran out on to the field thinking, 'I thought I'd left all this behind.' I had to exchange pads and stuff out in the middle with Bill Athey. It was a bit like a club game.

Taylor kept wicket for the rest of the day without blemish, although he did not get the chance to take a fairy-tale catch.

Taylor: I had only been retired a couple of years so I wasn't too stiff afterwards. I actually really enjoyed it but it was pretty quiet and I never had a chance of a catch.

Coney: Some said that it started a precedent and that if we let a substitute keeper on then when a bowler gets injured he could be replaced like for like. I did not feel that was the issue and what could have been gained from saying no? Bob might have felt a bit stiff afterwards but he was tidy as ever behind the stumps and I can't blame England for asking him.

Bobby Parks arrived from Hampshire the following day to replace Taylor, and French was well enough to return for the New Zealand second innings, making it four keepers during the match.

French: I still felt pretty queasy but it had got a bit embarrassing and I couldn't let a fifth keeper play.

With his work done Taylor returned to the sponsors' tent.

Coney: Bob probably had to go back and finish off that bottle. Some months later I received a case of Cricketers' gin in the post from a supporter in England. The note said what I'd done was an extremely sportsmanlike act and long may it continue. I enjoyed the gin very much.

Interviews by Nick Hoult

Lillee's clanger

Dennis Lillee wields his aluminium bat against England, Perth, 1979

It was grandly trumpeted as the 'three-way battle of the cricket gods'. In fact it was England's 1979–80 tour of Australia, with the hosts taking on West Indies too. The matches were part of the peace deal agreed by the governors of traditional cricket and Kerry Packer's World Series. Packer's stars had experienced two seasons of innovation, in-your-face marketing and player-power. All three factors probably had a hand in Dennis Lillee's decision to take to the pitch during the Perth Test against England with an aluminium bat.

Bob Willis (England bowler): The Australians were in the middle of an extraordinary summer; they beat us quite easily and at the same time they were getting hammered by the West Indies.

England were to play only three Tests against Australia, and the Test and County Cricket Board had let it be known that the Ashes would not be at stake. Australian officials growled that the decision gave the impression that the Poms were chicken.

Ian Chappell (former Australia captain and commentator): It shouldn't be up to one country to say: 'We think on this occasion we won't be playing for any trophies, so bad luck if you win.'

Mike Brearley (England captain): It was an interesting clash of cultures and personalities. We'd cobbled together a tour under pressure – not the sort of tour we wanted. Most of the regulations for the one-day internationals, of which Packer wanted to stage about 15, had not been settled by the time we got to Australia.

The first Test was played at Perth. Australia batted, and at the end of the first day were 232 for 8. Lillee was at the crease with Geoff Dymock and had scored 11 runs with a willow bat. The next morning he decided to show England his new toy.

Dennis Lillee (Australia bowler): The bat was not designed or made for first-class cricket. At half the price of a willow bat, we thought it would be useful for schools cricket, nets and for underdeveloped countries. People have asked me why I used it in a Test match – it was a marketing ploy. I'm not ashamed of that.

It was not, in fact, the bat's debut. It had been premiered by Lillee against West Indies in an earlier Test at Brisbane. Its appearance had been brief and uncontroversial, with Lillee lbw for a seven-ball duck.

Lillee: The first ball Joel Garner bowled to me, it went 'Clangggg!' and Desmond Haynes at short leg hit the ground laughing. I was out for a duck and there were no complaints – nothing was said, nothing was written.

It was a friend of Lillee's whose idea it was to make an aluminium bat. He'd been influenced by the growing number of cheap metal baseball bats sold in the USA. A local company took him up and the result was the 'Dennis Lillee Combat'.

Willis: The bat looked the same on both sides, with no spine down the back.

Lillee: I checked with the authorities before I played in Brisbane and they told me there was nothing in the laws to say I couldn't use an aluminium bat.

Ian Botham's first ball of the day hit Lillee's pads. Lillee blocked the second and left the third. The fourth was hit through extra cover for three.

Brearley: I didn't even know what it was to start with. It just sounded like an odd, old bat that made a funny noise.

The England captain was not happy and told the umpires so.

Willis: Mike decided – quite rightly – that the bat was damaging the ball. It wasn't ripping it to shreds or anything, just bruising the surface.

Lillee: I was annoyed because the bat was coated with enamel and our tests showed it did not damage the ball. There was a stand-off, with the umpires saying I must change the bat, and Brearley refusing to let his bowlers bowl to me.

What followed was a ten-minute break in play while the bat's qualities and disadvantages were debated robustly in the middle. According to Wisden it was an incident that 'served only to blacken Lillee's reputation and damage the image of the game'.

Brearley: The bat had made more of a mess of the new ball than an ordinary one would. It was a huge tantrum on Lillee's part.

The Australian captain, Greg Chappell, was looking on from the dressing room with increasing exasperation. Apart from anything else, he thought that if his bowler had hit his last scoring shot with a wooden bat, the result would have been a four rather than a three. The 12th man, Rodney Hogg, was sent on with an explicit command and a couple of traditional bats under his arm. Hogg was a reluctant messenger.

Rodney Hogg: I could see myself on national television, before a packed ground, and Dennis hitting me between the eyes with his metal bat.

Lillee: I told him to buzz off. Then Greg came out, grabbed the bat off Hoggy and marched towards me. I knew I was in trouble. Greg wouldn't allow me to use the bat, for the sake of good relations and the game itself.

Willis: Dennis, in his own inimitable style, decided he would respond by throwing the bat across the field. It was blatant advertising.

Lillee: I was not happy at being pushed into a corner, and I threw the bat in Greg's direction, hoping to make him jump. I now hold the record for throwing an aluminium bat the furthest in a Test match, and I know it will stand for ever.

Chappell: It was pretty silly on Dennis's part, the way he went about it. I think it's been proved by subsequent events that the aluminium bat hasn't taken off.

Derek Underwood (England spin bowler): It was apparently a sign of weakness for an Australian Test cricketer to apologise or in any way regret such acts.

The game started again and Lillee was soon dismissed, giving a traditional wooden-sounding nick to Bob Taylor behind the stumps. Lillee was furious.

Lillee: Greg admitted later he used the situation to wind me up, knowing I would be bowling soon afterwards. He said that he intended to let me use the bat for one over before replacing it. His plan worked because I dismissed both openers without scoring.

Derek Randall and Geoff Boycott were the two men who felt the force of Lillee's anger.

Brearley: Boycott reckoned I made a mistake in challenging Lillee's use of the bat; he thought it fired him up to an extra effort with the ball. We fell apart. It was probably one of our worst performances. There was a bit of fear about Lillee and apprehension about the pitch. Although he was a great bowler, he wasn't as fast as he had been and the pitch wasn't lethal. The team talked him up inwardly.

Lillee: I regret now holding a Test match up for so long, but at the time I was determined I was in the right and I was being set up.

As England tried forlornly to save the game in the second innings, Boycott was nearing a century when England's ninth wicket fell and Willis came to join him.

Willis: I decided that I was not up to the combination of Dennis and the Fremantle Doctor so I said, 'I'll take Geoff Dymock, you have Lillee.' Geoffrey tucked Lillee away for an easy three on 97 but I was like a traffic policeman at the non-striker's end after Geoffrey turned for the third: I just held up my hand. I'm afraid that before Geoffrey could score another run Dymock got me out.

Boycott became the first England opener to carry his bat in a Test innings without making a century. His was a slow walk back to the dressing room.

Willis: I don't think Geoffrey ever forgave me. Did we discuss it? No, I don't think that would have been helpful. I had showered, changed and was back at the hotel by the time he got off the pitch.

Within a couple of seasons, Willis himself was dabbling with unusual bats. Even though he was a copper-bottomed No. 11, Willis used something called the 'Run Reaper' – a bat drilled full of holes.

Willis: The theory was aerodynamics. The holes allowed the air to go through the bat so it moved more quickly. But it was in fact a disaster. Dennis Amiss tried it out in the nets at Edgbaston; he played one shot and it disintegrated in front of all the press men.

Back in Perth, tempers had cooled and the Test was over.

Lillee: At the end of the game I got each side to sign the bat, and Mike Brearley wrote, 'Good luck with the sales.' But we didn't sell a single bat because they were banned. The laws were changed to state that bats must be made out of wood.

The spoilsports at Lord's ensured that Lillee's experiment was not a commercial success. Even so, he remained hopeful that the controversy would one day pay off.

Lillee: Someone in India offered up to US$3,000 for every bat made, so who knows, there may be some money in it yet.

Interviews by Simon Lister

Additional research by James Coyne

It was the future once

The birth of 40-over cricket, 1969

Next season 40-over cricket will come to an end. After 40 years it will be no more. But back in 1969 it was the new thing, the Carnaby Street of cricket, and one county in particular was the hip cat of the Sunday League.

Brian Close (Yorkshire): Oh yes, Lancashire were a bloody good limited-overs side, bloody difficult to score off.

Jack Bond (Lancashire): You see, we had lads who'd been brought up in the Lancashire leagues. They were timed games but it was all over in a day and you had to learn to get runs quickly and to bowl sides out.

Barry Richards (Hampshire): I think the reaction was like the reaction to Twenty20 today. 'What's all this about?' It was fun but not everybody thought it was proper cricket. That was until the players realised that it was a way of making some more money. Then they took it seriously.

David Lloyd (Lancashire): At the very beginning some other sides were a bit iffy about the Sunday League. Especially coming to Old Trafford. Don't forget that we were a raw team with raw supporters. It'd be like going to Chelmsford today. Intimidating.

Jack Simmons (Lancashire): Of course we'd grown up playing competitive league cricket. But some counties, Yorkshire included, were less interested in the Sunday League. All Bondy told us was that our members would enjoy watching it, so we played as well as we could.

Bond: Oh, I think Brian didn't like it at all at the start, he thought it wasn't cricket.

Close: I had my reservations. All of a sudden you could win a game negatively. In first-class cricket, if you don't bowl the buggers out, you don't win. That was the way we played our cricket in Yorkshire.

County cricket in the late 1960s was suffering a crisis of confidence. Some counties wanted more three-day games, others wanted fewer. Some counties were plain broke and were searching for something to help them stay afloat. Step forward the John Player tobacco company, who agreed to sponsor a one-day competition to be played on a Sunday afternoon.

Trevor Jesty (Hampshire): It helped our season a lot. We still had something to look forward to for the weekend.

Lloyd: We had a great balance in the side. Me and Harry Pilling would set up the innings, Clive Lloyd, Farokh Engineer and Frank Hayes would take it away and Jack Simmons and David Hughes would finish it off.

Simmons: We brought people to Old Trafford. Twenty thousand on a Sunday afternoon. It became the thing to do.

Lancashire started the Sunday League with a win against Sussex. Then they came up against Essex at Chelmsford.

Bond: We got a real pasting. John Sullivan, our extra bowler, went for 70-odd off his eight overs. That made my mind up. 'Never again,' I said to myself, 'never again'. After that we always went in with five specialist bowlers, no matter what.

The strategy worked. Bond's side won eight John Player games in a row. Sunday cricket was being enjoyed in Lancashire, although it had caused the county's Methodist captain some sleepless nights.

Bond: Yes, I was concerned about playing on a Sunday, and it was something I thought about a lot. It seemed as if one went against the other. So I spoke to my minister at the church and he said: 'If Methodist bus drivers have to work on a Sunday, there's no reason why Methodist cricketers can't,' and that was good enough for me.

On Sunday mornings, while his players were having a lie-in before an away game, Jack Bond would look for a place to worship.

Bond: I remember one Sunday down in Southend-on-Sea. I got lost looking for the chapel and I came across this Salvation Army gathering. I said: 'Is the Methodist church nearby?' and they replied 'Oh yes, only a quarter of a mile or so, but now that you're here, why don't you stay with us?'

On the field Bond always knew exactly where he was.

Bond: There were no fielding restrictions but even so I liked to attack. We'd often start with two slips and a gully or a bat-pad.

Richards: It was a curious set-up in the first year because it was one-day cricket but with so few of the current regulations. So you had guys bowling bouncers, wide leg side dot balls and of course there were defensive fields from the off.

Bond: My midwicket and my extra cover were my attacking fielders. They were important because I thought saving runs in one-day cricket was all about getting your angles right.

Simmons: It was always a challenge, right from the off – especially for the bowlers. Even in those days you had people trying to hit you inside out, get you off your stride. Mike Procter, Barry

Richards. Bondy was very specific. He expected us to dive in the field. Each man, he said, was to save one run an innings. 11 runs that could win us the game.

Jesty: I think we had a side that was better disposed to one-day cricket rather than three-day cricket, but we weren't naturals. I don't think we caught on that quickly. Certainly not as quickly as Lancashire.

Simmons: Bondy told us that, if one of us came into the dressing room after fielding and we didn't have green on our knees, he wanted to know the reason why.

Lloyd: I do giggle when they talk about the fielding and the fitness being better today. Has there been a fitter man than Clive Lloyd? Has there been a better extra cover? Look at the pictures. We looked like a fit side. Walking, running for buses and carrying your own bag – that's what did it.

As the season went on, Lancashire kept winning. Hampshire stayed with them. Some cricketers were now playing seven days a week. Not that they minded at Old Trafford.

Simmons: No, never. Never, ever. It was never a grind. Even Ken Higgs, who was a bit set in his ways by then didn't mind it. It was fun. Saturday night was still party night and, even though we had to play Sundays, we still got a kip in the morning. Didn't have to be at the ground until noon.

Richards: We didn't earn that much and there were cricketers who played for 28 days straight. Because you weren't well off, you couldn't take time off. You just had to keep playing. Then I got back to South Africa and had to do it all over again. 'What do you mean you're tired?' they'd say. 'So and so has just bowled a thousand overs this season. Get out there and play!'

For most the extra prize money made little difference. Sunday League cash was on offer for an individual clutch of four wickets and there was a £1,000 pool for sixes. There were 355 hit that season and Keith Boyce of Essex took home £2 16 shillings and four pence for each of his 16 clean hits. He also won £250 for the fastest televised fifty, made in 23 minutes against Lancashire.

Simmons: We didn't see that much of the money. It was all pooled, then some went to the club and we were taxed on what was left. A few years later I got done by the Inland Revenue. They investigated three Lancashire players at random and decided we'd not paid the right amount on the number of sixes we'd all hit. I told 'em it was all taxed at source but they wouldn't have it. 'Hell's bells!' I thought. 'I've had to pay for those ruddy sixes twice over.'

Aside from the money the tobacco company did a bit of product-placement in the dressing rooms.

Bond: Oh yes, there were plenty of free cigarettes. Two hundred a side per game, I think. Or was it 400?

Jesty: Actually more of the Hampshire wives smoked than the players. So all the John Players used to disappear into the kit bags to be handed out later on.

With two games remaining Hampshire's chance of winning the league went up in smoke when they collapsed against Essex from 93 for 1 to 153 all out. Lancashire won at Nuneaton against Warwickshire and the new title was theirs.

Lloyd: It worked because we had an exceptional skipper. Visionary, unselfish, an excellent leader. And Jackie treated us like an extended family. Most of us were so young and he had the good sense to give us our head.

The league had been a success, at least at the turnstiles. The Sunday game had brought in 280,000 supporters in its first season. The aggregate for the County Championship in 1969 was just 327,000 paying at the gates. The 40-over game would stick around for a while yet.

Close: I think what did happen and actually the same is true today – is that the younger players benefited the least. Forty overs, 50 overs, 20 overs – it's no place to learn the game because the skills, to a certain extent, are artificial.

Lancashire's last game of that 1969 Sunday season was against Worcestershire. Having already won the league, Jack Bond hatched a plan to his players.

Bond: It was on the telly, so we decided we'd try to get the fastest televised fifty and the 250 quid. David Lloyd would open and keep one end safe and we'd all blaze away at the other.

Worcestershire made 156 and the Lancashire batsmen limbered up for their assault. The operation proved to be a disaster.

Bond: Oh, it were funny. Bumble was there, gamely patting it back, playing to the plan and everyone else came in, slogged and got out.

Simmons: We did laugh. The thing was the crowd had no idea and they thought Bumble was just batting for himself. We finished a couple of runs short and, oh dear, David was booed off the pitch.

Bond: Aye. (*laughing*) Booed off.

Lloyd: It wasn't the first time. Water off a duck's back to me, it was.

Close: No. Lancashire deserved it. They were a damn fine side when it came to one-day cricket. But don't forget Yorkshire won the County title six times that decade. I didn't think Lancashire were ever going to win the Championship.

Interviews by Simon Lister

CHAPTER 7

Upsets

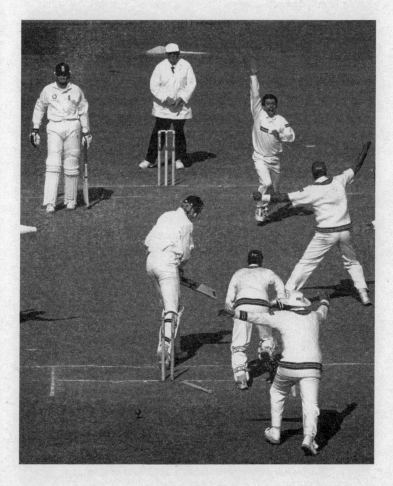

A week or so later I got a letter from a prep school headmaster. His team had been bowled out for 10, 20 and 23 and he wondered whether we would like a fixture.

Surrey captain Roger Knight on their humiliating defeat to Essex in 1983, during which they scored just 14 runs

overleaf:
Umpire David Shepherd looks on as Saqlain Mushtaq cleans up at Old Trafford during Pakistan's 2001 tour of England

The duck has its day

Essex dismiss Surrey for 14, 1983

Essex and Surrey were two sides tipped to win the Schweppes County Championship and this showdown at the start of the season offered a chance for one side to claim early ground. The match sprang to life on the evening of the second day when Surrey flirted with the least desirable record in the first-class game . . .

The first day had been largely lost to rain. Surrey won the toss and bowled Essex out on the second day for 287 with Keith Fletcher scoring 110.

Roger Knight (Surrey captain): I won the toss and put Essex in, in the hope we would bowl them out reasonably cheaply. We got them out at 5.10 p.m. and we had not done that badly. The ball had not done too much and I thought our bowling performance was a reasonable effort.

Neil Foster (Essex bowler): The general idea was to let them have a bit of a bat at the end of the day and perhaps we could chase a score on the last day. It was a good pitch and it was not very bouncy. The ball started swinging and they got a panic on for some reason.

With an hour to go until the close of play on the second day, Surrey opened with the experienced Alan Butcher and Grahame Clinton.

Knight: We started batting at 5.20 p.m. and had about an hour or so to survive before the close of play. I remember thinking that I wasn't too concerned about the number of runs we scored that evening but I didn't want to lose too many wickets. The pavilion at Chelmsford is side-on so we couldn't really see what was going on in the middle. I noticed there was quite a lot of leaving by our openers and that gave me an idea the ball was not staying on the straight.

Foster: We got both their openers out caught down the leg side so the ball was swinging a lot.

David East (Essex wicketkeeper): Nobby [allrounder Norbert Phillip] would set the ball out a foot outside off stump and I was taking it at first slip.

Butcher and Clinton were out with the score on 5. The next six batsmen failed to score as Surrey slumped to 8 for 8. Foster and Phillip were making the ball swing prodigiously.

Knight: We lost a couple of wickets and it soon became clear the ball was doing a lot more when they bowled than it had for us. I remember my own dismissal. I left a ball from Norbert Phillip. It was quite a wide delivery outside off stump but it came back in and I was not surprised to be given out lbw. Graham Monkhouse was dropped at slip and I knew we had a bit of a situation on our hands.

Foster: I've played in games where we had teams 20 for 7 and they have put on a bit of a revival but this time it just didn't happen. They went from being a bit unlucky to having a panic. They then tried to dig in and defend. No matter what they tried it just didn't work. We had seven or eight slips and didn't have anyone in front of the bat.

East: I've never seen the ball swing so much in my life. We gave them a nasty 45 minutes in difficult conditions and we nearly had them following on that night, which is astonishing. It was challenging to keep wicket in that situation. The stock ball was the away-swinger but the odd one would be flying down the leg side. It was going away from me all the time and every other ball they seemed to be getting an edge on.

Knight: If they bowled straight we missed it and if they bowled wide we nicked it. That was the way it went.

The lowest first-class score is 12 made by Oxford University against MCC in 1877 and by Northamptonshire against Gloucestershire in 1907.

Knight: I knew that 12 was the lowest score but it did not cross my mind at the time as things were happening too quickly.

Foster: The senior players were gobsmacked. I didn't think anything of it though. It just felt good. We were making inroads and I had no idea what any other low-score figures were. I didn't know the lowest score was 12.

With Surrey 10 for 8 West Indian fast bowler Sylvester Clarke took a slog at a ball off Foster which went for four to take them past 12.

Knight: Sylvester had a slog and it trickled over the midwicket boundary so we went from 10 for 8 to 14 for 8. Another wicket fell and next thing I remember is Sylvester and Pat Pocock having a discussion in the middle. Pat was remonstrating with Sylvester and obviously telling him to play sensibly. Next ball Sylvester lost his off stump.

Clarke was the last man out and Surrey had been dismissed for 14 in 14.3 overs. Phillip finished with 6 for 4 and Foster 4 for 10.

Knight: We were all out by 6.20 p.m. I don't think anyone played a poor shot and you have to give credit to the bowlers. It only takes 10 deliveries to bowl a team out but unfortunately we got them rather earlier in the innings than usual.

Foster: I was only 21 and had not played a lot of first-team cricket. I only realised the enormity of it when I stepped off the pitch. I didn't know what 14 meant, all I knew was that it wasn't a very good score. Nobby was an experienced player and he was the major threat and it was just a bonus that the young pup bowled well. We both kept them under pressure.

Knight: Micky Stewart [Surrey coach] was at Chelmsford for most of the day but he had set off to watch a second-team game the following day when we started our innings. When he heard the score he was so shocked he nearly drove his car off the road.

Six Surrey players were dismissed for 0 and Pocock was stranded without scoring – they became known as the Magnificent Seven on the county circuit. The Surrey players had ties designed to commemorate their failure.

Foster: Micky Stewart had a sense of humour failure at that.

Knight: I still wear it occasionally. I know Micky was not very happy about it and we were not allowed to wear them at The Oval.

East: It was a remarkable hour's cricket that I will never forget.

Surrey were humiliated and faced an innings defeat. With one day to go they hoped for better batting conditions in the morning.

Knight: I remember going back to our hotel and it was a mixture of disbelief, shock and eventually humour. We had a couple of drinks that night and there were a couple of good comments. The best came from Alan Butcher, who pointed out we needed six runs to avoid losing by an innings to their extras score. In that situation you either collapse in a heap or make light of it and pull yourself together. We got up in the morning and showed the other side of the Surrey team.

Essex expected an easy victory the next day but conditions favoured the batsmen. Knight made 101 as Surrey reached 185 for 2.

Foster: I did not bowl badly the following day and I thought it would go a similar way. I knew they would put up a tougher show but the ball didn't do a thing. I got a bit frustrated that I didn't bowl more. I was young and thought I would bowl them out and win the game.

Knight: We batted better the next day and painfully slowly. They never looked like getting us out. We picked up four points for bowling them out and they picked up three for their batting and four for bowling. So in the end it was only seven played four.

Essex went on to win the Championship for the second time in five years. Surrey bounced back by winning their next game by 10 wickets and finished eighth.

Knight: A week or so later I got a letter from a prep school headmaster. His team had been bowled out for 10, 20 and 23 and he wondered whether we would like a fixture.

Interviews by Nick Hoult

Cornered tigers burning bright

Imran Khan lifts the World Cup trophy, Melbourne, 1992

England, packed with all-round talent, won five of their first six group matches. Only the weather prevented them from knocking Pakistan out there and then and, though they lost to New Zealand and Zimbabwe, they beat South Africa, albeit controversially, in a semi-final to start the final as favourites. But Imran Khan's 'cornered tigers', with enthusiastic backing from the Australian crowd, had other ideas.

Graham Gooch (England captain): I was convinced we'd win this time. I thought it was the best one-day side England have had – lots of flexibility. I agree with Michael Vaughan's recent comments: there hasn't been a one-day side near that 1992 line-up since.

The night before the final England attended a banquet.

Ian Botham (England allrounder): It was the last thing we wanted. Some grotesque drag artist . . . started to take the mickey out of the Queen. I snapped. I pushed back my chair, fixed my eyes on the exit sign and headed straight for it.

Phil DeFreitas (England allrounder): It had been a long winter but at the start of that tournament we were outstanding. We qualified early doors but then our form dropped off.

Gooch: Naming the starting XI was one of the toughest decisions I made. Allan Lamb had been injured earlier on but he was one of England's greatest one-day players. Neil Fairbrother was also a superb finisher – England have never replaced them, except maybe with Paul Collingwood. Dermot Reeve was also a good finisher but it was hard leaving out Robin Smith.

Derek Pringle removed Aamir Sohail and Ramiz Raja in a miserly opening spell, then thought he had Javed Miandad, struggling with a back injury, lbw.

Derek Pringle (England allrounder): It looked stone dead but Steve Bucknor, having already fingered Ramiz, remained unmoved, something that could not be said for me. That decision probably cost England the match. Javed, the finest one-day technician (as opposed to hitter) the game has seen, went on to make 58.

In the dressing room afterwards Javed said: 'Bad luck,' gently tapping his leg halfway up. 'Allah smiled on me today.'

Aqib Javed (Pakistan bowler): Some were unhappy Imran had promoted himself to three as he hadn't scored many runs in the tournament. There was shouting in our dressing room: 'What is he doing?'

DeFreitas: I nearly had Imran caught but the ball dropped between mid-on and midwicket.

Gooch: I dropped a high swirler from Imran [on 9, off DeFreitas], which proved costly. They accelerated brilliantly later on.

DeFreitas: If we'd taken those chances we'd surely have been champions.

At one stage Imran and Javed scored only four in 60 balls. Were they leaving themselves too much to do? The answer was 'no'. Imran and Javed, the old protagonists, combined brilliantly, adding 139 in 31 overs. It was a masterclass on how to rebuild a limited-overs innings after a bad start. After 34 overs Pakistan were 113 for 2; in the next 16 they hit 136; in the last six 51. Inzamam smashed 42 from 35 balls, Wasim 33 from 19.

Gooch: Even though no World Cup final had been won by the chasing team, I still thought 250 eminently gettable if we batted decently.

But Botham fell for a duck. Pakistan batsman Aamir Sohail said to him: 'Why don't you send for your mother-in-law now? She couldn't do any worse.' Alec Stewart and Gooch soon followed . . .

Gooch: A dashing innings by Neil Fairbrother, in partnership with Allan Lamb [they added 72 in 14 overs], brought us back in with a chance but two quite brilliant deliveries from Wasim to bowl Lamb and then Chris Lewis next ball did for us.

DeFreitas: We were going well and were confident but runs on the board count double in those situations and Wasim ripped through us; it was a spell of magic.

Aqib: Those two deliveries were unplayable. It was perfect reverse swing. Wasim will remember that unique spell all his life. Extraordinary.

After Imran dismissed Richard Illingworth to win, the Pakistan players flung themselves down in prayers of thanks.

Gooch: We finished 22 short. I was choked, gutted. So was Botham. We all were. But the better team on the day won, no doubt about it. Perhaps we had just come off the boil.

Pringle: Like most England sides we were at our best playing to a plan, which is fine if your opponents oblige – something Imran's 'cornered tigers' didn't do. Having let another final slip, many of the England team wept openly.

Botham believed Gooch and coach Micky Stewart's rigorous training methods and the winter's hectic programme, including Tests and one-dayers in New Zealand, had taken their toll.

Botham: I believe that the overemphasis on physical training was directly responsible for our defeat.

Gooch: I still think we were the best team but we peaked a little too early. The tournament rules were also strange. In the group game against Pakistan, because there had been rain, our best bowling overs were knocked off, the maidens, etc. . . . so, after bowling them out for 74, we had to chase [64 in 16]. I also have no sympathy for South Africa [in the semi]. When Lewis and Reeve were scoring at 10 to 12 an over, South Africa slowed it right up. They paid the price. I've no real regrets in my career, but if I had to name one, it would be that I didn't win one of my three World Cup finals.

After Imran was presented with the trophy he forgot to mention his players as he dedicated the win to his cancer hospital in Lahore.

Imran: I want to give my commiserations to England. But I want them to know that by winning this, personally it means that one of my greatest obsessions, to build a cancer hospital, winning this will go a long way towards its completion.

Aqib: We didn't realise what we'd done until we returned to Pakistan. I've never seen our people so happy. There were 10 receptions in every city. It was the best time of my life.

DeFreitas: Australia is a great place to play . . . as long as you're winning.

Interviews by Huw Turbervill

Middlesex sham,
Irish rock

Ireland trounce a first-class county,
Benson & Hedges Cup, 1997

Middlesex might have been expecting a straightforward win, but Ireland were ready for them. Although they'd recently failed to qualify for the 1999 World Cup, Ireland had won a European competition and the Triple Crown for the first time, beating an England amateur side, Wales and Scotland. Their overseas pro for the Benson & Hedges Cup was the South African captain Hansie Cronje.

Angus Fraser (Middlesex bowler): I've spent 10 or 15 nights in Dublin as a cricketer and only been sober on two of them – the two nights of that match. Considering how the game went, it seems like it was a wasted opportunity for a good drink.

Mike Hendrick (Ireland coach 1995–2000): There was a little bit of arrogance about Middlesex when they arrived at the ground. I think the attitude may have been 'Let's stick 'em in, bowl 'em out and knock 'em off.' Hansie had been with us for about a week. I'd told the lads that he was one of the best players in the world, but I didn't want anyone hiding behind him.

Alan Lewis (Ireland batsman): When he arrived, Cronje said his goal was to win two of the four Benson & Hedges games. There were a few raised eyebrows in the dressing room when he said that.

We found he brought a fantastic simplicity to the way we played cricket. We looked professional and having him there helped that.

Hendrick: When it came out three years later that Cronje had been behind the match-fixing scandal I was staggered. He was the last bloke in the world I'd have thought would get involved in such a thing. Of the three overseas players Ireland had used – Steve Waugh and Jonty Rhodes being the others – Cronje was the best.

Cronje scored 94 not out and took three wickets but the man of the match was a Londonderry abattoir worker called Desmond 'Dekker' Curry.

Fraser: Middlesex weren't much of a sledging side and when we found out that this lad could probably break a sheep's neck with his bare hands, we certainly weren't going to say anything to annoy him.

Curry opened the batting and belted 75 in no time at all. Simon Cook was playing his first game for Middlesex. He went for 71 off nine overs.

Simon Cook (Middlesex bowler): I was 20 and had been signed at the end of the pre-season tour to Portugal. It had all happened very quickly. I'd never played anything other than club cricket; there'd been no 2nd XI games for Middlesex. I was in the middle of working a month's notice for a computer company in Oxford and had to take a few days' leave to play.

Lewis: We knew Simon Cook was on his debut. We wanted to have a real cut at him. Dekker set the whole momentum – he was a run machine.

Hendrick: In club cricket, Curry was scoring hundreds for fun. He liked to play on his own terms and didn't see the game the way I did. But when he was in the right frame of mind, he was a real asset.

Mike Gatting (Middlesex captain): Desmond had an interesting day. When he mishit anything it dropped short of our fielders, when he connected, the ball went out of the ground.

Hendrick: The third ball of the match, Desmond went down the track and hit a six straight back over the bowler's head. Hansie looked at me as if to say 'What's going on here?'

Cook: Gus Fraser had the whole thing worked out! The ground had a big slope running down towards the stumps at my end and the boundary behind me was tiny – it seemed like it was about 40 yards away. I was running into the wind. Gus, of course, bowled with the wind and the longer boundary behind him.

With Ireland 117 for 2, Cronje came to the crease. The game was set up for him to take Ireland to a big score.

Hendrick: When Hansie batted, he just looked so smooth. I remember glancing at the scoreboard and thinking: 'How on earth has he got to 40-odd already?'

Lewis: I was in with Hansie early on in his innings and after only a few balls he was hit on the pads right in front but the umpire gave him not out. Later he said to me: 'What should we do now?' and I thought 'What's he's asking me for?' I replied: 'Shall we move it along at around four an over for the next few?' Cronje said: 'No. I want five runs from you this over.'

Even though it was April and a green wicket, Middlesex played three spinners who bowled 21 overs between them.

Fraser: Cronje was always in control because he was such a good player of spin. He knew if he stayed in they'd get a minimum of 250 because they'd had such a good start.

Gatting: Cronje kept it ticking over and was safe at one end, so it allowed everyone else to come in and have a whack.

Cook: When I came back for my second spell they got after me. I was completely inexperienced; I didn't know how to take the pace off the ball or how to bowl yorkers. I was just turning around from my mark and running in. Cronje got stuck in and hit me for a couple of massive sixes.

The middle order weighed in and Ireland finished on 281 for 4 from their 50 overs.

Gatting: Before the match I hoped we'd bowl them out for about 180. But at the end they knocked it about and hit an extra 30 or so. I think I would have been happy if we'd had to score 240, maybe 250. That would have been OK. When it came to our batting, we didn't really get going. There were no real partnerships. We'd get established then lose a couple of wickets.

Mark Ramprakash top-scored for Middlesex with 34. When it rained late in the innings it meant play would be carried over to a second day. Overnight, Middlesex were 134 for 6 and a huge upset was on the cards.

Fraser: I was padded up, so that's a pretty good indication of how desperate the situation was.

Hendrick: All we had were medium-pacers but the pitch was slow so it didn't really come on to the bat and that didn't help Middlesex. We also took a couple of great catches. Overnight I was happy and we all went out for a meal together but there was no way I was getting too excited. I knew from experience that with Ireland, nothing was ever straightforward.

Gatting: It was a pretty tough situation at the end of the first day. We only had a few wickets left and I guessed that Phil Tufnell wasn't going to hit the winning runs for us.

Tufnell and Fraser put on 47 on the second morning to create some anxiety for the Irish but a required rate of more than eight an over was too much for the Middlesex lower order. They were bowled out for 235, losing by 46 runs.

Hendrick: When we eventually got that last wicket it was an absolutely brilliant feeling. I think someone had worked out that on average, county sides got beaten by amateurs once in about 200 fixtures – that was the scale of what we achieved. We enjoyed the moment in the dressing room. I had to get back to Belfast but there was no way I could drive. Someone else had to take me.

Lewis: It was a very significant moment in our history but I'm sure we'd have traded it for getting to the 1999 World Cup. Having said that, for Ireland to beat a first-class county for the first time was magnificent. It was my burning ambition and it had been realised.

Gatting: We had no overseas player and were probably stretched a bit thin but there was no reason why we should have lost. There were enough of us who knew how to play. Ireland deserved to win. They were the better side.

Cook: We were all very disappointed, not embarrassed but annoyed that as professionals, we hadn't nailed the job properly. When I was reading about it in the papers I realised that this was big stuff and I had to learn very fast.

Fraser: It was embarrassing. We were professionals and we'd got our arses kicked by an amateur side. At the airport, one of the players got hold of a newspaper and looked at the inside back pages and couldn't see a match report. He said to me: 'That's lucky Gus – I think we've got away with it.' I said to him: 'Don't be an idiot – have a look at the back page' – and there it was, the lead story splashed across all seven columns.

Interviews by Simon Lister

An almighty Din

Asif Din bats Warwickshire to victory, against all the odds, Lord's, 1993

It was the NatWest Trophy final, and Sussex had taken Warwickshire for 321 for 6, the highest score in any Lord's final.

Asif Din (Warwickshire batsman): In football terms, it was 4–0 to Sussex at half-time. We had the belief, but belief is one thing, reality is another and 95 times out of 100, Sussex would have won.

Neil Lenham (Sussex batsman): We thought we'd won. No one said anything, of course, but it should have been enough. Then they were 18 for 2, and we had it in the bag. We took our foot off the throttle a bit.

Dickie Bird (umpire): To be honest, I didn't think they'd get anywhere near, especially after they lost early wickets.

Roger Twose (Warwickshire batsman): We knew we had about a one-in-20 chance of winning. But as we progressed, the body language in the dressing room changed.

Asif: I had just nodded off in the dressing room when Dermot [Reeve] told me I'd been promoted from No. 7 to No. 5. I didn't have time to think, which probably helped.

Bird: I remember Asif Din coming in and saying to me, 'I'm just going to enjoy myself and we'll see what happens. You never know.'

Paul Smith was fourth out at 164 in the 36th over, when Reeve joined Din.

Lenham: We thought, 'They'll have to score their runs in boundaries.' But they ran very well between the wickets.

Asif: We started to believe we could do it when Dermot and I were in, and the Tannoy announced the scores after 45 overs. Both sides had made the same total [205 for 4]. We looked at each other and said, 'It's there for the taking.'

Bird: Nerves came into play, and Sussex panicked a bit. Looking into the faces of their fielders, you could see the tension.

Asif: They gave us too many singles. We were getting six an over without even trying.

Twose: The last half-hour was a bit of a blur. The pressure started to turn around.

Din fell for 104 and Warwickshire needed 15 off the last over bowled by Franklyn Stephenson. Reeve whittled it down to two off the last ball – but Twose was facing his first delivery.

Twose: It was the most nerve-racking delivery I've ever faced. It was dark and the keeper was standing up, which was a fair indication it was going to be a slower ball.

Lenham: Even then, we should have won.

Twose got bat to ball and scampered through for two. Amazingly, Warwickshire had done it.

Twose: I could easily have been caught at gully. God knows how I'd have felt if it had gone the other way.

Lenham: There was a deathly hush in the dressing room afterwards. Everyone was thinking 'What the hell happened here?'

Bird: It was one of the best games I ever stood in, up there with the 1975 World Cup final between Australia and West Indies. I'll never forget it.

Asif: It's what people remember me for. They still talk to me about it.

Interviews by Lawrence Booth

The whole thing was a mess

Ashes 1989 – Aussie dominance begins

The Ashes had remained on England's mantelpiece for most of the 1980s. When the Australians arrived in 1989 for the last series of the decade, few people here thought that they'd be taking the urn home with them. The Australians had different ideas.

Mark Taylor (Australia batsman): I'd not played much Test cricket. I didn't know how good England would be, but I did notice that as we left Australia some bookmakers had put us at 4-1 outsiders to win the series. I thought that was a bit strange.

Angus Fraser (England bowler): There were quite a few new faces in this Australian side and I think some of the newspapers had written them off before they'd got on the pitch. None of us knew how good they'd become.

Robin Smith (England batsman): We had a side with a lot of experienced players in – Botham, Lamb, Gower, Gooch. Now, I wouldn't say that we were complacent, but were probably confident of retaining the Ashes.

Ian Healy (Australia wicketkeeper): This may sound strange but actually, some of those players were our heroes, we looked up to them all. Of course on the pitch you sort of had to disrespect them.

Australia were tired of being beaten. So was their coach, Bob Simpson.

Simpson: I'd taken on the job in 1986. Before then, I'd watched the side on the tour of New Zealand. There were some pretty terrible things going on. There were guys who couldn't pick up and throw off the correct foot in the field. Blokes running blind when batting. Basic stuff that you would expect schoolboys to get right. A lot needed doing. By the time we came to England we were at least facing in the right direction.

The first Test was at Headingley where Australia hadn't won since 1964. The groundsman reckoned it was probably a good pitch to bat on. David Gower won the toss and England did get to bat – but not until the third day. By then, Australia had made 601 for 7 declared. Mark Taylor and Steve Waugh both scored their first Test hundreds. When Waugh passed Taylor's 136, he made the fact known to his mate.

Taylor: I remember it well. A little 'gotcha' to the balcony. He did the same back in '85 when we both made centuries for New South Wales against South Australia. That time he wouldn't let the skipper declare until he'd got more than me. So what I do is remind Stephen that he took more Tests to get his first hundred than I did.

Australia's first innings put the game beyond England – although a draw was still possible.

Healy: At lunch on the last day, we were cock-a-hoop because we knew we couldn't lose. I think at that stage, that was the limit of our expectations. Then it all changed.

Graham Gooch (England batsman): It looked like it was going to be a draw and then we lost six wickets between lunch and tea. It was very disappointing because the first Test of the series, even if you don't win it, you want to give a good performance. We let it slip.

The home side were 1-0 down.

Healy: Suddenly I realised the Ashes was a really, really big deal.
You could see it in the faces of our older players. Hohns,
Alderman, Lawson. We can win this series, we thought.

*The second Test was at Lord's, where England again saw a Test slipping
away from them. The Queen, who was to meet the players, had to come
early in case the game ended. The significant day was Saturday, where
another fine innings from Steve Waugh put Australia on top. Angus
Fraser was England's 12th man.*

Fraser: It was a pretty dispirited dressing room when I got into it. I
remember being given all my kit – a great moment. I got my shirts,
sweaters and cap. Then I was told I wasn't playing. I had to give it
all back and go and play for Middlesex.

*That meant Fraser missed a memorable event after play. Leaving a
pack of angry reporters in mid-quote, David Gower ended the Saturday
post-match news conference early, to go to the theatre.*

Gooch: That was David. Sometimes very calm and cool, sometimes
a very sharp temper if he thought people were being foolish.

Smith: He said 'I've got some friends waiting in a taxi'. In fact it
was myself and my wife. It was the opening of *Evita*, I think …

Cole Porter's Anything Goes, in fact. At the Prince Edward Theatre.

Smith: Oh yeah. Wasn't Elaine Page in it? Anyway. David got into
the cab a little bit flustered and he said: 'Oh, they were just
carrying on and I got fed up and frustrated.' But there's no malice
in David. When we're under pressure, we all do and say things we
regret.

*The England captain did say sorry afterwards. Then made up for it in
the best way by scoring a century of his own. But England still lost to go
2-0 down. Then at Edgbaston, it rained a lot. Angus Fraser got to keep
his jumper this time.*

Fraser: It was a ridiculously muggy day but I was so proud and didn't take it off the whole time. I was sweating buckets at the end. The other thing I remember is the pre-Test dinner. David wasn't happy with the wine, so he ordered a different bottle and said, "Anyone like a glass?" "That'd be nice," I said. Half an hour later he came up and went: 'That'll be 40 pounds please.' My jaw dropped. I knew I was on a decent wage, but I wasn't used to paying 40 quid for a glass of wine.

Fortunately for Fraser his coach Micky Stewart took pity on him. Soon, the young seamer paid him back in kind. He did something that no one else had managed in the series and got Steve Waugh out.

Fraser: My first Test wicket. Nipped back through the gate.

Up to that ball, Waugh had made 393 undefeated runs in four Test innings.

Healy: Like a few others, Stephen hadn't known this confidence before. But as the tour went on I have very strong memories of him sitting like a king on every balcony that summer. He padded up once and then said to me: 'Gee Heals, I feel great.'

The third match was drawn. For England, the situation was desperate but not hopeless. There were three matches left. Trouble was, England couldn't keep a settled team. Nineteen players had already been used. Then at Old Trafford, things got much worse.

Fraser: You have these visions of 'Land of Hope and Glory' and Churchillian speeches before you go out to play but there are a lot of blokes there for whom it's not a novelty. World-weary even. When the five-minute bell went, David Gower said: 'Right lads, that's the Worker', and that was about it.

Smith: The atmosphere changed and guys were having secret meetings and I wondered what it was all about. I thought we should have been focusing on the Ashes. Of course, they were planning to take a side to South Africa.

Gooch: I knew something was going on.

It was less 'Land of Hope and Glory', more Rand of Hope and Glory.

Fraser: There are several dressing rooms at Old Trafford and they'd chucked me and Mike Atherton, who was 12th man, in this little back room. It became the conference room for John Emburey and the others. I was nervously watching us bat on TV and blokes kept popping in and out to discuss whether or not they were going to go to South Africa.

Simpson: Well, players weren't paid so well in those days, and we'd had troubles of our own over South Africa, but as far as England were concerned it was just another distraction that they didn't need.

Taylor: It all added to how demoralised they were. South Africa. New players every Test. We talked about it a lot. All these outside influences certainly took their toll.

There was a first Test century waiting for Robin Smith in this match, and a maiden first-class century for Jack Russell. But with their minds elsewhere, England, yet again, played badly. Even the mid-series return of Ian Botham could not raise spirits. His dismissal for a duck in the first innings summed up England's troubles. When David Boon swept Nick Cook on the last day, the Ashes were on their way to Australia.

Taylor: It was a massive night. Wild scenes in the dressing room.

Fraser: We had communal showers for both sides. The Aussies were singing 'Under the Southern Cross' and I had to see it all, wishing I was in their bloody dressing room, not ours. They seemed a close-knit side who enjoyed each others' success yet we were a pretty disparate lot.

Taylor: We had a county game at Nottingham the next day. I went to bed about 4am. Geoff Marsh was the skipper and when he tossed, there were about three blokes in the dressing room who could stand up. If we'd had to bowl, I think we'd have had to forfeit the game.

For Graham Gooch, enough was enough. Australia's opening bowler Terry Alderman seemed to be able to dismiss him at will. The England batsman asked not to be picked for the fifth Test at Trent Bridge.

Gooch: I just didn't think I was batting well. Terry Alderman got me with a few lbws and my game deteriorated. I thought I wasn't doing the team justice, you know?

Healy: Terry was a delight to keep to. You always knew where it was coming. He had this crafty sense of variation too. But in fact he didn't swing it away too much. I remember Dean Jones saying once that Terry didn't swing a single ball away on that tour. He bowled good corridor, outside off stump and then brought one back. That was all. He had extreme control.

Gooch: It's a myth to say that he swung the ball away and got wickets. His danger ball was a bit more of an effort ball, one that nipped back. I was getting too far to the off side and playing across the line too much. It wasn't a memorable time for me, but having said that, I thank Terry Alderman a lot. He exposed a technical fault in my game, I put it right and the rest is history.

That was all to come. With or without Gooch, England were still wretched. Allan Border's Australians were without remorse. This time they put on 329 for the first wicket.

Fraser: I remember them being so hard on the field. And there wasn't a great deal of socialising. I think they'd been undone by Botham in the past. He was their best mate in the evening, then he'd tear into them on the pitch, swear at them and get them out. I think Border wanted to put a stop to all that.

Simpson: Allan was determined, patriotic and he hated losing. That made a big difference. We worked well together.

Smith: All series the sledging was like nothing I had known. At Nottingham I was batting and through etiquette, I asked Border if I could have a glass of water and he walked straight up, looked me in the eye and said: 'No mate. What do you think this is, an effing picnic?' At Lord's I left my crease wanting to pat down the wicket. I looked around and asked Allan if it was OK. This time he came up and said: 'You little c***. We're not trying to run you out, we're trying to f***ing knock you out.'

Blimey. That was tough.

Taylor: I remember running down the track and getting stumped in this game. Mind you, I had got a double-century. The first person in the dressing room was AB and he said, 'Well batted, but are you tired?' and I said, 'No, not really'. 'Why did you give it away then?' I said that I was trying to do something a bit different and hit the ball over cover. Allan told me that I'd missed a great opportunity to get a triple century. That's how much winning meant to him. He wanted all of us to drive England into the dust, whatever the circumstances. I'd never played that bloody shot before and I never played it again.

This time, England lost by an innings and 180 runs – their heaviest home defeat to Australia. And even the draw in the final Test at The Oval almost became a fifth Aussie victory. 'An autumnal gloom descended on Kennington SE11 like a symbolic final curtain to close yet another English summer of despair and emphatic failure,' brooded Wisden.

Smith: You might say it had all been going well until we lost the first Test match at Headingley.

Taylor: This series shaped the next decade for us. No doubt. We knew then we could compete overseas. In England the new players found their feet. We had belief. From then on the only objective was to beat the best – the West Indies.

Fraser: No matter where England go again, it's difficult to believe that they'll ever get so lowly again. The whole thing was a total mess. The summer started with everybody taking the mickey out of the Aussies, yet within a couple of months English cricket seemed in turmoil and Australia were embarking on a wonderful new era.

Interviews by Simon Lister

Bounce back inability

Sri Lanka's first Test in England, Lord's, 1984

The summer of 1984. West Indies in England and the 5–0 'Blackwash'. When it was all over, Sri Lanka arrived at Lord's for a one-off Test match. It was a chance for England to restore some pride and pick up a straightforward victory. At least that was the plan . . .

Chris Broad (England batsman): We'd lost 5–0 to the West Indies, so there was a feeling of relief that for once we wouldn't have to face all those fast bowlers. I think some people thought it would be easy.

Jonathan Agnew (England bowler): My debut had been earlier in the summer against the West Indies. The series had been pretty ghastly. Winning hadn't entered into it.

David Gower (England captain): A couple of the Tests could have gone either way but then the West Indies got past us.

Agnew: I'd played against Sri Lanka several times for Leicestershire, so I knew they'd be a decent proposition. At the team dinner beforehand there was a feeling that we'd crush them with fast bowling.

Allan Lamb (England batsman): We all thought it would be easy.

Aravinda de Silva (Sri Lanka batsman): England underestimated us but we proved them wrong.

Paul Downton (England wicketkeeper): We weren't looking forward to it. It had been a long season and we had been given a beating. Sri Lanka was a hiding to nothing. It was their first Test in England, so we were expected to win by a large margin.

Gower: Was it a respite? It was meant to be.

De Silva: I was 18. It was a remarkable Test match for Sri Lanka. Every guy who went in made a decent score except me. I was the one who was a bit disappointed.

David Gower won the toss and decided to bowl. Two days later his England side were still in the field.

Agnew: It was a nice summer's day. It was without doubt a bat-first pitch. But for some reason I've never got to the bottom of why David decided to put them in.

Broad: I don't quite know what was going through David's mind. Pitches at Lord's in late August are usually pretty good to bat on.

Lamb: We had spent the summer being pasted all over by the West Indies and then, against Sri Lanka who had only just come into the cricketing fold, we stuck them in on a flat wicket.

Gower: The toss? Oh, God [sighs]. When we got to the ground, Peter May, chairman of selectors, had an idea it might be a swinging day.

Downton: It was a classic London morning: overcast, a patchy forecast and the pitch looked a little green. If things went right they could have been four or five down by lunchtime. But we were fooled by the conditions.

Gower: As captain I had the right to overrule Peter May but in a summer where we'd been beaten into submission my confidence in my own abilities was a little low.

Downton: Literally as we walked out, the clouds parted and the sun shone. There was no swing and the ball wouldn't go past the bat.

Agnew: Things got off to a bad start when some Tamil political protesters ran on to the ground just as I was about to bowl the first ball. Dickie Bird was umpiring and he made a huge song and dance, almost lying on the pitch to protect it.

For some England fans it was the highlight of the day. Despite taking two wickets before lunch, England were blunted by the mild pitch. The Sri Lankan opener Sidath Wettimuny benefited the most. According to Wisden, England had 'many dreadfully inept moments' and Gower's captaincy was 'short of imagination'. At the end of the first day, with his side on 226 for 3, Wettimuny was 116 not out.

Downton: It was, of course, the very worst sort of wicket to prepare for a team such as Sri Lanka. They should have had something with much more pace. I remember the captain, Duleep Mendis, got some runs. He was very unathletic-looking. That made it even more frustrating. They did play well, though. They batted out of their skins but the whole thing was so slow.

It wasn't that slow. Mendis made 111 off 143 balls. At the time it was the fastest Test century scored by a Sri Lankan. His innings included 11 fours and three sixes.

Agnew: Ian Botham decided we could bounce them out. So we spent most of the day picking the ball out of the Mound Stand.

Day two was no better. Sri Lanka – and Wettimuny – just batted and batted.

Agnew: The final ignominy was that on the Friday night, when Sri Lanka were still going strong, we were in the field desperately trying to convince the umpires that we should go off for bad light as another ball sped past us. I was at square leg with Dickie Bird, trying to persuade him.

Sri Lanka were offered the light – twice. Both times they refused. There were more runs to be had.

Broad: Sides coming to Lord's were usually inspired because they knew they might not be back. We had a bad record there, perhaps because of all the county games. There wasn't such a sense of it being a special occasion.

De Silva: It was so special for most of the Sri Lankans and especially for me, being my debut. It was a heartening Test for all of us.

When England did get to bat, they made it past the follow-on target but were bowled out for 370, saved only by Lamb's fourth Test century of the summer.

Lamb: Nothing against Sri Lanka but I wouldn't class it as my greatest hundred. Some of the guys in the side were under a little bit of pressure to get on the tour of India that winter.

Downton: Even though it was Sri Lanka that were the opposition, the selectors wanted to use that final Test to help them decide who was going on tour.

Agnew: It was a shambles, rather sad in fact because many of us were playing for our place to India. I remember dear old Chris Tavaré, like me, was one of those uncertain of a tour spot and he played a ghastly knock.

By Saturday afternoon 'the ground rang with shouts of derision', remembered Wisden. At a press conference on Saturday night Gower even apologised to spectators, saying, 'that kind of cricket is no fun to watch and it is certainly worse to play like it'.

Downton: Tavaré managed to bat himself out of the England side. It was his last Test for five years and he couldn't get it off the square.

Sri Lanka began their second innings with a lead of 121. This time Amal Silva got a ton and the skipper Mendis made more quick runs.

Agnew: Just before we were coming out to bowl, I saw Peter West and Richie Benaud commentating on the television saying, 'Agnew is certainly one of those who has got to make an impression for the India tour.' I thought 'thanks a lot, guys'. As a result I tried far too hard and had no success.

Neither did the rest of England's seam attack. It was time for desperate measures.

Lamb: Botham was pleading to bowl off-spin. Swing had failed, seam had failed. He thought it was the only way to get them out. When I saw that I definitely knew the standard of the game had dropped.

Downton: Reduced to Botham's off-breaks. Quite extraordinary.

Agnew: It was hideous. We were going through new balls like there was no tomorrow. I think even our regular off-spinner Pat Pocock took one of them.

Lamb: The Sri Lankans were fine players of spin and I knew we were taking the piss when Botham started tweaking it.

Downton: Probably he did it in a fit of pique, probably there was a hint of tongue in cheek. Whatever the reason, it didn't work at all.

Broad: We were lucky to get away with the draw.

Downton: By the end it had become rather a futile game; there was very little chance of a result. In fact it was really dull. But Sri Lanka had achieved their task. They had come to Lord's and not lost the Test. They were delighted.

Agnew: Looking back, the game could be used as a classic case to illustrate how different things are today. I felt a complete outsider, not part of the set-up. I think the feeling in the dressing room was that the game had been a bit of a cock-up.

Gower: I suppose we were setting out to prove we weren't a bad side but it didn't work out that way.

Interviews by Simon Lister

A step too far

Did England fall to Saqlain's no-balls?
England v Pakistan, Old Trafford, 2002

By the early summer of 2001 England had started to feel good about themselves again. Australia lay in wait but there had been uplifting winter victories against Sri Lanka and Pakistan. Back home, England had to continue the momentum. The first Test against Pakistan at Lord's was won by an innings and by tea on the final day at Old Trafford the draw that would secure the series was on the horizon. Then the wheels fell off.

Rashid Latif (Pakistan wicketkeeper): Saqlain really bowled some magic. He was at his peak then and his doosra was turning and better disguised than that of most off-spinners you see today.

Saqlain Mushtaq (Pakistan spin bowler): Waqar told me, 'Look. You're going to have to bowl. You might have to bowl all day. The breeze will help you with some loop.'

Marcus Trescothick and Graham Thorpe came out after tea. England had eight wickets in hand and needed another 174 to win. It was a remote target but it seemed more likely than a Pakistani victory.

Mike Atherton (England batsman): A lot of people supposed that we were playing for a draw but that's not how I remember it.

There was no conscious decision to bat it out. The reality was that Pakistan bowled pretty well.

Alec Stewart (England captain): We were confident from Lord's. It had been English-friendly conditions there but the one place you don't want to play Pakistan is at Old Trafford. The square is abrasive so the ball reverses and the pitch turns too.

Saqlain: We'd lost the first Test when the ball moved about a lot on the first day, but we were still confident that we would come back. At first it was difficult. It was chilly and windy too. Trescothick and Thorpe were batting well and the ball was new.

Atherton: We were going well on that last day but the Old Trafford pitch was bare and the ball had started reversing.

Waqar Younis got one of those balls to swerve into Thorpe's stumps. The next hour or so was one of the most memorable that Pakistan fans watching a Test in England can have experienced. First, Nick Knight was lbw to a Wasim Akram no-ball. Then, as the Wisden Almanack *remembers it: 'With successive deliveries Saqlain had Ward caught behind cutting and Caddick dumbfounded by the doosra.'*

Rashid: A hangover from the first Test was a spat with Andrew Caddick. He'd sledged us a little at Lord's. In the second innings we really let loose on him. When he was batting against Saqlain, he was literally quivering. His hands and legs, he couldn't hold the bat properly and was dismissed pretty quickly.

England had lost four wickets for just one run in 13 balls. The trouble was, Knight, Andrew Caddick and Ian Ward had all been dismissed by no-balls.

Atherton: My own reaction to the no-balls? I didn't give a shit about it to be honest. If the bowler's foot was one centimetre over the line or one centimetre behind I can't see it making any difference.

Stewart: I'd been at the non-striker's end earlier and – as was my habit if I thought it was necessary – I would not-so-subtly make a mark with the toe-end of my bat along the popping crease where the line had worn away. I did it a couple of times.

Another wicket fell. Cork lbw. Another Saqlain no-ball. Like the previous two, it wasn't noticed by the umpire David Shepherd.

Saqlain: I didn't know about the no-balls at the time. I mean if you bowl one, you always check your run-up and it happens every now and again. We're not engines, you know.

Rashid: There was a lot of pressure on the umpires. It was such a tight Test that you can't really blame them. They had to watch the bowler coming in and the crease for no-balls and then for any decisions they had to make.

The third umpire watching everything unfold via a television screen was Ray Julian. He could see that England wickets were falling to no-balls.

Ray Julian: What you've got to remember is that as the bowler delivers the ball, the umpire's got to think of four things almost at once. Is he stepping over the side? Is he stepping over the front? Is he following through on the pitch? Is the ball pitching in line for lbw?

Atherton: There was usually a TV on in the dressing room with the sound turned down, so the players would have known what was happening.

Stewart: Saqlain's front foot goes down straight and then he'll pivot and the heel shoots out to the left. So he's always very close to the line and when does he actually let go of the ball? It's very difficult to tell if he's overstepped or not.

Julian: The referee Brian Hastings said to me, 'Can we get a message to David, to mention the no-balls?' I said, 'That's your job,' so in the end I think the fourth umpire Mark Benson got the opportunity to go out to the middle and quietly said something when he was there.

Stewart: Saqlain was a world-class spinner and on a turner it was always going to be hard. I rate Shep as being the best English umpire, if not the best in the world, in the period that I played Test cricket. I hold him in such high regard so I won't criticise him.

Julian: Shep was very upset afterwards, nearly in tears, the lad was. I said to him, 'We're all in it together mate, you're a human being. You've been too good a servant to the game to give it up now.'

Rashid: You shouldn't blame the umpires because even we, as the fielding side, were completely unsure of some decisions, of whether to appeal or not. It happens in that sort of situation where everyone is a little excitable and things are happening every over.

Stewart: Shep held his hands up, he was distraught and wanted to pack it in but I'm glad common sense prevailed and he stayed on. It was frustrating but for the sake of a couple of centimetres we shouldn't forget we were outdone by world-class bowlers.

Atherton: I know that David Shepherd was very upset about it all because he'd missed them. I spoke to him afterwards and told him it was irrelevant.

England had lost eight wickets for 60 runs in 23 overs. The game was over. The Australian team watching on television in London must have been almost as pleased as the Pakistanis.

Stewart: We were a side that had showed we could stay in a game, but we didn't play attacking cricket. The Australians were much better than us in 2001. I was skipper in the one-day games later in the summer and I remember when I handed my team sheet over to Steve Waugh and looked at his XI, it was men against boys.

Atherton: I think Steve Waugh made some comments after the match that we had lost momentum. The truth was we'd been beaten by a good side.

Saqlain: I was so excited that we'd drawn the series. Some friends came up from London and we went out to dinner to celebrate. It wasn't until the next day that I heard that three of the wickets came from no-balls. What was my reaction then? I said, 'Thanks be to God for this good fortune!'

Interviews by Simon Lister and Osman Samiuddin

Donald denied by Dunkirk defiance

South Africa arrive in England in 1998, expecting victory...

A team of confident South African cricketers arrived in England in the summer of 1998, expecting victory. They were right to be looking forward to the contest. England had not won a five-Test series for more than a decade.

Allan Donald (South Africa): 3-0: that was our captain Hansie Cronje's prediction. Now we had to back those comments and we had the players to do it.

Mike Atherton (England): I was in shocking form. I really needed to give myself time to do something about it. So I worked my nuts off for three days before the first Test in front of a bowling machine.

For the first time in five years Atherton had a little more time on his hands. He had resigned the captaincy and been succeeded by Alec Stewart.

Atherton: It didn't bother me at all. I'd had my time. I told Alec that I was there if he needed me but really there's nothing worse than a former captain getting involved when he's no longer in charge.

The first Test at Edgbaston was drawn but Atherton's time with the bowling machine had paid off. He scored his first Test century for more than a year. Rain on the last day stopped England setting South Africa a target. It was a time of change. There were speed guns at the matches and England had employed a psychologist.

Steve Bull (England psychologist): David Lloyd, the coach, had appointed me. People often get the wrong idea of the psychologist's job. There was no white coat, no office. Neither did I 'psych the players up' or 'motivate' them. It was about suggesting, not telling. My role was to contribute to the development of independent-minded cricketers.

Despite England's new addition, the psychological edge soon belonged to South Africa. During the second Test at Lord's Donald bowled beautifully. Beautifully fast.

Angus Fraser (England): He's a magnificent athlete, isn't he? There are some of us who make even the easiest tasks look bloody difficult and then you've got this bloke who was a superstar.

Donald: There was a big 'oooh' from the crowd and I didn't know what it was. Shaun Pollock was at mid-off and said, 'That's not bad gas, that.' The board showed 94.7mph or something. I thought, 'Yeah, that's pretty sharp.'

Fraser: It became a bit of a macho thing. Darren Gough was always looking at it. But it wasn't helpful when you're not taking wickets and your last ball was only 79mph.

Donald did take wickets. His five-for in the first innings caused England to follow on. Before long, South Africa were 1-0 up in the series.

Jacques Kallis (South Africa): All cricketers love to do well at Lord's and now we had our foot in the door.

Donald: After Lord's we felt that our house was in order and that we were playing the way we should. Never for once did I think we were over-confident, we just had a great deal of self-belief and thought we'd win the series well.

The third Test was at Old Trafford and South Africa squeezed England further. They batted, batted and then batted some more. A score of 552 took them to the third morning.

Donald: That was a mistake. We should have declared on that second night. Even though it was a big score, I saw it as too cautious.

Atherton: South Africa batted too slowly. It was typical of their approach under Cronje. His was a conservative side.

Yet it seemed to be enough. For the second Test in a row England followed on. Their 183 had barely taken a bite out of the deficit but in the second innings they were hungrier. Captains old and new, Atherton and Stewart, put on 226.

Alec Stewart (England): It's nice to think that it was a captain's innings. Yes, we weren't going to win but we had to stay in the game and, if a little opening came our way, we had to take it.

On the last day, South Africa needed eight wickets to take a 2-0 lead.

Donald: We thought the job was done. Then England put up a hell of a fight.

Kallis: Atherton and Stewart played well and it showed the guts that English cricket has. It really shows why England are so tough to beat at home.

Fraser: Yeah, they both batted very well but I remember being livid that each of them got out hooking when we were trying to save the sodding game. I know you don't render yourself shot-less but still …

Stewart: That's typical Gus, isn't it? He's only happy when he's miserable. If we weren't allowed to hook we wouldn't have got two-thirds of the runs we did. I scored thousands of runs playing it. Typical bowler-talk that is.

The home side kept scrapping. Wisden called it a 'Dunkirk style evacuation of the kind much beloved of English cricket followers'. Leading the flotilla was England's off-spinner, Robert Croft.

Robert Croft (England): It was a real 'fight for the badge' Test, this one. I reckoned we had a one in 10 shot of pulling it off.

Croft had come in at No.8 and had put on runs with Mark Ramprakash, Ashley Giles and Darren Gough.

Croft: We had to score a few but play out time too. I wasn't thinking about wanting to be there in an hour and a half. I just thought about the first 10 minutes, then the next and then the next.

England were six, seven, then eight wickets down but, with time running out, the volume of the South Africans' frustrations increased.

Croft: The chat hadn't been too bad but all of a sudden it got very spicy, about the time Darren Gough started batting. He took one look at Brian McMillan, who'd come from the dressing room to field at slip, and said: 'Why's the bloody bus driver playing?'

Gough took the flak for more than an hour before he became Donald's sixth wicket of the innings. England still needed two more runs to make South Africa bat again when Fraser, last man in, walked to the middle.

Fraser: I'd been quietly cacking myself on the balcony with the coach, David Lloyd, sitting next to me agonising over every ball. He'd got himself worked up into such a bloody state and there I was – next man in – having to calm him down.

Bull: Resilience, mental strength. Fraser's approach was critical.

Fraser: When I got out there I tried to speak and I had no spit in my mouth because I was so nervous. Crofty said: 'Ntini is quite difficult to see coming out of the Red Rose Suite, so I'll take him and you have Donald.' I thought 'Thanks a bloody lot, mate.'

Fraser survived one delivery, then another. Croft continued to bat in a Test as he never had before. South Africa were straining for a decisive victory. One ball would do it.

Stewart: It was edge-of-the-seat stuff.

Fraser: You just throw your body in front of the ball. Get forward, cover your stumps, get your pad outside the line and, if it's short and it hits your chest, so be it.

The longer Fraser stayed there, the more curious he became to know when it was supposed to end.

Fraser: There was all sorts of confusion. Was it overs? Would there be a 10-minute break between innings? If the scores were level, was that enough? I spoke to the umpire Peter Willey and said, 'What's going on?' And he said, 'I haven't got a clue, just keep batting.'

Donald was approaching his 40th over of the innings and had all but bowled himself into the ground. He summoned up the energy for one more yorker. The scores were level. He ran in and hit Fraser on the foot to bring screams for an lbw from his whole side.

Fraser: Everyone says I was plumb but it didn't hit me on the front toe, it got me on the back leg, on my heel. I was so far over, it would have slid down the leg side.

Donald: Gus is probably right. When I appealed, I thought it's maybe done too much. Well worth a shout, though.

It was the game's last act. England had escaped with a most unlikely draw.

Donald: At the end I was on my haunches and I don't think I've ever been so tired. The series should have been nailed right there. That's where doubts started creeping in.

Atherton: We had a beer in their dressing room and I saw Allan's feet. He'd planted them in a bucket of iced water and they were covered in blisters.

Donald: Some of the guys questioned the captain's declaration but Cronje hated negativity, absolutely hated it. He told us we were to forget it, get back on the horse at Trent Bridge and smack 'em there.

But had the horse already bolted? Propelled by their escapologist's trick at Old Trafford, England played aggressively in the fourth Test. Fraser, who was not even certain he would be picked, took 10 wickets. But the match will forever be remembered for something else ...

Fraser: (chuckles) Ten bloody wickets and all people talk about is Atherton and Donald.

On the fourth evening, chasing 247 to win, England had lost one wicket and Atherton was batting with Nasser Hussain. Donald was again leading the South African bowlers.

Bull: It was a psychologist's dream. I still use the footage today. It was an utterly pivotal moment.

A fast short ball, Atherton defends and the keeper yells for joy. Caught behind? Atherton stands his ground.

Atherton: I was an avowed non-walker. It's as simple as that and I've never made any apology for it.

Donald: The umpire has to make the decision. Out or not out. Atherton made the right call because the Test series was going to swing there and then and, if he had walked, it could soon have been three, four or five down. What followed is perhaps the fondest moment of my career. Really.

Coming round the wicket, Donald bowled a series of short-pitched, extremely fast deliveries. Atherton ducked, hooked and took the blows. He would not yield. Neither would Donald.

Bull: Yes. The eye contact. Very interesting.

Donald: He just stood there and I could have glared at him for 10 minutes but I knew I had to turn first. That was round one to Atherton. The guys were telling him in the clearest terms that he had been quite fortunate. Hansie was getting stuck in.

Kallis: I felt for Atherton. The batsman's wondering, 'When's it going to end, when's it going to end?' It was unbelievable viewing; I was standing at slip and balls were flying past ears and heads and he was playing and missing.

Stewart: It was one of the best pieces of Test cricket I watched as a player. You had a world-class bowler against a world-class batsman and they were both playing with a bit of meaning.

Atherton: It was a particularly fierce and red-blooded passage of play. What was significant was that it was going to take the series one way or the other. It was their big push.

Donald: I have never, ever been more focused on an individual. But I had to do it in a controlled fashion, not reckless and angry. I took a huge breath and I thought, 'If I lose it here, we could lose the game tonight.' Nothing short and wide.

Bull: It was spectacular. Mike was, in my view, the epitome of controlled belligerence. In moments of great pressure distraction comes very quickly to most people but he never wavered from believing he would win that contest. He oozed self-control.

Atherton survived – and so did Hussain after being dropped at the wicket. Donald turned to the skies and howled.

Donald: That just blew me away and I think my frustration told it all. That was my last punch. I thought perhaps this was not meant to be.

He was right. The next day England won the game by eight wickets and Donald received a consolation gift.

Donald: Yeah. Mike gave me his batting glove. He signed it on the red mark that the ball had left.

The series was now 1-1 with one to play and at Headingley a low-scoring thriller unfolded in which Fraser and Donald again took five wickets in an innings. At the close of the fourth evening South Africa, chasing 219 to win, needed another 34 runs but had only two wickets left.

Stewart: For the last morning they gave the seats away free and because it was Yorkshire it was full up. But it was a very special atmosphere.

A crowd of 10,000 witnessed half an hour's play. The series was being decided.

Fraser: Goughy and I went out for a loosener and the ground was three-quarters full. Back inside we told the lads and then all of us went out to a noisy crowd and an exciting atmosphere that got us all going.

Donald: I felt very low coming to the ground on that last morning.

Donald's anxiety was well-founded. He was soon dismissed by Fraser, and on the 43rd ball of the morning, Makhaya Ntini was lbw to Gough for a duck. England had won the series.

Donald: Later I saw a photo of Hansie watching England running off the field and he was just out of it. We knew we would win that Test series. We just knew it. But England fought hard, came back brilliantly and, when they had a sniff, they went for it.

Stewart: We saved it and then we won it.

Donald: Winning here in this country is massive. I don't think English people realise how big it is for touring sides. It's *the* accolade. It's absolutely humungous, priority number one. And for a short while we had it in our hands.

Fraser: The cameras came into the dressing room almost straight away and Gough and Cork were hogging it as they do and I just remember going around the corner and putting a towel over my head. Then I started crying. Throughout the 1990s we had under-achieved hugely. This was the biggest moment in my career. The tears were for the victory, for having played a part in it and for beating South Africa. After all, they were a bloody good side.

Interviews by Simon Lister

CHAPTER 8

Extreme Conditions

You weak Victorian. I want a tough
Australian out there.. I want a
Queenslander.

**Australia captain Allan Border to Dean Jones in the 40° heat of
Madras, September 1986**

overleaf:
**Lancashire players (left to right) Peter Lever, Clive Lloyd, Frank
Hayes and David Lloyd inspect the pitch with umpire Dickie Bird
(second from right) when snow stopped play at Buxton in 1975**

'Weather: unbelievable'

When snow stopped play
in Buxton, 1975

The summer of 1975 was a sunny one. The first World Cup was blessed by a fortnight of long, hot days and clear evenings. But days before the competition started Derbyshire played Lancashire at Buxton in a county game. No one had remembered to pack mittens.

Dickie Bird (umpire): Oh yes, it'd been a gay day on Saturday and Sunday. Lovely weather.

Clive Lloyd (Lancashire batsman): I was having a fine summer and had already made a few hundreds. So I was in form and Buxton is not the biggest ground a man will ever play at.

Bird: That's right. It was only small. Very pretty, looking right down into the valley.

Geoff Miller (Derbyshire bowler): It was very flat that year. A belter. Glorious day on the Saturday.

The crowd had come to see a Championship tie starting on the last Saturday in May. A John Player League game was to be played on the Sunday and then the sides would carry on with their three-day match on Monday, 2 June. Lancashire took charge straightaway.

Bob Taylor (Derbyshire wicketkeeper): I was captain. We'd lost the toss but, to be honest, I thought we hadn't done too badly. We went for under five runs an over.

Lancashire made 477 for 5 on the first day. The rules at the time restricted a side's first innings to 100 overs. Just as well for a Derbyshire bowling attack that had lost its two fast bowlers not long after the match began.

Taylor: What was wrong with them? I think they both had altitude sickness. You know that Buxton is the highest ground in the country, don't you? I was left with two spinners and a man bowling off-cutters to David Lloyd, Frank Hayes, Clive Lloyd and Jack Simmons.

Miller: He's not joking. They were both there panting in the dressing room, honestly. As I said, it was a very hot day, Keith Stevenson and Michael Glenn were young lads who'd not played there before and it was too much. Gasping for breath they were.

Clive Lloyd was seeing the ball particularly well.

Jack Simmons (Lancashire spin bowler): When I went in we'd made 300 or so and Clive was close to 50. By the time he'd reached his century, I'd got 40-odd, so that was OK. But then he went from a ton to 160, while I scored another 10 runs. He hit six after six and they were going into the bowling green beyond the ground.

Lloyd's unbeaten 167 took exactly 167 minutes. At one stage he hit seven sixes out of 50 runs scored.

Miller: I did hear that they were playing bowls and they had to abandon the game because they were getting peppered. Clive was hitting it dead straight. It was as if an air-raid warning had gone off.

Simmons: The other umpire was 'Dusty' Rhodes and he started moving further back at the bowler's end when Clive was batting. I said, 'What are you doing, Dusty, you're 12 feet from the stumps.'

Dusty said, 'He's hitting it so damn hard and straight, I'm just giving myself some time to react.' I said, 'What if the bowler bowls a no-ball? You won't see it.' And Dusty replied: 'Somehow I don't think Clive will be too bothered about that.'

By the end of the day Derbyshire were 25 for 2, still more than 450 runs behind their opponents.

Taylor: On the Sunday we won a John Player League game against Glamorgan at Buxton with pretty much the same side and then we all went home.

Lancashire had driven to Essex and back for their one-day game. It was late and dark when they arrived back in the Peak District. Monday dawned.

Simmons: I shared a room with David Hughes and in the morning the waiter, who was foreign, came in with the tea and I said, 'What's the weather like?' and he said, 'It's snowing.' Well, I thought he had misunderstood me and I got up and had a look for myself. I was astonished.

The foreign waiter was right. Buxton was covered in snow.

Lloyd: I pulled back the curtains. The old Railway Hotel, I recall, and there was snow everywhere. In June. I was rubbing my eyes in disbelief.

Taylor: I lived in Staffordshire, you see, not too far away. All the other lads were in Derby – about 50 miles. Where I was in Leek, well, it's just over the top really, so despite all the snow, I made it to the ground. Snow covered the whole pitch and of course there was no way we were going to get the game on.

Miller: I came from Chesterfield, which was clear. Of course everything's uphill on the way to Buxton, and as I got nearer I saw the snow on the ground and was thinking: 'What's going on here?'

Bird: Six inches deep it must have been. Unbelievable. No chance of play.

The recollection of the Wisden Cricketers' Almanack *is a little more restrained. 'No play was possible on June 2,' it noted, 'because of snow which covered the ground to a depth of an inch.'*

Simmons: About noon we were in the dressing room and it got darker and darker and then for about 20 minutes we were in one of the heaviest snowstorms I'd seen. You couldn't see the other side of the ground. Clive was as excited as a kid, running around trying to find a photographer to take pictures of him in the snow.

Lloyd: I think I'm right in saying there are no ski resorts in Guyana, so I had never really seen snow before. I glimpsed it through a window in Moscow one night in '66 when we refuelled there on the way to India but I'd never made a snowball in my own hands.

Miller: Cricket wasn't as intense a game in those days. We were all having a good laugh about the snow. Some TV crews turned up, I remember. It was a phenomenon.

Bird: It took a battering, did the ground. Buxton were snowed in.

Taylor: There was a front-page picture on a newspaper that I've kept to this day. I think it was the *Express*. Anyhow it showed two spectators at the ground on the Monday, the whole place covered in snow. Usually the paper had a little thing on the front saying 'Weather: Sunny' or 'Mild' or whatever. On this edition it said 'Weather: Unbelievable'.

The cause, according to the Meteorological Office, had been a depression moving down from the Arctic, bringing very cold air with it. The Times *on the Tuesday printed a picture of the snow-bound ground complete with forlorn spectators on its front page. Snow had not fallen so late in an English summer since 1888. 'East Midland farmers,' the paper told its readers, 'said supplies of new potatoes would be delayed by several weeks.'*

Lloyd: That would have caused some trouble. My memory of the lunches at Buxton is that the potatoes were the only warm dish on the menu. It was not a ground where you went for the food.

Taylor: By Tuesday the snow was going fast but I still thought the game would be called off. I said to Dickie, 'There's no chance is there?' and he said, 'Bob, you'll be starting on time.' I said: 'What about all this melted snow?!'

Bird: It had all gone overnight. Red-hot it was, the next day, but of course the wickets in those days were uncovered from start to finish. Left to the elements.

Lloyd: It looked pretty dangerous to me.

Bird: Well, we gave it a lot of thought. There were lots of spectators waiting to see the game start.

It did. And Derbyshire, already hundreds behind, were caught on a foul, drying wicket.

Bird: Those poor Derby boys had no chance. The ball was flying all over. Taking divots out. Popping, stopping, jumping.

Miller: Don't forget that Buxton was a league pitch. The wicket had been beautiful but couldn't cope with such an unusual occurrence. So suddenly you had England bowlers playing on an uncovered league wicket. It was lethal. A recipe for disaster.

Lloyd: I have a very strong memory that Peter Lever, our quick, didn't want to bowl. He was fast and I think he was very concerned that he might hurt someone. So he came in off a very gentle run-up.

Taylor: Oh yes, Peter was certainly afraid of bowling. I had been with him in New Zealand earlier in the year when he had accidentally hit Ewen Chatfield on the head and we thought he'd been killed. There was no way that Peter was going to bowl fast on that wicket.

Derbyshire watched from the dressing room with mounting trepidation. By the time Ashley Harvey-Walker came to the wicket at No. 5, the pitch was all but unplayable.

Simmons: The first one went straight past his nose off a length as he played forward.

Taylor: Ashley wasn't the bravest but he was a big hitter.

He may have been lacking in courage but he certainly had plenty of sense. He set off towards the umpire.

Lloyd: So this guy heads for Dickie and he looks like he's carrying something in his hand.

He was. His false teeth.

Bird: I was at square leg. And Ashley started to walk towards me. I said, 'What are you coming here for, man? The pitch is over there.' He said: 'I've got something for you to hold on to.' Anyway he popped them straight out, there and then.

Miller: The set he'd had since childhood had been knocked out about three years previously. So he said to Dickie: 'I paid a fortune for these. Don't lose them.'

Taylor: Dickie made him wrap them up in a handkerchief before he'd put them in his umpire's pocket.

Bird: Then he said, 'Don't worry, Dickie. I won't be long. I'll collect them from you shortly.'

Ashley Harvey-Walker was as good as his word.

Simmons: A few balls later Peter Lee bowled to him and he popped it up and David Lloyd took the catch. Harvey didn't see any of this and he was turning round saying: 'Did you catch it? You did? Thank God for that.' Then he went for his teeth.

Bird: He put them back in and walked off. That was that.

Miller: I was very fond of Ashley. He was best man at my wedding, and when I was a young lad in the 2nd XI he always looked after me.

The Derbyshire innings was equally toothless. They were bowled out on the last morning for 42 – a deficit of 435. They then batted again, following on, and were dismissed for 87. It was one of the biggest defeats – by an innings and 348 runs – in County Championship history.

Miller: It's like I always say in my after-dinner speech. We might have been bowled out for 42 the first time around but in the second innings we played twice as well.

Taylor: I'll never forget it – the snow, the defeat. Not long afterwards we were down playing Sussex and spent the day sunbathing on the beach at Hove. Eighty degrees it was.

Bird: You needed a fine technique to play on a wicket that was snow-affected. I'd like to see some of today's boys getting runs on such a pitch.

Interviews by Simon Lister

Out of darkness into light

England's victorious tour of Pakistan, 2000–01

It was England's first tour to Pakistan since Mike Gatting's row with Shakoor Rana in 1987–88 and the ball-tampering accusations of the early 1990s. England had to repair broken relations as well as combat alien conditions and continue their rebuilding under Nasser Hussain and Duncan Fletcher.

Nasser Hussain (England captain): I was fortunate as I had captained England A there a couple of years before so I knew what to expect. It was also a bridge-building tour. Whatever happened we could not go down the road of a siege mentality or confrontation. We had to be open and go out and taste the culture rather than moan about being there.

Graham Thorpe (England batsman): Remember we were down to lose in Pakistan and Sri Lanka that winter. 3–0, 3–0 was what people were saying. But we thought we could deal with it. We had that little bit of belief you needed.

England had little time to acclimatise. They lost the one-day series 2–1 amid insect swarms at Lahore and rioting at Rawalpindi.

Craig White (England allrounder): Lahore was the worst conditions I've ever played in. You were running in to bowl and the flies would be in your mouth. They would stick to your shirt and when you took it off they would be crawling through the hairs on your chest. In Pindi I remember looking through a gap in the wall and seeing people being chased away by police with batons. The tear gas came wafting over and the guys batting were struggling. It was unbelievable.

Preparations were further disrupted for England during the Rawalpindi one-day international when an Indian bookmaker claimed he had paid Alec Stewart £5,000 for team and pitch information in 1992.

Thorpe: We were shocked about Stewie. It was very tough for him but he managed it well. The team rallied around and things carried on as normal. There were a few jokes played. People left brown envelopes out for him and stuff like that.

Hussain: It brought us together. That was important in Pakistan. Our hotel-room doors were always open. The PlayStation culture grew up with Craig White and Michael Vaughan having football competitions. Nobody had a moan or whinge about being there. We enjoyed each other's company.

England players took the opportunity to sample the culture. A trip up the Khyber Pass was organised with the players chaperoned by an armed escort.

White: They took us right to the Afghan border. It was amazing to see how people lived up there. They were living on the edge of a war zone. You would see the shops selling knives and machine guns. People would go outside the shop and shoot bullets in the air to test the guns. It was pretty frightening.

It was Duncan Fletcher's second tour as England coach and his emphasis on physical training and methodical preparation had filtered through to the team.

Hussain: Thorpey and me would rough up the wickets in the nets. The ground staff looked at us in disbelief but we knew they would prepare one pitch for net practice and a different one for the Tests.

The planning and preparation paid off in the first Test. Even though Saqlain Mushtaq took eight wickets, Thorpe countered with an innings of exemplary patience and concentration. He became the first player to reach a Test hundred having scored only one boundary.

Thorpe: I came off and they told me I had hit only one boundary. I said 'Really?' I hadn't noticed. They're pretty big boundaries in Lahore, especially for a bloke like me.

Hussain: I knew having been there before and through my Asian roots that the crowds would get at them. It put them under immense pressure if they did not get off to a flier. I knew if we lost only 1–0, then we would be treated like heroes. If they only won 1–0, then Moin Khan would be sacked.

White provided Thorpe support with an innings of 93, then his highest Test score. England drew the Test and morale was high.

White: I just tried to be positive against Saqlain in everything I did, whether it was defence or attack. The ball was not spinning quickly and it did not bounce much, which was the problem for them.

The second Test in Faisalabad was a truncated affair with morning dew and fading light eating into the playing time. The tour moved to Karachi for the final Test. Pakistan brought back Waqar Younis for his first Test of the series. England sensed they had a chance.

White: They were crapping themselves going into that Test. We could see how they were changing.

Thorpe: With one Test to go it was at the back of our minds that if we played a great game we could get a win.

With Pakistan passing 400 in their first innings at Karachi and England close to matching their score thanks to a nine-and-a-half-

hour hundred from Mike Atherton, a draw seemed likely. But Ashley Giles dismissed Inzamam to leave Pakistan starting the final day with a lead of 88.

Thorpe: On that fourth evening we got in amongst them. I took the best catch of my life on the boundary to get Saeed Anwar and then Gilo got Inzy. That was massive for us.

Pakistan collapsed on the final day. Giles finished with 17 wickets in the series. But England had a choice to make: to go for their target of 176 in 44 overs or bat out for a draw.

Thorpe: The light was fading and Nasser said we could win but that we had to be a bit careful. I can remember him not wanting to open with Atherton and wanting to put me down the order. I remember saying that Saqlain was coming around the wicket and it was perfect for me. 'You have got to get a leftie out there,' I said.

Hussain: I said to Duncan we have nothing to lose. If we are doing well and they offer the light, we turn it down; if we start losing wickets, then we would take the light. We had eight people padded up in all.

It was a situation made for Thorpe. England had lost early wickets but he was at his nuggety best, forced to scamper singles as the light faded.

Thorpe: I got out there and they kept the fielders out and let us pick up runs. They did not apply any pressure. I found it simple to work the ball around. It was like matchplay cricket all of a sudden. I always thrived in that situation. It was about who was going to withstand the pressure.

Pakistan took 40 minutes to bowl seven overs and the match referee warned Moin Khan about slow play as the situation became more tense.

Thorpe: I always felt it was a bad idea to annoy Steve Bucknor. I became aware of that as Moin carried on. I kept checking with

Steve that he was not going to take us off. We needed about 30 to win and I knew the light was getting very bad. Moin was saying his fielders couldn't see the ball. Bucknor just shrugged his shoulders.

White: They would have come off in club cricket, it was that bad.

When Hussain joined Thorpe England needed a further 20 to win. It was after 5 p.m., the time when every other day's cricket had ended.

Thorpe: It was up to me to win it. Waqar came on and it was tough to see the ball. It was tough for the guy coming in. Nasser came in and played like he couldn't see it. Then again he'd been playing like that for the whole tour.

Hussain: Thorpey said he'd take Saqlain and I could take Waqar. It was pitch black, like playing at night-time. We shouldn't have been out there.

Thorpe managed to inside-edge Waqar to win the match and seal England's first series win in Pakistan since 1961–62.

White: We deserved to win. They were making excuses and saying we robbed them but we deserved it. It was a fantastic result.

Thorpe: I had adjusted and luckily I'd played a lot of club cricket when you turn on the headlights to see.

England returned home that night. In 1987–88 the England players cheered as the flight took off. This time there were celebrations of a different kind.

Thorpe: We were whistling *The Great Escape* as the plane took off.

White: I will never forget whistling that. It will live with me for ever.

Interviews by Nick Hoult

A tale of two pitches

Nottinghamshire's spicy pitch wears thin, 1989

In the 1980s Nottinghamshire were famed for their 'sporty' pitch. To some it was brazenly tailored for the home seamers. To others it was an honest square that guaranteed four innings. Whatever the truth, it all went a bit wrong when Derbyshire arrived at the end of the 1989 season.

Ron Allsopp (Trent Bridge groundsman): Crikey. I thought I'd left this behind. It's the first time I've really talked about it in 20 years.

Tim Lamb (TCCB cricket secretary): There'd long been a feeling that there was no effective sanction against sub-standard pitches. You'll recall also that there was a perception, an allegation, that Nottinghamshire cultivated their pitches to suit their bowlers. And I refer to two gentlemen in particular: Richard Hadlee and Clive Rice.

The two great overseas players had actually retired at the end of the 1987 season but the legend of the spicy pitches they bowled on was still alive.

Tim Robinson (Nottinghamshire captain): Teams would arrive, take a look and immediately be at a psychological disadvantage.

They'd stand around tutting, then ask if the strip had been cut yet because it was so green. I remember once, Barry Wood was captaining Derby and he was so worried he wanted the match abandoned before a ball had been bowled.

It was August and Derbyshire were back once more, a three-day County Championship match starting on the Saturday. A Test had finished at Trent Bridge five days earlier.

Chris Broad (Nottinghamshire): Ron was an outstanding groundsman. After all, he'd kept Clive Rice happy and there aren't many who can say that over the years. It was a very difficult balance and he almost always got it right.

Robinson: Ron loved his Test wickets and worked very hard on them. This match was straight after and I think he'd be the first to admit that the county wicket was underprepared.

Michael Holding (Derbyshire): Underprepared? You mean unprepared.

Allsopp: Oh dear. Where should I begin? The wicket had first been used in the game against Essex a fortnight earlier. Yes, it was a green-top and OK, I suppose it was a little bit fiery but it was all right. I thought: 'I can titivate this one and we can play Derby on it.' I mean it would probably be a result wicket but we were used to that.

Barrie Meyer (umpire): Peter Wight and I went to the middle for a look on the first morning. I was unhappy. But we said: 'Let's see what happens when play starts.'

Allsopp's problems had begun earlier in the week. He had been asked by England to protect the Test wicket so they could stay in Nottingham and use it for practice after the Test had ended.

Allsopp: So that evening there was a huge storm. Torrential. Like a prat I ran on with a sheet and kept the Test track perfectly dry because I'd been asked to. It was a right downpour and the wicket for the Derby game was flooded. 'Oh, bloody hell,' I thought.

Lamb: This, I think, was the first season of the 25-point penalty for sub-standard pitches. I had overall responsibility for the day-to-day running of the first-class game in England. My job was to convene the pitches committee.

Allsopp: I visited the TCCB pitch inspectors quite often you know. Most times I think Clive Rice should have gone along too. Anyway I had three days and I knew there was no chance. I was dying to roll it but it wouldn't take the roller – too wet. 'Oh, I'm in a mess now,' I said to myself. There I was, looking after England and I should have looked after myself.

Broad: Clearly Ron hadn't had enough time. It was dry …

Holding: … very dry. Dodgy.

Kim Barnett (Derbyshire captain): There were some holes in it and bits and bobs were missing.

Allsopp: Don't forget I was Groundsman of the Year three times.

Meyer: It was soft and clearly going on the top.

Allsopp: I wasn't thinking straight and I eventually did get the roller on and that cocked it right up. All that happened is that the pitch got a great crust on it. It was obvious what was going to happen.

Until the match started reservations about the pitch were audible but restrained. Nottinghamshire won the toss and batted. Devon Malcolm opened the bowling.

Barnett: It was poor from ball one. Flying off a length. It was pretty unpleasant to bat on.

Holding: From my first over the ball was exploding everywhere.

Despite the surface Broad and Paul Pollard put on 87 for the first wicket.

Broad: I batted it out and took a few bruises on the chest and arms.

Barnett: I remember Broady actually running down the wicket to Holding – outside the line of course – and having a swish at him. Mikey pointed out fairly directly that he thought he ought to remain in the crease.

As the pitch opened up further, Nottinghamshire lost more wickets. They were 114 for 5 and bowled out for 185 after lunch. Then it was Derbyshire's turn.

Broad: It was pitching on a good length and going over the batsman's head. Actually it was rubbish. Like club cricket.

Allsopp: It was bloody worrying. I just closed my eyes. Very unpleasant.

Derbyshire batted with the same hesitancy as their opponents. By the close of the first day their innings had ended for 165 and 19 wickets had fallen. It would surely have been 20 if Devon Malcolm had not hurt his back in the field. 'By this time,' noted Wisden, 'the umpires had already reported the pitch to the TCCB.'

Holding: The game should have been abandoned and Derbyshire awarded all of the points.

That would have been the easy way out. Play resumed on the second morning when Nottinghamshire went in to bat again.

Meyer: Michael would have killed somebody. It was clear that this was not an acceptable pitch on which first-class cricket could be played.

After 40 minutes' play, having been hit several times and had the visor of his helmet broken, Broad was caught off Holding at short leg.

Broad: As I left I shook the fielder's hand.

Meyer: He did. And he said: 'Thank God I can go now.'

It looked like being the game's last incident. The umpires intervened.

Meyer: I went over to square leg and said to Peter: 'I've seen enough and I'm going to stop it. Are you coming with me?' Then we phoned Lord's.

Broad: I got to the dressing room and Reg Simpson, who was chairman of the cricket committee, had some flunky sent up to deliver a message about me shaking hands with the fielder. 'I don't want to see anything like that on a cricket pitch ever again.' I sent the flunky back down with my reply: 'I don't ever want to see a cricket pitch like that again.'

It was expected that the game would be abandoned. But then – from Lord's – extraordinary news.

Robinson: There were lots of phone calls and meetings, then Lord's said: 'Resume on the old Test wicket.'

Meyer: It wasn't our doing. They told us to get on with it. We wanted to abandon the game but I think HQ wanted a result. They asked: 'Isn't there something you can do?'

Barnett: We were amazed when the match was moved to the other wicket. We assumed it was all over.

Lamb: We wanted to a) avoid serious physical injury and b) get the game completed. I would agree that these were, indeed, extraordinary circumstances and that the notion of a reserve pitch wasn't great but a completed game is better than no game at all.

One player disagreed. Holding was not prepared to bowl again.

Holding: I was furious. It was very unprofessional. No way was I going to take part in a farce. I told Kim: 'I'm not doing this.' He was on my side. 'Mikey,' he said, 'I'm leaving it to you.'

Barnett: He went home. It was the principle of the thing. I actually agreed but I had to stick it out.

Allsopp: I shouldn't wonder he wanted to stay on the first track and get more wickets.

Holding: No! Absolutely not! I was simply not interested in playing cricket on a pitch like that.

Barnett: After he left I went to Tim Robinson and explained what had happened. I asked him, seeing as we were down to 10, if Notts could provide an emergency fielder. 'Holding's gone home?' he said. 'If that's true, you can have anyone you want, even Derek Randall.'

With the players preparing to go back out and the pitch inspectors motoring north from St John's Wood, Allsopp was desperately trying to spruce up a week-old wicket that had endured four days of Test cricket.

Allsopp: I had to dig the ends out. 'Would they hold up?' I wondered.

The game resumed on the new pitch. Kim Barnett bowled the rest of Holding's over and stayed on. On a tatty and tired turner he took four wickets with his leg-spin.

Barnett: This pitch wasn't dangerous, it was just awkward. It had worn a lot.

Nottinghamshire were bowled out for 114 this time, meaning that Derbyshire needed 135 to win. They got nowhere near – 64 all out.

Robinson: It had become obvious that we were going to be docked 25 points for the pitch, so I thought we had to get something from the situation. The best thing to minimise the pain was to win.

'On the second pitch,' recorded Wisden, 'the batsmen in fact fared worse than on Saturday and wickets continued to fall at a steady rate. The match was over before the end of the second day, when D.B. Carr, chairman on the county pitches committee, and Lamb arrived from London to inspect the ground.'

Lamb: When I saw it, we hardly needed to classify the pitch as unfit. It contained a hole the size of a plate that had opened up on a length. The umpires themselves had deemed the pitch to be unsuitable, so it hardly left us with a difficult decision to make.

Tim Robinson's prediction was well-founded. His county got 21 points for the victory and were later fined 25 for their pitch.

Lamb: The second wicket wasn't much better. But we certainly couldn't deduct 50 points. I stand by the decision to bring in such a draconian penalty, though. We did much to prevent any continuing of the alleged Hadlee-and-Rice syndrome.

Allsopp: Bloody hell …

Robinson: Ron got a lot of flak, and I expect if he had his time again he'd do it differently but he was one of the best. He had a knack for producing good wickets with pace and bounce. He was up there with the best, I'd say.

Allsopp: When it was all over, people showed me a lot of kindness. I felt terrible. Kim Barnett took me for a drink in the Tavern. It's true. I admit it, I dropped a clanger and I've never told the story until now. But what can they do to me? I've long retired and they're already paying me a club pension!

Robinson: You know the thing with Ron? His pet hate was boring draws. He made sure that they never happened.

Interviews by Simon Lister

'You weak Victorian'

Dean Jones hospitalised with exhaustion after 210, Australia's tour of India, 1986

In 110 years of Test cricket, the Australia–West Indies game at Brisbane in 1960–61 had been, famously, the only tied Test. But in 1986, Australia, under new coach Bobby Simpson, and India, fresh from a 2–0 win in England, were to prove so well matched that at the finish in Madras, the players did not even know the result.

When Australia arrived in India they had not won a Test series for over two years. Coach Bobby Simpson and captain Allan Border were intent on reversing their fortunes. India were on the rise after a series win in England.

Bobby Simpson (Australia coach): It was my first time away with the team and I was very keen to get them winning again. We set out to win the first Test as it was important we established a winning habit.

Dean Jones (Australia batsman): Allan Border had played 70 Test matches and I think the next best was seven. It was a very inexperienced team. Allan Border laid standards down on dress, preparation, everything.

The temperature in Madras was around 40°C with 80% humidity.

Simpson: They were the worst conditions I've ever known a Test match to be played in. The ground was very bare and dusty. There was also a canal running by the side of the ground and when the wind blew the wrong way the stench was outrageous.

Greg Matthews (Australia spin bowler): I used to wear a hankie around my face and nose because the smell from the canal would come in and used to make me cry. The stadium was just a concrete bowl and radiated heat.

Border won a crucial toss on a good pitch and Australia got off to a great start, with David Boon making 122. But it was the performance of Dean Jones, in his first Test for three years that was the cornerstone of the innings.

Simpson: I have not seen a braver innings that Dean's. He was running on adrenalin. During breaks we would have one bloke waiting to take off his pads and another would strip him and put him in an ice bath just to try and revitalise him. It was immensely courageous.

Matthews: Dean's eyes were sunk back in his head and he was playing by memory. I felt that the real hero was Ray Bright. He scored 30 as nightwatchman before nearly collapsing halfway back to the pavilion when he was out. His toes were dragging on the ground as he walked off and I couldn't help but think this poor bloke has got to go out and bowl as well.

Jones: I was a mess. On about 170, I wanted to go off because I was stopping the game every over to be sick. And Allan Border said, 'You weak Victorian. I want a tough Australian out there. I want a Queenslander.' So I stayed. My last hundred I got in 66 balls because I couldn't run at all. I said 'block, block, I'm going to slog this for four'. Then I'd block until I had enough energy for another go.

Jones was hospitalised with exhaustion after his 210.

Jones: When I came off the ground they put me in an ice bath. People were talking to me, and I was quite coherent, I thought I was OK. Then when I got out of the bath I completely passed out and woke up in the hospital at one o'clock in the morning.

With Border making 106 Australia could declare on 574. India lost two early wickets but rallied through their captain Kapil Dev.

Matthews: Ray Bright was not young and fit like Dean Jones. He got the 12th man to ask AB if he needed him in the field after he had gone off with exhaustion. AB told him to 'get his arse out here'. When he came out I would have started crying if I'd had any moisture left. I was real stoked and it gave me a big lift. I then asked for a jumper to bowl in. I wanted to show we could take it and I wore that jumper for the rest of the session. I knew I was in the zone. I was swearing at AB if he tried to take me off. I know my bowling record isn't great but I knew that match was mine.

Matthews took 5 for 103, his first five-for in Test cricket, as India were dismissed for 397. Jones batted again in the second innings and Border declared overnight to set India 348 for victory.

Matthews: The only way they were going to win was if they raced out of the blocks. They took 16 off the first over.

Ravi Shastri (India spin bowler): The last day started with about 10,000 fans in the ground. By the end there were 50,000. We were always going to go for it. When Kapil got out in the second innings I made sure that I didn't pass him on my way to the middle because I did not want him to say to me that we were no longer going for it. I really felt we could do it. I hit my first ball to the boundary and AB knew it was game on.

Simpson: The real amazing performance was by Greg Matthews. He bowled unchanged for the whole day. He had a little stool on the boundary which he would sit on between overs. We always made sure he was fielding in the shade as well.

By tea India were 193 for 2 and needed 155 from 30 overs. They were cruising towards victory when they lost three wickets for 13 runs.

Shastri: The last two hours were simply fascinating. The players were getting very heated and the umpires had to calm us down. The over rate dropped to a bare minimum. I remember the umpires telling AB to get on with it.

Last man Maninder Singh and Shastri needed four from the final over, bowled by Matthews.

Matthews: I always say Steve Waugh cost us that Test. His misfield allowed Ravi to get two off the first ball of that over. He then settled for a single next ball and that got Maninder on strike with one needed. He went back and across to one and it hit him on the back leg bang in front of middle.

Shastri: I remember putting my hands up and shouting no for a single. AB raced around to get the ball and didn't even appeal. Then I turned round and saw the umpire's finger go up.

Jones: There's two scoreboards at Madras, one said we were in front by one, and one said scores were level. And when the wicket was given, we were running off the ground and I thought it was a draw. Then we got told by Bob Simpson, who had played in the first tied Test, 'No, it's a tie.' And we just said, 'Is that good?'

Matthews: I remember two things. One, is that most of the lads didn't realise it was a tied Test and the other is packing my kit up next to AB. He had the match ball in his left hand and he said, 'You've earned this.'

Jones: The bonding that we had between the two teams was fantastic after that. We flew that night to Hyderabad and when we walked into the hotel there were 30 waiters, all with a tray and a bottle of Veuve Clicquot. We hadn't had a drink in a month and the manager of the hotel says, 'Free champagne for everyone!' Both teams celebrated like you wouldn't believe. Next morning a bill was put under our Australian cricket manager's room for $13,500. We only got paid $9,000 for the tour!

The rest of the series failed to live up to the Madras Test, with two rain-affected draws. But Australia had turned a corner.

Simpson: We got a lot out of that tour. The Marsh/Boon opening combination really worked for us in the future and we had a core of players that we could build on. The match set Dean's career going. He was a great talent but people were wondering whether he was a bit touchy as far as his cricket was concerned.

Jones: I think this particular Test was the renaissance of Australian cricket. And I personally started to believe I was good enough to play at that level and be on the same ground as Sunny Gavaskar and co. It was my Mount Everest of cricket. Even to this day I have a psychological problem that if it's 36 or 37 degrees my body starts to shake.

Interviews by Nick Hoult and Emma John

The longest day

Lancashire chase the darkness in the Gillette Cup semi-final, Old Trafford, 1971

It became known as the 'Lamplight Game'. Lancashire played Gloucestershire at Old Trafford in the 1971 Gillette Cup semi-final and the match did not finish until five to nine. A tie that hung in the balance was decided by a young Lancastrian who in one over took on the gloaming and the Gloucester attack to bring his county one of their fondest victories.

Roger Knight (Gloucestershire batsman): It was so dark by the end – but captivating. I remember at about half past eight there was an announcement: 'The last train to Bristol will be leaving shortly.' Well, absolutely nobody moved. I've no idea how all the Gloucester supporters got home.

John Mortimore (Gloucestershire spin bowler): They kept delaying the train but eventually people just waved it goodbye from inside the ground.

Jack Bond (Lancashire captain): I was batting when the umpires asked us if we wanted to come off and I thought, 'Well, there's been 27,000 people here all day and if we go off now, they'll only be wondering why they've been here so long.'

Tony Brown (Gloucestershire captain): I think it was from this game that the immortal discussion between Jack Bond and the

umpire Arthur Jepson came: Jack was complaining about the light
and Arthur said, 'What's that?' pointing to the sky. 'The moon,'
said Jackie. 'Well, how bloody far do you want to see?' said Arthur.

*The late finish was caused by rain interruptions around lunchtime
when an hour or so was lost. The consequence was that Gloucestershire
had to do their fielding in one stint – three hours and 57 minutes
of it.*

Brown: My family told me afterwards that the BBC news went live
to the game at the beginning of the bulletin because no match had
ever gone on so long.

David Hughes (Lancashire allrounder): They took the sightscreens
away to get more people in the ground. It was heaving. People
were all over the grass, and the gangways and aisles were full of
spectators too.

*Gloucestershire were defending a score of 229 made in their 60 overs.
They were quite happy with their efforts.*

Knight: It was a reasonable total. We were especially pleased to get
Clive Lloyd out cheaply. Mortimore bowled him and one of my
strongest memories of that day is David Shepherd, who was at
deep square leg, coming steaming in from the boundary to join in
the celebrations. It took him a while to arrive.

*At half past seven Jepson and the other umpire Dickie Bird decided
that the match should be played to a finish. Lancashire, with six wickets
down, needed 94 runs in 24 overs. Bond and Jack Simmons edged their
side closer. Then, with the darkness gathering fast and the run rate
rising, Simmons was bowled by Mortimore.*

Hughes: I came in at No. 9 and before long the equation was 25
off five overs. It was very gloomy and the lights from Warwick
Road station looked very bright. Of course, 30-odd years later it
gets darker every time I talk about it.

Knight: There were five overs left. Mike Procter had two, Jack Davey had two and Morty had one. Tony Brown had to decide whether or not to get Morty's out of the way or give him the last over.

Hughes: I think if they'd made the tactical decision to bowl the four overs of seam at us, because of the dark, they'd have won the game.

Brown: Morty had actually bowled extremely well against some bloody good cricketers and got the wickets of Clive Lloyd and Farokh Engineer. Before his last over started I said, 'Keep it flat and if we restrict them to nine or ten then we'll still be right in it.'

Morty did not keep it flat. Hughes went inside out to hit the first ball for four through extra cover and then, after several changes to the field, he put the second delivery over long on for six.

Knight: Morty thought he'd toss the second one up a bit higher and drop it a bit shorter. The result was that it went a bit further.

Hughes: Apparently, after I hit the first two balls of the over for 10, Jack Simmons had come out on to the balcony shouting 'Just push for singles, push for singles now.' I couldn't see or hear him.

A pair of twos followed, which the Gloucestershire outfielders could barely pick up in the gloom.

Brown: I think the darkness was probably more of a disadvantage to us because we had no idea about the path of the ball. The batsmen at least knew where it was coming from. For Morty's over I was at long off and could see nothing. One of the sixes went straight over my head. The off-side cordon were shouting to each other 'It's over by you.'

Bond: Look at it this way. There was only one Lancashire player trying to see the ball; there were 11 Gloucestershire players trying to see the ball. It was an 11–1 chance and I like those odds.

Knight: I remember haring around to try to cut off a boundary – and I've seen some television footage of this – when two boys had come over the rope to field the ball. It looks like I knee the first boy and drop the shoulder like a Maori wing-forward into the second one in an effort to cut the ball off. I'm not actually certain there was any significant contact.

Brown: When we batted the rope was right up against the fence. I do remember that as the game went on and the spectators ringed the boundary, the rope crept in. A couple of our fielders reckoned it had shrunk by a good 10 yards in some places.

To finish with, Hughes clattered another four and then a six. Twenty-five to win from five overs had become one from four.

Mortimore: He decided to give it a go. Sometimes it comes off, sometimes it doesn't. That day it came off.

Brown: Morty was a very phlegmatic character, a very sensible bloke. His reaction was not too different if he had got a seven-for or gone for 30 in an over. Of course he was disappointed and we all commiserated. I wouldn't have expected Garry Sobers, never mind David Hughes, bless him, to score 24 off an over from John Mortimore. I think he probably could have bowled it flatter but they were determined to have a go at him.

Knight: It was an extraordinary day because few sides chased around five an over with any success in those days. The game was going our way and suddenly we had all but lost the match in an over.

It was left to Bond to hit the winning single in the next over bowled by Procter. As the crowd ran on, the BBC commentator, Brian Johnston, remarked that he hadn't seen anything like it since England had won the Ashes at The Oval in 1953. It was 'one of the most extraordinary cricket matches' he had ever witnessed.

Hughes: The Lancashire side had changed a lot in recent years. We were a young side, many of whom had come up from the leagues, which meant two things: we feared no one's reputation and knew how to play the one-day game.

Brown: It was a glorious game of cricket and it took several seasons for us to get our revenge. Mike Procter was captain and we beat Lancashire after lots of rain because we had a better run rate. Proccy said, 'I don't believe it. I've wanted this for years, and when it came, we won it by sitting in the bloody pavilion.'

Hughes: The next morning the groundsman, Bert Flack, went to dismantle some of the temporary turnstiles that had been put up. As he was taking the frame of one of them down, a huge cloth bag full of 50-pence pieces fell and hit him on the head. It had been put up there for safe keeping by a gateman the day before who'd forgotten about it in all the excitement.

Interviews by Simon Lister

The *Wisden Cricketer* is the world's highest-selling monthly cricket magazine. Launched in 2003, it was the result of a merger between *Wisden Cricket Monthly* and the *Cricketer*. Edited by John Stern, it carries features, interviews and analysis on all aspects of cricket.

For more information visit:
www.thewisdencricketer.com

Simon Lister, author of the foreword to this book, is a regular contributor to the *Wisden Cricketer* and the author of *Supercat: The Authorised Biography of Clive Lloyd*.